Understanding China

Series Editors

Emmie Yang
Business, Economics China, Springer-Verlag Asia
Beijing, China, People's Republic

Niels Peter Thomas
Heidelberg, Germany

For further volumes:
http://www.springer.com/series/11772

Peng He

Chinese Lawmaking: From Non-communicative to Communicative

Springer

Peng He
Law School
Zhongnan University of Economics
and Law
Wuhan, People's Republic, China

ISSN 2196-3134 ISSN 2196-3142 (electronic)
ISBN 978-3-642-39506-2 ISBN 978-3-642-39507-9 (eBook)
DOI 10.1007/978-3-642-39507-9
Springer Heidelberg New York Dordrecht London

Library of Congress Control Number: 2013947191

Printed on acid-free paper

Springer is part of Springer Science+Business Media (www.springer.com)

Foreword

Much work in legal theory has been concerned with law and its operation, its connection with morality and the interpretation of the law through the courts and the judges. Law as a process of legislation has not been touched upon much. There is now a developing literature in the Western world on the theory of legislation and the process of lawmaking. This tries both to recover what Waldron has called 'the dignity of legislation' and what has more generically been termed 'legisprudence'. What is important here is the study of the philosophy and context of good legislation. Rather than concentrating on legal reasoning by the judges, the emphasis is on the protocols of lawmaking and the reasoning necessary for good legislators and legislation.

Dr. Peng He in her book addresses some of these issues drawing on Western and Chinese sources for her argument for a 'communicative' theory of lawmaking. This book is timely and important in the Chinese context. Her argument depends upon the insight that what is important in societies is not just representative democracy but 'voice' – the ability of other actors to be heard and of bringing their input into official systems. She shows how law can be seen not just as the one official system, but rather as a system in interaction with many systems of rules outside of it. This helps to facilitate the many voices that exist outside of the official legal system in society, and can do so without subverting it. This for Dr. He counters the 'top-down' view that too many think of as the most appropriate way of lawmaking. Moreover, she argues that this can also take further the idea of living under the rules as something that is not to be seen as a narrow legalism but as something more akin to living 'righteously' – a view which is resonant with some parts of Chinese legal thought.

This book is important in the present Chinese context in yet another way. The developing economy necessitates substantial legal reform. But the application of Western models to China can often be naive and not fully fulfil their intended purpose. Peng He's work addresses this by looking at the process of legislation in connection with law reform. It is grounded in a sound theoretical reflection of both the process of legal transplantation and the process of lawmaking and looks both at Western and Chinese sources. Such an approach needs to draw from several intellectual traditions, and it is this interdisciplinary, foundational research that is the task Dr. He has set herself in her project. Her theory will provide an abstract theoretical framework that is more sensitive to local conditions, while at the same time incorporating insights from a broad range of disciplines on law reform. Her research is of direct practical relevance for reforming the legislative process in China.

On a personal note, the thesis upon which this book is based was completed at Edinburgh University where I was a supervisor. It was for me a fruitful experience, and I am pleased to see the culmination of Dr. He's work in published form. I learnt a lot concerning Chinese legal thought during her time with us, which perhaps contributed to subverting my prejudice of the top-down hegemony of Western legal theory!

Edinburgh, UK
28 February 2013

Zenon Bańkowski

Abstract

In this book, I will discuss and criticize different legitimation for lawmaking, including ancient and contemporary Chinese theories, and Western representative perspectives on lawmaking. I will disclose the disadvantages of the Chinese lawmaking system. As a new research project of Chinese law, I argue that both the traditional and contemporary Chinese lawmaking lacked elements of communication. The top-down lawmaking mode was the reality as well as the dominant theoretical justifications of legislation in China. I believe that the top-down lawmaking mode in China was insufficient in its justifications for legitimacy, neither was it beneficial for increasing the degree of individual freedom and rights. Therefore, it is better to absorb positive Western lawmaking elements, especially taking a shift from a non-communicative mode to a more interactive and cooperative mode.

Western theories of lawmaking could contribute to Chinese future legal reform. Theories of communication have positive contributions to this proposed change. After my introduction and analysis of Western theories, I have attempted to escape from pure theoretical discussion about law and legality and tried to provide a practical application of communicative lawmaking in China. Relying on the contributions of Western lawmaking theories, but at the same time realizing the difficulties in their application in Chinese contexts, I believe that Confucianism, a Chinese philosophy of love and law, could contribute to a discourse theory of lawmaking. The core of Confucianism, *Ren* (loving people, humanism), provided a possible theoretical background for a discourse theory. Professor Bankowski's argument for the interplay of law and love, the inside and the outside systems, also initiated a debate for the communicative decision-making and is, thus, employed to solve the difficulty of applying Western theories into Chinese contexts.

The 'appropriate' lawmaking in this book refers to a communicative lawmaking mode, in contrast to the non-communicative mode that is defended by Chinese legalism and contemporary justifications of lawmaking. I attempt to introduce this interactive and cooperative lawmaking structure to balance individual rights and state interests. This structure would go against the grain of the traditional top-down legislation. In this new structure, individuals' voice would be heard and paid attention to, which is a way of achieving *Ren* (humanism).

Acknowledgement

This book is based on my doctoral thesis that was supervised by Professor Zenon Bankowski at the University of Edinburgh. I would like to thank him for carrying the weight of a long-lasting supervision. It was very kind of him to introduce to me Professor Neil MacCormick and Professor Luc J Wintgens, from whom I derived inspiring ideas. With their encouragement, I overcame the difficulties I faced in research. Their research on legislature was a useful resource I got access to through Professor Bankowski. I also express my gratitude to Professor Bankowski who prayed for my mother during difficult times, which means a lot to me and my family.

Professor Bankowski also offered me ideas from his books and papers to structure the whole thesis. The brief introduction on Habermas was also added under his suggestions. He helped me to develop my analysis and criticisms on my chosen Western theories. Understanding my limits of expression, he even wrote down for me the ways to use quotes and to lead and assist readers to understand my thinking. He was a very strict supervisor. Sometimes when I could not understand his criticism, I spent time watching the Big Bang Theory in which Jim Parsons plays the character of Sheldon Cooper, because I thought my supervisor was also much like Sheldon in the series, who was a smart person but could hardly understand less talented persons. I had to exert my utmost efforts to write this thesis. Sometimes I had to struggle to extend my limits, but my supervisor 'kicked' me to go further. With his strict ways, he helped me to grow up, to find my place in the academic world and to form a strong but humble character. I could not imagine how difficult it was for him to bear with a stubborn and emotional student like me until I became a teacher myself, which is when I started to understand why a teacher would be so strict with a student: It is because the teacher thinks the student can do better.

I also thank my Chinese teachers Professor Handong Wu, Professor Zhongxin Fan and Professor Jingliang Chen. My colleagues and friends Dr. Chunxia Gong, Dr. Jian Huang and Dr. Jian Yang have been in contact with me and offered me inspiration and information on comparisons of Chinese history and English legal history. Thanks to the inspiring discussion with them, my comparative study *Chinese legalism and*

Western legalism that was published in *Frontiers of Law in China* (April 2011) became the foundation of Chap. 4 in this thesis. Dr. James Harrison helped me at the start of my Ph.D. project. He offered information on legislation in the UK, especially the Legislative and Regulatory Reform Act 2006. With his help, I began to read the statutory instruments of the UK and trace the history of secondary legislation in the UK. I also thank him for proofreading my first year report, which developed into Chaps. 5 and 6 of this thesis.

My sincere friends Emily, Pierre, Michael and David did English proofreading for the first draft of the dissertation 2 years ago. I especially thank my colleague Ms. Annie Morris who did the proofreading for the last draft of my thesis. It was not an easy task, but they kindly and patiently accomplished the work. I would also like to specially thank those who have continuously encouraged and supported me during my stay in the UK, especially Emily, Hao, Ogla and Yangyang. With their company and help, life here has been much easier for me.

I thank the University of Edinburgh which offered me the Overseas Research Student Award, which lightened the financial burden on my family members, all of whom appreciate that very much. My mother, Defang Tan, my sister, Ling He, my aunt, Hong Tan, and all other family members sacrificed a lot to support me to chase my dream of studying at Edinburgh. Without them, I could not have come this far to see a whole new world.

I thank the Zhongnan University of Economics and Law, which offered and maintained my position during my study at the UK. The Law School of the University also provided me the Fundamental Research Funds for the Central Universities of China (31540910610) to encourage me to continue the research.

This book is supported by The Humanities and Social Science Project of the Chinese Ministry of Education (No. 13YJC820030).

I especially thank editor Ms. Emmie Yang who kindly helped me in publishing this book with Springer.

My husband Hao Chen and my parents-in-law, Jingfang Li and Ming Chen, took care of me after my mother's death in 2009. No words can fully express my gratitude for their love.

I dedicate the work I put into this thesis to my parents, Rusheng He and Defang Tan, who loved me very much and taught me to be strong, independent and open-minded.

23 May 2013 Peng He

Contents

Abbreviations

ADB	Asia Development Bank
BCG	Boston Consulting Group
caf	Conceptions About Freedom
cof	Conceptions of Freedom
CPC	The Communist Part of China
LAP1996	The Law of the People's Republic of China on Administrative Punishments 1996
LLC2000	Legislation Law 2000: The Legislation Law of the People's Republic of China 2000
LRTS2003	The Law of the People's Republic of China on Road Traffic Safety 2003
Measures 1982	The Administrative Measures of Accept and Dismiss Vagrants and Beggars with No Means of Support in Cities 1982
MLSUR	System of Minimum Living Standard Security of the Urban Residents
NPC	National People's Congress of China
PPC	The Paris Peace Conference
Regulation 2001	The Regulation Governing Building Demolition and Resettlement
SCNPC	The Standing Committee of the National People's Congress of China

Chapter 1
Introduction

The theory of communicative democracy was not popular in Chinese debates of lawmaking theories. As I will discuss in this book, the theory of democracy is translated into a representative system, a system that the minority is subordinate to the majority. It is a rule-based system and actors in this system are under an obligation to follow the rules, and they take little participation in making rules. However, as Professor Zenon Bankowski argued in his book, ***'Democracy should be seen as to do with communication and not necessarily with representation'***.[1] Representative lawmaking is not equal to democratic lawmaking unless it makes communications possible. My book is to argue for a communicative lawmaking mode, in which people should be part of the construction of the 'Enterprise of Law'. The traditional non-interactive and top-down lawmaking mode made contributions to the maintenance of the social order in traditional China. It also promoted efficiency in the execution of law. It, however, faces difficulties in the justification of the authority and legitimacy of law, especially 'the law of the society' in contrast to the official law. The traditional Chinese legal system was a closed system that made rule-following the primary obligation of people. It, however, failed to justify the morality of rule-following. In the old system, rule-following was a plain fact of obligation rather than an individual's moral decisions. Lawmaking therefore led to a fact of *passive* acceptance of law. The communicative lawmaking mode in this book aims at transforming this passive acceptance into an active 'exchange' mode. In this dynamic mode, lawmaking and 'the empire of law' should not be a closed but an open system.

Ideas from Professor Bankowski's *Living Lawfully* [8] and *Bringing the Outside In* [9] are employed in this book to support my argument. In his legal theory, the moral autonomy could and should contribute to the construction of a legal system. The idea of living in a morally correct way was what legality should mean. In contrast with legality, legalism was a rigid rule-bound way of living without concern with the meaning of living under the law. Legalism was described as the legalistic

[1] Zenon Bankowski. 2001. Living Lawfully-Love in Law and Law in Love. 221. Dordrecht: Kluwer.

P. He, *Chinese Lawmaking: From Non-communicative to Communicative*, Understanding China, DOI 10.1007/978-3-642-39507-9_1, © Springer-Verlag Berlin Heidelberg 2014

attitude, and normative behavior to be a matter of rule-following. In legalism, law merely was a heteronomous system of rules.[2] It was not only 'an ideology internal to the legal profession as a social whole' or 'the operative ideology of lawyers' and of those who have a 'rule-oriented thinking', but also a background theory of law, which implied a rule-based way of looking at things and a tendency to treat law as just 'there' and separated of non-law.[3] Professor Bankowski described this attitude as 'it is the rules that are important, not how they are arrived at'.[4] '*No matter where the rules come from, the effect of legalism is to make them appear objective and unchangeable.*'[5] He criticized legalism, in which law was a net of rules, or heteronomy fact. In legalism, law was a closed system and in such a system, '*you do not ask people not to break the law, you make it impossible for them to break it*'.[6] It was a system where people take the fact that the law was as an automatic reason for behaviors, and in so doing they behave like automatons or robots. In such a system, law became 'monological': '*it receives nothing except on its own terms and within its own protocols. There is no interactivity and no input from the outside*'.[7] As a contrast, *Living lawfully* was an enterprise through which people live a righteous life. Such conclusions in *Living Lawfully,* although not specifically referring to Chinese legal system, depicted an appropriate image of traditional Chinese legal system that I will criticize in this book.

Three themes in *Living Lawfully* are related to my thesis, firstly, different sorts of system of rules can interact; and secondly, a normative system's construction can depend on interactions; and finally there is law and love. The first theme indicates the possibility of exchange between official rules and other rules. The second theme refers to the practical solutions of building a system better than the system of rules or the 'empire of law'. The third theme which is also the core theme pictures an image of life which is not under the net of rules but refers to a virtuous way of living under the rules. These three themes are inseparably interconnected. Professor Bankowski criticized the trend that legal scholars reduced life to the life under the rules. He disagreed with the legal scholars egocentric way of description and prescription. Their world was a closed system and they looked the world from the 'inside'. In his valedictory lecture he reminded us that ' *(in Law's Empire) Law is everything and it swallows everything back into itself. There is no external*

---

[2] Ibid. 43.

[3] J.N. Shklar. 1986. Legalism, Law, Morals and Political Trials, Cambridge, Mass.: Harvard University Press, vii-viii, ix-x, 2–3, 5, 35. also see Bankowski's introduction of Shklar's legalism in Zenon Bankowski. 2001. Living Lawfully—Love in Law and Law in Love. 44. Dordrecht: Kluwer.

[4] Zenon Bankowski. 2001. Living Lawfully—Love in Law and Law in Love. 48. Dordrecht: Kluwer.

[5] Ibid. 59.

[6] Zenon Bankowski. 2007. Bringing the Outside in: The Ethical Life of legal Institutions. Law and legal Cultures in the 21st Century: Unity and Diversity. Wolters Kluwer Polska. 193–217.

[7] Ibid.

skepticism.'[8] The deficiency of the character (selfishness) and cognition (egocentricity) caused the problem of 'incommensurable discourses', and '*the world breaks down into self absorbed circles, secure and confident in their righteousness*'.[9] To solve the problem, he thus proposed an open and dynamic perspective of the world, where life is re-evaluated by the outside.

A life in law was not necessarily a closed prison of rules because to Bankowski a life in law did not reject a life in love. In *Living Lawfully,* he attempted to rediscover the relation between ethical life and a society under the law. He argued that the ethical life should be seen as not one or the other way of law and love, but interlinking and tension between them.[10] In this way, he pointed out the possibility of 'continually recreating law' by 'being inside and dragging the outside in'.[11] As we saw, the inside here referred to the empire of law, and the outside, love. The conception of 'exchange' was further proposed to connect the inside with the outside. 'Exchange' was also the main line shared by the three themes stated above. 'Exchange' was seen as a sort of 'give and take' process, 'which opens us to creative transformation and our ethical lives and those of our societies become dynamic and can grow'.[12] In this sense, the above three themes were coherent because they were all about the construction of a dynamic system. 'Bringing the outside in', and then people can live lawfully in a dynamic exchange system of love and law.

I discovered that the relationship between law and love in *Living Lawfully* was debated in another way in ancient Chinese schools of philosophy, represented by Chinese legalism and Confucianism. I thus found it interesting to re-interpret ancient Chinese philosophies through a Western perspective. Although in *Living Lawfully* communicative lawmaking was not the theme, it implied that a righteous life under the law should tolerate people's participation in lawmaking. Especially in *Bringing the Outside In*, Bankowski softened the strict boundary of the inside and outside systems of law, which was also helpful for my argument for a communicative lawmaking.

In this book, I will disclose the disadvantage of a closed system by using the Chinese mode as a case study. It is a new research project of Chinese law and could also be seen as a further compliment and concretization of Professor Bankowski's project on legality. I, therefore, inevitably use Bankowski's legal theory as my theoretical base and support. In my thesis, his theory of legality (or living lawfully) inspired me to re-discover the positive value of Confucianism and the meaning of Ren (仁,means humanity; love) in Confucianism.

[8] Zenon Bankowski. 2011. The Long Goodbye: (a) Life in and out of the Law, in Bankowski's Valedictory Lecture. I thanks Professor Bankowski for sending his lecture to me. It lightened my burden of listening comprehension and helped me to understand the lecture better through reading it.

[9] Ibid.

[10] Ibid.

[11] Ibid.

[12] Ibid.

As a new research project of Chinese law, I disclosed that both the traditional and contemporary Chinese lawmaking lacked elements of communication. They were justified by requirements of efficient economic policies and administrative governance. Although lawmaking was for the goal of common prosperity in Chinese official announcements, as will be criticized in this book, it led to the unfortunate result that laws authorized and justified *in-equality* in opportunity among different groups of people. A top-down lawmaking mode was the reality as well as the dominant theoretical justifications of legislation in China. In this traditional mode, lawmaking transformed social problems into making legal rights and duties; the actual problems were not necessarily solved. Such a rule 'transformation', however, as Bankowski argued in *Living Lawfully*, was problematic:

> *[T]he law translated questions of morals and politics into questions of legal validity...the law would translate a social problem into a series of legal problems which did not necessarily get at the actual problem. Thus problems of poverty and bad housing conditions were translated into questions of the rights of tenants. This did not address the question of lack of housing stock and the means to buy or rent it. Problems of crime and vandalism are seen as something to do with lack of enforcement of the law. This disregards the various social conditions that might be said to be important contributing factors.*[13]

As we can see in the quote, in such a 'rule transformation', complex social problems were reduced to relatively simple solutions (legal rights and duties). Simplification promoted efficiency in problem-solving but it sometimes deviated from the truth. This deviation rather the simplification per se need us to pay attention. In other words, when legal arrangements could not solve the social problem, i.e., they deviated the purpose of having them, we should remain vigilant of the problem of the 'rule transformation': the simplification and deviation from the truth. The problem of the 'rule transformation' also existed in China. As I will disclose in this book, in China, the actual problems that lawmaking was supposed to solve were still there; while at the same time, other new problems appeared after the new laws were made in such a non-communicative system. Chinese lawmaking theories claimed the importance of economic reform and efficient administration. Real demands of the public, however, were hardly substantiated by the method and result of the contemporary lawmaking mode. A discourse theory, in my point of view, could contribute to solve the problem of 'the rule transformation' that Bankowski mentioned in his criticism of legalism. It provided a route of how to 'bring the outside in'. In lawmaking a discourse arena would assist the people to express their genuine needs when making new rules, rather than accept what law tells them to do passively. Here I am not making an arbitrary conclusion that a discourse theory *will* directly lead to social justice. If I understand right, a theory is an internally consistent 'art of debate'; the effect it will cause to the reality, however, is difficult to justify during the debate because it needs further tests. China has not used the discourse theory for its lawmaking practice. Representative democracy overacted; deliberative democracy, however, was not absorbed.

[13] Zenon Bankowski. 2001. Living Lawfully—Love in Law and Law in Love. 57. Dordrecht: Kluwer.

Although at present it is hard to test whether this theory is 'better' than the existing ideologies, it offers another perspective and another practical route for China's further legal reform. This theory aims at disclosing the realistic problems as well as the defects of old Chinese legitimation theories. It attempts to provide another solution or 'way of thinking'. It does not belong to the camp of 'total Westernization' but argues for the absorption of the Western elements *on the premise of* respecting the existing Chinese legal system. I agree with Bankowski's solution for social problems: '*We can…learn to interact with the institutions that we find ourselves in and not stand against them, seeking to construct them anew*'.[14] This book is such an attempt to offer different perspectives and solutions *within* the Chinese lawmaking system, rather than to argue for a substitution of a whole new Western congress system.

When the tension between autonomy and heteronomy, love and law, freedom and regulation was softened, another problem of law and lawmaking appeared: It seemed that people could choose when to follow and when to disobey rules. If so, the Rule of Law became problematic because people's behaviours were a kind of 'speculation'. Decision-making became a gambling house for self-interests. The result of unscrupulous lawmaking was not what we were looking forward to. As Bankowski also argued in *Living Lawfully*, '*if we move to saying we will know when to apply the rule by looking at the circumstances of the particular case, then we start to lose connection with the meaning of the law.*'[15] He used the metaphor of the tension between the Antigone and Creon in the Greek tragedy *the Antigone of Sophocles* to describe the dilemma.

The tension between Antigone and Creon in the tragedy was whether Polyneice, the rebel, the enemy of the city, ought to be given burial rituals; whether Antigone, the sister of the rebel, who buried Polyneice in defiance of state ought to be punished; and whether Creon, uncle of Polyneice and Antigone, the new ruler of the city, was entitled to the throne. The contrasting views of Creon and Antigone with regard to laws higher than those of state inform their different conclusions about civil disobedience. Creon demanded obedience to the law above all else, right or wrong. He believed that there was nothing worse than disobedience to authority. Antigone responded with the idea that state law was not absolute, and that it could be broken in civil disobedience in extreme cases, such as honoring the gods, whose rule and authority outweighs Creon's. As Bankowski observed, they were both blind of the other's world: '*They both try to protect themselves in the armour of the law but in doing so they lose the humanness that they are supposed to preserve.*'[16] Bankowski used the play to disclose the fact that in many times people like Antigone and Creon seek to follow their own rigid rule system but refuse to see the reason or values of the 'outside' rules. Antigone and Creon both claimed to be the sole judge of them—

[14] Zenon Bankowski. 2001. Living Lawfully—Love in Law and Law in Love. 84. Dordrecht: Kluwer.

[15] ibid. 139.

[16] Ibid. 32.

[T]hey both read them off from a set of values, a set of rules that are structured there for them; the rules of the city or the rules of the Gods. There is no conflict, there is no tension between law and love—there are just rules. They both live the nomian life. So keen are they to avoid contingency, and the uncertainty and unpredictability of life, that they close it down and make things clear and predictable. They hide and cut out contingency, the things that welfare and love add in.[17]

As we can see from the above quote, the rules of the city were seen as the opposite of the god's rules. Conflicts existed between the two systems of rules and there lacked 'exchange' or 'communicate' between each other. We saw a set of closed systems in the play: Firstly, the systems of rules were closed (therefore they both emphasized the strict submission to their own rules). Secondly, their love (love of law or love of family) were also closed to each other (and they both were blind to the other's plight). And finally, law and love could not 'exchange' in the play. The question Bankowski asked in *Living Lawfully* was more than the morality of disobedience to law, but the possibilities of breaking the boundaries of these systems, and the exchange between law and love.

It reminds me of a classical Chinese play, *Chi Sang Zhen* (a name of a small village) the story of Mian Bao in Song dynasty (960–1279), which appeared to be about the opposition between law and love, between rigidly following official laws and family love. It was quite similar to the play of Antigone and Creon that was discussed in *Living Lawfully*. In Chinese tradition, family love and filial piety were the core value of being a good person, or living rightfully. Family love in China was endowed with transcendent values: a good example was that Chinese people prayed to dead family members as they were their gods who could protect later generations. *Chi Sang Zhen*, or the Case of Mian Bao, was written in this special cultural background.

The main protagonists, Zheng Bao (the other famous name is Bao Gong) and Mian Bao, were uncle and nephew. Zheng Bao was the famous (in many Chinese stories the most) upright judge in Chinese history.[18] Zheng Bao was an orphan and was raised up by his sister-in-law Miaozhen Wu, the mother of Mian Bao. Mian Bao, Miaozhen's son and Zheng Bao's nephew, however, took bribes and broke the law when he was a county magistrate. Zheng Bao as the upright judge sentenced Mian Bao to death, according to the official law.

The play began with the cry of Miaozhen Wu, the mother of Mian Bao, the sister-in-law and 'foster mother' of Zheng Bao. In Miaozhen Wu's perspective Zheng Bao forgot family love and evaded his responsibility to his family. Miaozhen Wu blamed Zheng Bao because he as the judge could give Mian Bao a light sentence rather than death. Zheng Bao claimed that he as the judge should rigidly apply the law. In the climax of the play, Zheng Bao and Miaozhen Wu had an argument of 'whether upbringing was the reason of obedience'. Miaozhen Wu criticized that Zheng Bao

[17] Zenon Bankowski. 2001. Law, Love and Legality. International Journal of the Semiotics of Law 14:199–213.

[18] Judge Bao (Bao Gong) is almost totally unknown in Western literature. But there are a series of novels by Robert Van Gulik, with a fictionalized Judge Dee as its central character, which is very loosely based on the real Judge Bao. Most Chinese have never heard of the character Judge Dee. About Zheng Bao, see http://www.chinapage.com/biography/baogong/baogong.html. Accessed 06 March 6, 2013.

was ungrateful to her kindness. She regretted parenting Zheng Bao. Zheng Bao answered that he was grateful to her love in his persistence of her earnest teachings. He said it was Miaozhen Wu who taught him to be an upright person and not to pervert the law. In the end of the play, Miaozhen Wu realized that Zheng Bao was right and she accepted his judgment. But Miaozhen Wu was so grieved because she had no son to support her in her weakness and illness, and to handle her own funeral affairs.[19] Zheng Bao comforted Miaozhen Wu by saying that he would take all the family responsibilities like her son to support her. Therefore the relation between Zheng Bao and Miaozhen Wu was seen as son and mother, and Zheng Bao and Mian Bao as brothers. Establishing such close relations was very important in China, and in this way Zheng Bao showed final filial obedience to his 'mother' Miaozhen Wu by taking care of her and fulfilling his 'brother's family responsibilities.

This classical Chinese play was popular and handed down to this day because it revealed a conflict of love and law in Chinese culture. From the case of Mian Bao we found that different rules did exist in reality (family rules and legal rules). Although following law or obedience to law was 'right' in ordinary circumstances, we may be blind to recognizing other rules that were also important. Or vice versa, we may be too biased to deny the justice of law when we found it had conflicts with our other values. Many laws were not perfect; imperfect laws needed to be improved by absorbing elements of other rules. The core of the play *Chi Sang Zhen* was to find solutions for the family. Zheng Bao changed his family status and responsibilities to take care of his sister-in-law and nephew, and in this way he obeyed both law and love. This play was about Miaozhen Wu's compromise to the law, through a communication with the representative of the law (Zheng Bao). It was also about Zheng Bao's recognition of the deficiency of the law, after the communication with his family. An exchange between law and love existed in the play, but the expedient solution Zheng Bao offered was still not enough for constructing an open and dynamic legal system.

1.1 Major Arguments and Backgrounds of the Study

The possibility of the exchange between the law and love, between law and other systems of rules, between strict official norms and social customs and traditions, makes a communicative lawmaking possible. But we need to clarify this question first: When is it appropriate (or right) to break laws? Shall we leave it to any individual's own conscience? If we leave this to anyone's conscience, shall we tolerate decisions of the extreme self-interested antisocialists? Or, do we only consider requests from the 'good' people, or (at the least) from the 'ordinary' people? Practically speaking it would be difficult to justify individuals' anti-law requests. We therefore need a standard, or 'rule of recognition' in Hart's *the Concept of Law*, to discover and confirm people's real and just requests.

[19] In Chinese culture, raising children for old age and for the funeral ceremony was extremely important to a person.

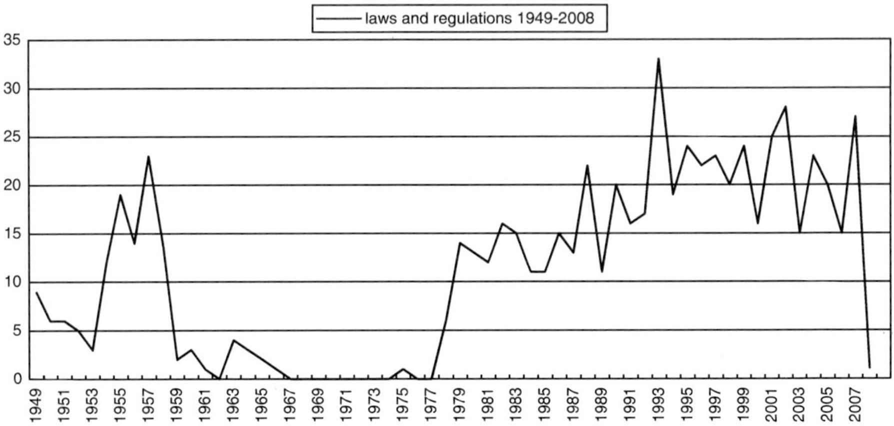

Fig. 1.1 Chinese laws and regulations 1949–2008 (9 6 6 5 3 12 19 14 23 14 2 3 1 0 4 3 2 1 0 0 0 0 0 0 0 0 1 0 0 6 14 13 12 16 15 11 11 15 13 22 11 20 16 17 33 19 24 22 23 20 24 16 25 28 15 23 20 15 27 1)

In this book, communication is the key word to understand such criterion for identifying real requests of the people. The 'appropriate' lawmaking in this book refers to a communicative lawmaking mode, in contrast to non-communicative mode. That means we need to break the boundaries between Creon and Antigone, and Zheng Bao and Miaozhen Wu, to let them communicate and pay attention to others' voices and requests. In contrast to the studies on the legitimacy of non-interactive lawmaking represented by Chinese legalism and contemporary justifications of lawmaking, I argue for an interactive and cooperative lawmaking mode. Before I come to this conclusion, I will structure my arguments through the following sequence:

1. The 'old' Chinese lawmaking mode lacked communication. Compared to the traditional Chinese lawmaking mode, contemporary Chinese lawmaking had absorbed Western ideas of democracy and the Rule of Law. It, however, was still a one dimensional pattern. Both the legitimacy of Chinese lawmaking and the authority of law were defended by a collective-interest-oriented theory. The Theory of Xiaoping Deng was a significant justification for the 30 year economic reform since 1979. Bureaucratic capability and economic efficiency were the most focused values of Chinese lawmaking. A golden age of lawmaking appeared since 1976, right after the age of 'vacuum lawmaking' in the Great Cultural Revolution period (see Fig. 1.1).[20] (Certain ideas are difficult to express in linear

[20] Statistics in Fig. 1.1 from 1949 to 1999 are from Youmin Yu and Xiaoyang Qiao ed. 2000. A Bulletin of 50 Years Law (1949.9–1999.12). Beijing: Chinese Democracy and Rule of Law Publishing House. 1–65. Statistics of 1999 to 2008 are from the Law Committee of the Standing Committee of the National People's Congress ed., Statistics of Lawmaking of the People's Republic of China. 2008. Beijing: Chinese Democracy and Rule of Law Publishing House. 269–270.

textual form. This book will therefore systematically try to translate some core ideas into graphical representations that are better suited to express multidimensional, dynamic interactions between key elements.)

2. Questions of the legitimacy of the legal and economic reform, however, were not debated hitherto in Chinese literatures. Most literatures stood by the official legitimation of lawmaking in Chinese Marxism represented by Deng's theory. This book attempted to discuss the legitimacy of lawmaking from a jurisprudential perspective based on the analysis of realistic problems of Chinese lawmaking and its justifications. I will employ empirical studies to disclose the image of the top-down and irreversible mode. In the old mode, common people's livelihoods, individual rights and the degree of democracy influenced or shaped by lawmaking were not satisfying. I believe that although the reform achievements worth compliments, the legitimation thesis it based on, however, needs further discussions. Chapter 2 is an empirical analysis of the contemporary lawmaking. It aims to disclose the reality and problem of non-communicative lawmaking mode.
3. I discover that the problem of Chinese lawmaking existed in the imperfection of subjective legitimacy, i.e., whether the *de facto* authority is sufficient to justify lawmaking. I discover that there is an irreconcilable conflict between the means and ends of Chinese lawmaking. The ultimate purpose of Chinese socialistic lawmaking is the 'common prosperity'; the approach, however, narrowed down the meaning of democracy.
4. In Chap. 4, I will continue the discussion of Chinese justifications of lawmaking and focus on Chinese legalism. The traditional Chinese lawmaking, which was based on Confucianism and Chinese legalism, was a typical top-down and irreversible mode. In this mode, the control of the ruler and submission of the ruled were the core lawmaking purpose and the function of law. The crisis of faith of the Rule of Law also reflected the imperfect legitimacy of law and lawmaking in China. Formalism and instrumentalism imbedded in Chinese legalism and lawmaking should be responsible for the crisis of legitimacy. Chinese legalism also exposed an ideology of solving all kinds of social problems through formal laws without referring to moral norms.[21] Law in those theories was described as the plain fact of social control and obligations. Governance was interpreted as Rule by Law rather than as a contract for automatic self-governance. The Chinese lawmaking mode could therefore be fit in with a typical 'repressive law' mode that introduced in Nonet and Selznick (1978).[22]
5. In Chap. 5, I will go to Western jurisprudence for possible solutions for Chinese lawmaking problems. Western legal positivism was similar to Chinese legalism.

[21] Fuguo Wang and Qixiang Sun. 2003. On the Deficiencies and Contributing Factors of the Current 'Pan-Legalism' Trend of Thought. Journal of Fujian Education Institute 4:79–81. see also Yanying Zhu and Xiaobo Deng. 2003. An Analysis of the Influence of Modern Pan-lawism. Journal of Yuxi Teachers College 19:48–51.

[22] About repressive law, see the introduction in Zenon Bankowski. 2001. Living Lawfully—Love in Law and Law in Love. 61–62. Dordrecht: Kluwer. Nonet P. and Selznick P. 1978. Law and Society in Transition: Towards Responsive Law. NewYork: Harper and Row.

In Chinese legalism, law was amoral official decisions and depended on the leadership's policies. In Western legal positivism, law was the result of the authorities' decision and the existence of law and legislature already justified its legality. The normative system of law or the legitimacy of law was self-sufficient; or depended on the rule of recognition or the existence of a particular political culture. Moral justifications were also not necessary in legal positivism. Legal positivism, however, led to the crisis of faith in law. Benthamnian utilitarianism influenced Chinese lawmaking and caused the problem of justification of law. Whether laws were 'appropriate' was reduced to a calculation of the collective good. People had an obligation to accept and follow law, and it caused that the legitimacy of law was unrelated to their rational choices. All were about the obedience to law. The legitimacy of lawmaking was reduced to the result that lawmaking could achieve.

6. Different from legitimation theses in authoritarian theories, libertarian theories offered another route for justification. Hayekian dual conception of law was provided to interpret the crisis of trust in law. As a contrast to the recognition of the official law, the subjectivity of the common people was re-discovered. Spontaneous rules or customary law were defined as the real law in contrast with legislation. Law was the derivative of human interactions, rather than a plain fact of control and submission. Jeremy Waldron, another scholar who emphasized the process of lawmaking, argued that disagreements constructed the dignity of legislature. In their perspectives, law should not interfere actively with agencies' self-decision-making progress. Interactional sociology and communicative reason also re-defined the social function of lawmaking: lawmaking should not be the instrument of control but an arena for discourse. The liberal contractualist theory therefore could support a communicative lawmaking mode. However, as I will discuss in Chap. 5, theories of Hayek and Waldron had their limits in Chinese contexts. Hayek did not discuss the possibility of communications between the official and the customary law; while Waldron avoided discussing the importance of agreements. Their theories thus could not be sufficient for a communicative theory of lawmaking for China.
7. Another liberal contractualist theory represented by Luc J. Wintgens was different from Hayek and Waldron in his deliberation on an alternative social contract theory. The subjectivity of lawmakers was pre-supposed differently in libertarian theories. Following the Kantian metaphysical hypothesis, a moral subject was seen as a conceptual individual with unlimited free will. Legisprudence developed by Wintgens confirmed the fact of external limitations of a subject, but based justifications on arguing for conceptual individuals' unlimited freedom. Legisprudence was therefore critical in describing reality while at the same time metaphysical in a construction of the legitimation chain of lawmaking. Realistic suggestions for lawmaking were interwoven with the metaphysical discussion of universal truth. Thus legisprudence was insufficient in solving problems in Chinese contexts, since the reality and the hypothesis in Chinese lawmaking were the opposite of those in legisprudence. I find it difficult to use the philosophical freedom as the *principum* of Chinese law-

making because in a collective morality context like China, there did not exist an isolated 'conception of freedom'. I therefore choose another route for Chinese lawmaking: a discourse thesis. In this route of argument the subject was concrete and restricted.

8. To argue for a discourse thesis of lawmaking, i.e., to defend that the process of lawmaking should include more elements of communication and negotiation, we would inevitably be involved into a differentiation between 'autonomous law' (where law is a differentiated institution capable of taming repression and protecting its own integrity) and 'responsive law' (where law facilitates the response to social needs and purposes)(both oppose to 'repressive law', where law is a servant of repressive power).[23] The question would be rephrased like this: whether I would agree with the 'liberating lawmaking from politics' as implied in Hayek's argument for the free market; or would I agree with the 'interactional sociology' in Fuller's the Morality of Law.[24] As discussed in Bankowski's book, in autonomous law, the independence of the judiciary needed a sharp line between legislative and judicial systems; 'procedure' was the heart of law.[25] I did intend to argue for procedural justice in my previous dissertation; however, I found it difficult in practice. The Chinese legal system did not involve a constitutional court or a judicial review procedure and the court system was not independent as in the Western legal system. Therefore 'pure procedural justice' was difficult to justify in the Chinese legal system.

Another difficulty existed in conflicts between the requirement of substantive justice and the pursuit of procedural justice. The autonomous law could demand lawyers' fidelity to the law. But it could not justify its requirement of people's unconditional obedience to the law. Different from autonomous law, responsive law 'tries to get a kind of openness in institutions with its integrity by looking to social interests'.[26] However, since in China law was from a non-interactive and strict top-down lawmaking mode, rather than stemming from common people's interactions, the idea of 'responsive law' was not 'realistic'. We should then return to the starting point of 'repressive law'. 'Repressive law' and 'responsive law' had essential differences. From the perspective of a 'law-addressee', repressive law meant primary heteronomy while responsive law embraced certain degrees of autonomy.

Fuller's suggestion of law as being interactive and communicative between citizens and between law receivers and law-givers therefore could contribute to the Chinese legal reform because old Chinese lawmaking mode emphasized too

[23] About the autonomous law, responsive law and repressive law, see Nonet and Zelznick. 1978. quoted from Zenon Bankowski. 2001. Living Lawfully—Love in Law and Law in Love. 61–62. Dordrecht: Kluwer.

[24] See 'interactional sociology' from Fuller LL. 1969. The Morality of Law. Princeton: Yale University.195.

[25] Zenon Bankowski. 2001. Living Lawfully—Love in Law and Law in Love. 63. Dordrecht: Kluwer.

[26] Ibid. 65.

much on heteronomy, and was a lack of autonomy. If we agreed that law needs both of heteronomous and autonomous elements, we would agree to introduce more of autonomous elements into the Chinese mode. In *Morality of Law,* Fuller described law as interactive and communicative in contrast to law in positivism. In the communicative mode, the law-giver interacted with the law-receiver and therefore they no longer constituted an irreversible giver-taker relationship. They both contributed to the enterprise of 'putting ourselves under the governance of rules'. As Bankowski emphasized, the concept 'enterprise' was important since '*it has the connotations of a common journey, of something that we all take part in, more than just the technical rational framework for all of us to achieve our individual goods but becomes part of our common good as well.*'[27] In this sense, Fuller transformed an abstract and outside law system into a concrete and inside way of living, or what Bankowski specified, *living lawfully*. Chinese legal reform could benefit from such a specification of law and its meaning because the interactive theory would introduce a way to combine autonomy with heteronomy, and the inside morality with the outside rule.

Arguing for a communicative lawmaking mode, we should not ignore the communicative reason or communicative rationality deliberated by Habermas.[28] Communicative reason was employed in this book to interpret the possibility of a shift from a subject-object lawmaking mode to an inter-subjective mode. Lawmaking in the subject-object mode was a purposive action, which was supported by instrumental reason. In an inter-subjective mode, however, lawmaking becomes a purposive and interactive action, which transfers an instrumental reason to communicative reason. In Habermas' discourse theory, what the idea of communicative ethics entails is something more than a mere respect for the autonomy of will formation and a public check on the imbalances of power. Communication is an approach to guarantee participation. In this book, Habermas's communicative reason is positive to the Chinese lawmaking practice because it offers a possibility of applying democratic processes to the codification of laws without excluding morality from law arbitrarily.

The principle of discourse implies that the validity of a decision is related to a 'rational consensus'. And norms are valid only if those affected can agree to them as participants in a rational consensus (Habermas 1998, p. 138). The legitimacy of law is accordingly based on a communicative mechanism. In this book, the discourse principle is employed to rectify the inequality caused in the old Chinese top-down and non-interactive mode. I will discuss how and why the old lawmaking mode generated and tolerated inequality. I will argue that communicative interactivity can contribute to social justice and should be introduced to Chinese new lawmaking mode.

---

[27] Zenon Bankowski. 2007. Bringing the Outside in: The Ethical Life of legal Institutions. Law and legal Cultures in the 21st Century: Unity and Diversity. Wolters Kluwer Polska. 193–217.

[28] JÜrgen Habermas. 1984. The Theory of Communicative Action. Trans. Thomas McCathy. Boston: Beacon Press. see also Michel Rosenfeld and Andrew Arato ed. 1998. Habermas on Law and Democracy: Critical Exchanges. Berkeley: University of California Press. JÜrgen Habermas. 1998. On the Pragmatics of Communication. MIT Press.

1.2 Chinese Contemporary Research on Lawmaking

Chinese literatures on lawmaking seldom discussed the legitimacy of legislature, or the procedural justice of the legislative progress. Plenty books referred to the Studies of Legislation (Li Fa Xue). They were, however, descriptive works about the legislative sources and techniques.[29] Before 1990s, books about comparative legislative studies, socialistic lawmaking, and studies on legislative power and procedures discussed Chinese lawmaking from different perspectives.[30] A synthetic monograph on lawmaking appeared later as a branch of knowledge called Li Fa Xue.[31] Since then, the focus on socialistic lawmaking shifted to the discussion of the basic concepts of lawmaking.[32] A historic review of the development of lawmaking was also a part of Li Fa Xue.[33] Li Fa Xue included a comparative study of legislatures as well.[34] Discussion on the legislative values and problems of globalization and lawmaking was a recent trend of Li Fa Xue.[35] Other works on Chinese lawmaking were either specializing in comments on the legislative law [232], or discussing the creation of specific branches of law [163].[36] Chinese texts books of lawmaking were similar in contents and structures and all of them were descriptive in the principles, institutions and procedures.[37] None of these books focused on a general jurisprudential argument of the legitimacy of lawmaking.

---

[29] Representative works are: Hehai Liu and Yufu Li ed. 2001. Li Fa Xue (A Study of Lawmaking). Beijing,: Zhongguo Jiancha Publishing House. See also Anliang Gu. 1993. Li Fa Xue. Beijing: Law Press. See also Keyu Qiao and Xinyao Wu. 1993. Li Fa Xue. Beijing: China University of Political Science and Law Press. And Jianfei Li. 1992. Li Fa Xue. Chongqing: Chongqing publishing house.

[30] Wangsheng Zhou. 1988. A Study of Chinese Lawmaking. Beijing: Beijing University Press.12.

[31] Wangsheng Zhou. 1988. To Set Up A Study on Chinese Socialistic Lawmaking. Law Review 6:21–26.

[32] Wangsheng Zhou. 1994. On Legislation. Beijing: Beijing University Press. see also Zhou Wangsheng. 1994. (We) Should Pay Attention to the Basic Concepts of Lawmaking. Law Review 3:1–7.

[33] Wangsheng Zhou. 2000. 50 Years Lawmaking of China 1949–1999. Legislation Review of China 1:1–22.

[34] Lin Li. 1991. A Comparative Study on Legislatures. Beijing: People Daily Press.

[35] Lin Li. 2005. The theory and System of Legislation. (Lifa Lilun Yu Zhidu). chapters 1 and 9. Beijing: China Legal Publishing House.

[36] Xin Liu. 2008. Legislative Law. Beijing: Beijing University Press. See also Wan Qigang. 2006. Lifa Linian Yu Shijian. chapters 17 and 18. Beijing: Beijing University Press.

[37] Liyu Zhu and Shuguang Zhang. 2001. A Study of Lawmaking (Li Fa Xue). Beijing: China Renmin University Press. See also Wangsheng Zhou. 2006. Li Fa Xue. Beijing: Law Press. See also Huang Wenyi. 2008. Li Fa Xue. Beijing: High Education Press. And Zhang Yonghe. 2009. Li Fa Xue. Beijing: Law Press.

Related articles were either about specific branches of laws or local lawmaking practices.[38] Few articles discussed the topic of legitimate lawmaking.[39] The concept of legitimacy was analyzed by referring to Western theories exclusively.[40] Or traditional Chinese orthodoxy of legislation was analyzed by referring to Confucianism exclusively.[41] The relationship between government control and the free market as a justification for economic lawmaking was discussed.[42] Contemporary Chinese law's legitimation, however, was not debated.

Even on the websites of three major domestic research institutions of legislation, we had limited resources of lawmaking.[43] On the website of the Peiking Legislation Centre, courses of lawmaking and fruits of research were 'in construction'; abstracts of the articles of the four volumes of Legislation Review of China were reduced to titles and subtitles. On the website of the Theoretic Legal Study of Jilin University, the names of the researchers, topics they were doing and the fruits of their research were vacant. And there was only one page of introduction of the subject on the Jilin website. The best website of the three research centers was literally the Xiamen University research centre, on which the research fruits, including translations of Western researchers' works, were published. However, six of the seven researches did not specialize in lawmaking and the 16 published articles were not sufficient to cover the wide range of the subject.

The above facts showed that contemporary articles, monographs, text books and research centers on Chinese lawmaking did not focus on theoretical debates on the legitimacy of lawmaking, including topics about people's recognition of law, democracy and representativeness. The moral ground for justification of the state

---

[38] See articles about the creation of branches of law include Xiaoming Dong. 2009. A Study on Lawmaking of Civil Public Welfare Lawsuit. MA thesis of Qingdao University. Yong Pi. 2009. On Cyber-Crime Legislation in China. Hebei Law Science 27:49–57. Guoming Du. 2008. Legislative Studies of Quality and Safety of Agricultural Products. Hebei Law Science 26:107–111. Wanyi Zhao, Dawu Hu. 2008. A Study of Legislation of Protection of Credit Right. Modern Law Science 30:165–171. Min Niu, Jie Jiang. 2008. The Legislative Study on the Law on Protecting Against Weather Disasters. Future and Development 29:45–47. Articles about local lawmaking practices see: Guanghui Wang. 1996. the Basic Principles of Local Lawmaking. Studies in Law and Business 6:81–85. Zhong Yu. 2002. Concept and Idea of City Lawmaking. Journal of Sichuan University (Humanities and Social Science) 1:124–129. Zhijian Liu. 2001. A Study of Creative Local Lawmaking, People's Congress Studying 8: 18–21.

[39] Only three articles are about the legitimacy of lawmaking in my search of articles in journals, MA and PhD resources from 1979 to 2010 in China National Knowledge Internet. Accessed 02 Feb 2012.

[40] Gang Cao. 2002. The Legitimacy of Legislation and its Rationalization. Journal of Remin University of China 4:85–90.

[41] Gang Cao. 2003. Royal Legislation and its Moral Limits, A Look at the Orthodoxy of Legislation in History. Ethics Research 2: 58–62.

[42] Jianshun Yang. 2008. On the Legitimacy of Legislation of Economic Regulations. Jurist Review 5: 48–59.

[43] The three research centers websites are: http://w3.pku.edu.cn/academic/legislation/index_Chinese.htm; http://www.legal-theory.org/?mod=info&act=view&id=269, and http://amoylegis.xmu.edu.cn/. Accessed 02 Feb 2012.

authority was largely neglected in the academic discourse. This book aims at filling this gap in the research of Chinese lawmaking. It is a critical but also constructive study aiming at providing a realistic and practical route for common Chinese people's participation in lawmaking. Conflicts between different social classes increased and became acute in recent years. This project therefore has a positive meaning to Chinese future legislative reform.

This book is based on an analysis of historical literatures as well as recent statistics, so that it differs from traditional jurisprudence that exclusively focuses on theoretic arguments. The method of logical deductions and analysis of empirical cases would be employed to support my arguments. Contemporary Chinese lawmaking had realistic problems in legitimation of the authority, procedure and purpose. In both of domestic and international research, Chinese theories were rarely studied in a topic of legitimation. Descriptions of Chinese historical and contemporary lawmaking reality and problems as well as interpretations of the ancient Chinese literatures of lawmaking were also rare in English literatures. This book thus provides a literature bridge for both the Western and domestic scholars to understand and study Chinese lawmaking.

1.3 Structure of the Book

My argument for interactive and cooperative Chinese lawmaking is constructed in eight chapters, including the introductive first chapter, six core chapters and the last chapter of the conclusion. The second chapter aims to analyze the major characteristics and problems of the contemporary Chinese lawmaking. In that chapter, the significance of economic and administrative lawmaking will be analyzed. Macro-economic policies, the efficient lawmaking purpose and bureaucratic lawmaking characteristics will be criticized with the recognition of the requirements of improving common people's livelihoods, democratic participation and representation as well as individual rights. The third chapter aims to interpret the background legitimation theses of contemporary lawmaking as well as to offer a critical discussion of the design and purpose of those theses. It will interpret the route from Confucianism to Chinese Marxism, to picture the characteristic features of Chinese legitimation theses. Four justifications of the contemporary dominant theory of legitimation will be expanded and criticized. In Chap. 4, Chinese legalism as a background ideology of Chinese lawmaking will be discussed. I will also disclose the similarities and differences between Chinese legalism and Western legalism in that chapter. Chapters 5 and 6 provide comments and critiques on Western lawmaking theories represented by utilitarianism (Bentham), liberalism (Hayek), structuralism (Waldron) and soft legalism (Wintgens). Bentham's theory was widely accepted in China since the modern legislative reform started in late 1900s and it had deeply influenced Chinese legitimation of lawmaking since then. The contemporary Chinese lawmaking mode and its purpose also reflected the principle of utility, though in the perspective of Chinese socialism. As a contrast, Hayek's theory was a recent popular topic in China which had increased

Chinese scholars' interests in a debate of liberalistic legislation. Chinese academies were not familiar with Waldron's and Wintgens' jurisprudence of lawmaking. A critique on legisprudence will be especially expanded in Chap. 6 because the discussion of the conceptual freedom, equality, social contract, principles of justifications and the legitimation chain were core to Western legitimation of lawmaking, but alien in Chinese legitimation. A Chinese translation on legisprudence[44] regretfully did not lead to a thorough debate of the argumentations in China. Relying on the analysis of their works on lawmaking, and my criticisms of Chinese realities and difficulties that discussed in previous chapters, in the final two chapters I conclude that a communicative lawmaking mode can transform the 'closed' Chinese legal system to a more 'open' system. Communicative lawmaking is believed to make a positive contribution to Chinese legal reform.

In short, I argue for a communicative structure for Chinese lawmaking because that would make the 'closed' legal system more 'open' to the people, and thereby contribute to the legitimacy of law by ensuring that some laws are created and helped by people, rather than by the authority exclusively. Lawmaking should be an enterprise that absorbs people's input. This would go against the grain of the top-down legislation that is deeply embedded in Chinese legal theories and practices. I analyze and criticize Chinese theories and realities to initiate a new theoretical research on legislation in China. Western theories are employed to provide an 'outside' perspective of Chinese lawmaking mode. After my analysis of Chinese realities and theories, and through a study of contemporary Western jurisprudence on legislation, I structure my argument through an analysis-criticism-construction sequence. My thesis is a new theoretical study of Chinese lawmaking. It also contributes to a deepened study and concretization of the theory of a righteous life under the law. Through the empirical and theoretical study of the Chinese lawmaking, this book attempts to avoid the mistake of jumping directly from legislation to legality. It uses the theory of legality as the background and base of argument rather than reducing a study of legislation to legality, and is thus different from other theories on lawmaking.

[44] Luc J. Wintgens. 2008. Legisprudence as a New Theory of Legislation. Trans. Baomin Wang. Journal of Comparative Law 4: 144–160.

Chapter 2
Chinese Contemporary Lawmaking: Reality and Problems

—The English word 'cosmos' came from Greek 'kosmos', which originally means 'order', in contrast with 'chaos'. Cosmos was not only the result of stepping off chaos, but the process of transforming chaos to order. It was a verb also: kosmos means the action of lightening the darkness. Without light and order, cosmos did not exist.

Wendao Liang, ātma-grāha

2.1 Introduction

I aim to introduce the reality and problems of contemporary Chinese lawmaking in this chapter. This chapter is the empirical background and starting point of my theory. It initiates my research interests on an argument for a communicative lawmaking mode. I will analyze why the current mode is not a communicative mode. I believe the 'old' mode is problematic in softening the tension between the 'inside' and 'outside' of the legislature. In this chapter, I will disclose realistic and theoretical problems that exist in Chinese lawmaking.

At the beginning of this task, I would like to introduce Chinese legal system as the background information. Contemporary Chinese legal system is constituted by the following major 'branches of law': the constitutional law, administrative law, civil and commercial law, economic law, criminal law, labor law, social security law, law for protection of natural resources and environment, and the laws of civil,criminal and administrative procedures. Until March 2010, Chinese legal system was constituted by 231 laws, more than 690 administrative regulations, and more than 8,800 local decrees.[1] Apart from that, hundreds of administrative local

[1] Bangguo Wu's 'Report on the Work of the Government about Administrative Regulations and Local Decrees' made at the third session of the eleventh NPC, 09 March 2010. http://news.xinhuanet.com/politics/2010-03/09/content_13133496.htm; see also http://www.chinadaily.com.cn/zgzx/2009npc/2009-03/09/content_7556715.htm. Accessed 02 Feb 2012.

P. He, *Chinese Lawmaking: From Non-communicative to Communicative*, Understanding China, DOI 10.1007/978-3-642-39507-9_2, © Springer-Verlag Berlin Heidelberg 2014

	constitutional		civil and commercial		administrative		economic		others		total
	no.	%	no.	%	no.	%	no.	%	no.	%	
laws	39	16.88	33	14.29	80	34.63	54	23.38	25	10.82	231
regulations	13	1.88	47	6.81	251	36.38	308	44.64	71	10.29	690
total	52	5.65	80	8.69	331	35.94	362	39.31	96	10.42	921

Fig. 2.1 Basic laws of China until March 2010

Fig. 2.2 Components of basic laws and regulations of China until March 2010

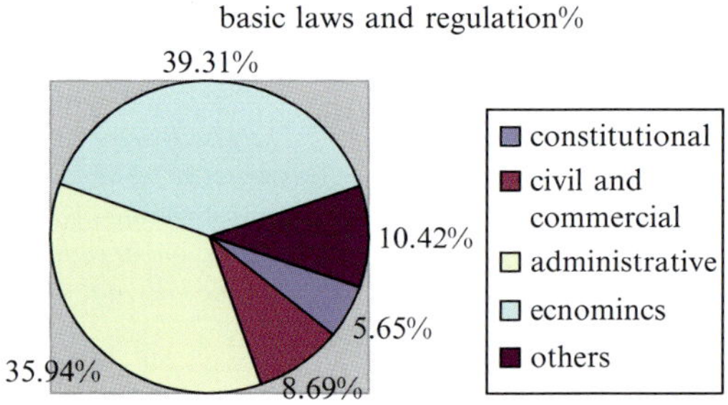

rules, autonomous decrees, special decrees and the international treaties that China has acceded to were also sources of law. Among 231 basic Chinese laws, one third were administrative laws and more than one fifth were economic laws (see Fig. 2.1). Administrative and economic laws were more than 50 % of the total laws; with regulations together were already more than 75 % of the total (see Fig. 2.2).[2] Contemporary Chinese lawmaking therefore gave an obvious priority to administrative and economic laws. This characteristic of contemporary Chinese lawmaking was caused by the economic reform since 1979. As I will discuss later, it led to social and economic inequality.

2.2 Chinese Contemporary Lawmaking

Since 1949, China had 62 years of history of legislation. Economic policy was not obviously prior to other goals in the first 30 years (1949–1979). Economic laws were not acknowledged by Chinese scholars until the economic and legal reform started

[2] Numbers of laws and regulations, see the Legislative Affairs Work Committee of SCNPC ed. 2008. Statistics of Legislation of People's Republic of China. 490–570. Beijing: Chinese Democracy and Rule of Law Publishing House.

from 1979.[3] Legislations for economic laws appeared since then.[4] Economic laws were not officially recognized important until the Chinese economic reform under Xiaoping Deng's leadership.[5] From 1949 to 1979, socialistic planning economy was the major policy of China. During Deng's decades, Western market economy was firstly officially acknowledged. Deng confirmed the meaning of market forces:

> *Planning and market forces are not the essential difference between socialism and capitalism. A planned economy is not the definition of socialism, because there is planning under capitalism; the market economy happens under socialism too. Planning and market forces are both ways of controlling economic activity.*[6]

Chinese lawmaking shifted from planning economy to market economics in Deng's reform. The economic reform caused an increase of economic laws directly. The amount of economic laws was continuously increasing. It reached to the peak in the period 1993–1997 (see Fig. 2.3). Average speedy rates of the increase for the period were 49 %.[7]

Administrative rules were the major body of Chinese legal system. The dominant role of administrative laws in Chinese legal system was rooted in the tradition. One typical example of ancient Chinese codes was the Tang Dynasty Code, *Tang Lu,* or *Tang Lu Shu Yi,*[8] or *Yong Hui Lu Shu*, promulgated in A.D. 563, which summarized the achievements of previous codes derived from the anterior dynasties.[9] Tang Code was based on public law primarily including administrative law, criminal law and

---

[3] Wenhua Liu. 1999. Economic Laws Are the Result of the Thought of Economic Reform. Juridical Science Journal 2:4–5.

[4] Handong Wu ed. 2008. General Theories of Law. 384. Beijing: Beijing University Press.

[5] Deng Xiaoping, the leader of the CPC after Mao's age, served as the paramount leader of China from 1978 to the early 1990s. Deng was named as 'the great designer' or 'the general designer' of the economic and legal reform, see Wang Xiangping, Why did the International News Media named Deng Xiaoping the general designer of China, CCP's news, http://news.xinhuanet.com/politics/2009-02/19/content_10847245.htm. Accessed 02 Feb 2012.

[6] See Deng's talks in http://cpc.people.com.cn/GB/69112/69113/69116/5396465.html. Accessed 02 Feb 2012. From 15th February to 22nd March 1991, Shanghai Liberation Daily published three editorials of Deng's speech in Shanghai, and discussed Deng's understanding of the essential differences between capitalism and socialism. Deng's future speech in January and February of 1991 was published in Shenzhen Special Zone Daily and caused nationwide discussion on the economic reform.

[7] Statistics of economic laws were analyzed based on Li Lin's research, 60 Years Legislation of the New China, from http://www.iolaw.org.cn/showArticle.asp?id=2563. Accessed 02 Feb 2012.

[8] *Tang Lu Shu Yi* is combined with the law (*Tang Lu*, the law of the Tang Dynasty) and the legal interpretations (*Shu* is the legal interpretations of the law, *Yi* is the explanations of *Shu*). The Tang Dynasty Code had 12 sections (*Pian*), 30 tomes and 502 items. Sections include: 'the general rules' (*Ming Li*, 57 items); the safety of the empire (*Wei Jin*, 33 items); the setup of national institutions and offices (*Zhi Zhi*, 59 items); residence and marriages (*Hu Hun*, 46 items); livestock stalls and storage of weaponry (*Jiu Ku*, 28 items); the master of the army and the construction of public works (*Shan Xing*, 24 items); theft and robbery (*Ze Dao*, 53 items); unlawful fights and litigant proceedings (*Dou Song*, 60 items); fraud and forgery (*Zha Wei*, 27 items); 'other items' (*Za Lv*, 62 items); the arrest of escaped criminals or soldiers (*Bu Wang*, 18 items); and the rules of trial and prison management (*Duan Yu*, 34 items).

[9] Shude Cheng. 1927. Laws of Nine Dynasties. 3. Beijing: Zhonghua Book Company.

Fig. 2.3 Chinese economic laws made from 1979 to 2010

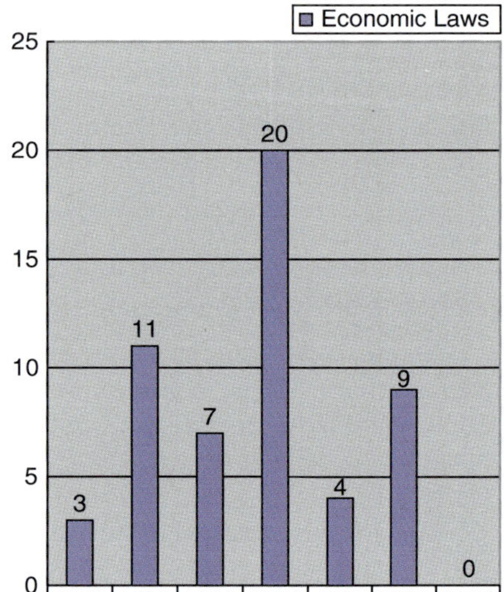

	1978 - 1982	1983 - 1987	1988 - 1992	1993 - 1997	1998 - 2002	2003 - 2007	2008 - 2012
Economic Laws	3	11	7	20	4	9	0

procedural law.[10] In addition, Tang Dynasty had series of mature administrative law codes, i.e., *Tang Liu Dian* (six codes of administrative law).[11] Laws in Tang Dynasty were also the paradigm of Chinese traditional laws. They influenced the lawmaking characteristics of the subsequent empires greatly.[12] From the Tang Dynasty to the Ch'ing dynasty (from the first to the last empire of 'old' China), the form and content of subsequent codes did not alter much. The significant role of administrative law was a representative characteristic of Chinese legal system.

However, administrative law's dominant role disappeared at the beginning of the 'new' China that started from 1949. The power of the administration was relatively weak during 1900–1949 because of the chaos caused by wars and the unstable governments. Administrative laws were one sixth of the legal system of the Republic of China during 1900–1949.[13] After 1949, administrative laws and regulations increased

[10] In contrast, the famous coetaneous code, Corpus Juris Civilis (529–534), was based primarily on private law.

[11] Six Codes of Tang Dynasty (Tang Liu Dian). 1983. Beijing: Zhonghua Book Company.

[12] Shude Cheng. 1927. Laws of Nine Dynasties. 3. Beijing: Zhonghua Book Company.

[13] In this period, new laws were codified in a short period of time to adjust the urgent need to learn from the west and be strong: the Regius Constitutional Precis 1908 (the first constitutional law of China), the 19 Constitutional Credendum 1911, the Existing Criminal Law of the Qing Dynasty 1910 (it is actually a re-edition of the Code of the Qing Dynasty), the New Criminal Law of the Qing Dynasty 1911 (the first modern criminal law of China), the Draft of the Civil Law of the Qing Dynasty 1911 (using the German Civil Law as reference), the Draft of the Commercial Law 1908, the Law of the Framework of *Da Li Yuan* (the supreme court) 1906, and the Law of the Framework

for a short period, and then the amount dropped drastically because of the unstable political situation during 1966–1976, in the Great Cultural Revolution movement. In 1958, the amount of promulgated administrative laws and regulations was 147, and then most of them were abolished and dropped to 50 in 1960, 8 in 1966, 1 in 1975, 0 from 1966 to 1974, and 0 in 1976.[14]

After the Great Cultural Revolution period, from 1978 the amount of administrative laws and regulations had been continuously rising and reached to 921 in 2010. The economic reform re-stressed effective administrative power in law. From Chinese modern history we can see that political stability and economic development contributed to the strengthening of administrative power. The free market economy was acknowledged and accepted in Chinese law gradually. Macro-policies and administrative laws in turn promoted the development of the economy. From the 5th to the 8th National People's Congresses, after 19 years economic reform, administrative regulations made by the State Council were over 750; local decrees made by local people's congresses exceeded 5,300; rules made by committees and ministries were more than 8,000; and local government regulations exceeded 17,000.[15] Administrative and economic laws were obviously increased.

Some problems appeared, however: Over speed lawmaking caused legislative inflation and imprudent legislation; bureaucratic lawmaking ignored common people's participation in the lawmaking procedure; the legitimacy of administrative legislation had conflicts with democracy. In the 8th National People's Congress (*hereinafter* NPC), on 28 February 1995, seven laws were passed in 1 day. During that year, NPC and the Standing Committee of the NPC's (*hereinafter* SCNPC) average rate for passing a law was 13-day; the State Council made a regulation in 6 days.[16] Large amounts of laws were made during the short period of time, which caused a limitation for a relatively prudent deliberation. Legislative inflation although did not necessarily mean low quality of law, the over speed lawmaking caused that some laws, regulations, decrees and rules were in conflicts with each

---

of the Court 1910 appeared successively. After the Qing Empire being rapidly overthrown by revolutionists because of the desperate diplomatic political situation of the time, another new legal system was instituted by the Nanjin Government in 1927, named as a six-law-system, which contained six major branches of law: constitutional law, criminal law, civil law, commercial law, civil procedure law, and the criminal procedure law. In less than 30 years, in 1949, the new government of the whole country announced the abolishment of the six codes made by the Nanjin Government.

[14] Jun Feng. 2003. A Brief Summary of The Three Stages of Development of the Administrative Laws in China. selected from Yong Xia, Guangxing Zhang, Jun Feng, Mingyuan Wang and Yuzhang Wu, etc. The Report on the Development of Chinese Rule of Law. 2005. The General Report.10. Social Science Academic Press.

[15] Jun Yu. 1999. The Introduction of the Cost-benefit Ratio of Law. Journal of Gansu Social Science 5:62–72. see also Chuntian Jiang. 2007. A Study on Contemporary Chinese Social Transformation and Legislative Transformation. 16. MA thesis of East China University of Political Science and Law.

[16] Bin Wang. 1995. The Market Economic Legal System is Becoming Complete. Legal Daily, October 19.

other.[17] The courts were also in a dilemma situation applying conflicting laws. Since conflicting laws should not be applied, part of those laws became invalid. It was a waste of the legislative resources. It also weakened the authority and credibility of law. Executive institutions faced difficulties too. Large amounts of new laws were made in a short period and left them with limited time to prepare for changes. Their understanding of the law could not keep up with the speed of lawmaking, not to speak to support them to execute the law accurately. Conflicts also existed between macro-economic policy and common people's livelihoods; between efficient lawmaking and democratic representation system; and between bureaucratic lawmaking and individual rights.

2.3 Marcor-Economic Policy

'Keep economic construction as the central task' was written in *The Legislation Law of the People's Republic of China 2000* (*hereinafter the LLC2000*). This rule implied that legislative work should serve the aim of economic development. In Chinese Legislation Law, lawmaking was a safeguard measure for macro-economic reform. Chinese lawmaking emphasized on the state rather than on individuals. The interest of the whole country was prior to that of the individual. Collective interests substituted individuals' diverse interests. It thus shaped a bureaucratic and utilitarian lawmaking. It became a problem to balance the macro-economic policy and specific individual rights.

Absolute equality, i.e., egalitarianism was once the dominating ideology of China. In 1958, the People's Communes appeared and developed rapidly in China. At that time, there was a popular saying 'communism is the heaven; the People's Communes are the bridge to heaven'.[18] In the system of People's Communes, 500 million peasants in a million villages had free meals.[19] Egalitarianism, however, caused universal poverty in China. From 1958 to 1959, Hubei, Guangdong, Hebei, Shangdong, and Henan provinces appeared widespread famine one after another. The national famine that happened during 1958–1961 was one of the serious famine disasters in human history. It caused 30 million deaths [5, 156]. Some scholars believed that the great famine was caused by the decrease of crops and natural disasters including drought and flood (Yifu Lin 1994). Nobelist Amartya Sen argued that unreasonable mode of distribution was the significant cause.[20] Xiaoping Deng also linked the cause of

[17] In the last section of this chapter, cases will be analyzed to disclose conflicts between laws. An obvious example was that The Regulation Governing Building Demolition and Resettlement 2001 was in conflict with the Constitution and the Property Law of China 2007.

[18] Laiqing Wang. 2010. The Rise and Decline of the First People's Communes. Centuries Appearance 1:35.

[19] Yi Xin. 2008. A Historic Examination of 'Great Leap' and People's Commune. Hebei Academic Journal 28:74.

[20] Ziying Fan and Lingjie Meng. 2006. New Explanations and Test to Sen's Entitlements: Evidence from China. Economic Studies 8:104–113. see also Xin Zi Peng. 1987. Demographic Consequences of the Great Leap Forward in China's Provinces. Population and Development Review 13: 639–670.

national poverty to egalitarianism: '*We used to practice egalitarianism, with everyone eating from the same big pot. In fact, that practice meant common backwardness and poverty, which caused suffering*'.[21] And Deng believed that we should abandon egalitarianism: '*The reason we should not practice egalitarianism was that it would never be possible to raise the people's standard of living and stimulate their initiative*'.[22]

A theory to reconcile macro-economic policy with individual requirements was proposed in 1983. In the new theory, it was reasonable for some people to become richer than other people. In Deng's economic and legal reform, economic inequality was permitted:

> *'The purpose of allowing some regions and some people to become prosperous before others is to enable all of them to prosper eventually. We have to make sure that there is no polarization of society—that is what socialism means'.*[23] *'When some people and some regions get rich first, others will be brought along and through this process, common prosperity of the entire population will be gradually achieved...this is our policy. And it will be the responsibility for the first prosperous regions to bring along other less developed places.'*[24] *'I have consistently maintained that some people and some regions should be allowed to prosper before others, always with the goal of common prosperity'.*[25]

In this 'let some people become rich first' theory, the purpose (the ends) was the common prosperity. The means was allowing or confirming economic inequality. The idea of economic inequality was officially acceptable after the People's Commune movement. Deng criticized the People's Commune movement and stated that if equality meant everyone was suffering in poverty, it was worse than (partial) inequality. He also proposed that when China would realize the common prosperity, economic inequality was acceptable and necessary for the development of productive forces.

The realization of common prosperity was proposed in three steps: Firstly, to allow part of the people become rich. Secondly, to let the rich people bring along others and help others getting rich. And thirdly, to realize the whole nation's common prosperity. From recent 30 years reform, Chinese lawmaking since 1979 had contributed to the first step of Deng's theory: Some persons and some regions of China became rich. But how to implement the second step, i.e., let the rich bring along the poor, by law? Was it right to let the law play an active role of adjusting people's wealth in the second step?

---

see also Ashton, B., K. Hill, A. Pizza & R. Zeinz. 1984. Famine in China, 1958–1961. Population and Development Review 10:4. see also Yifu Lin, Fang Cai, and Zhou Li. 1994. The Chinese Miracle: The Development Strategy and Economic Reform. Shanghai: Sanlian publishing house..

[21] Xiaoping Deng. 2001. Selected Words of Deng Xiaoping 3:155. Beijing: The People's Publishing House.

[22] Ibid.

[23] See Deng's speech in meeting with a delegation including senior American entrepreneurs organized by Time Inc. on 23 October 1985. Deng Xiaoping. Selected Words of Deng Xiaoping. 2001. 3:142. Beijing: The People's Publishing House.

[24] See Deng's speech in his interview with Prime Minister David Lange of New Zealand on 28 March 1986. ibid.

[25] See Deng's talk in his visit at Tianjin during 19–21 of August 1986. Deng Xiaoping. 2001. Selected Words of Deng Xiaoping. Beijing: The People's Publishing House.

In the beginning of the economic reform, Deng's theory affirmed free market's positive function and criticized the planned economy. Law was put into a passive position when individuals' livelihoods were concerned. In the first step, individual autonomy was the driving force for becoming rich. The legal system was designed to protect such autonomic self-arrangement of life. If in the second step, the value of individual autonomy were still in the core of lawmaking, i.e., law should remain silent in economic inequality, the adjustment of social wealth therefore would rely on the rich persons' moral obligation.

Following this logic, law should not interfere into the rich person's right of donation; and rich persons could refuse to assist the poor since they did not have a *legal* obligation to. In this perspective, the second step of Deng's reform should rely on the kindness of the rich. Was such morality of the rich persons what Deng's theory about? At least from Deng's literatures, it was not obvious. To Deng, economic inequality was a means to the end, (common prosperity as the end). Deng criticized extreme inequality and polarization of society.[26] In his design of the new structure of the society he stressed that 'it will be the *responsibility* for the first prosperous regions to bring along other less developed places.'[27] How to understand the concept of 'responsibility' in this statement? Considering Deng's 'partial rich' suggestion with his purpose of 'common prosperity' (or 'collective prosperity'), the responsibility should be an obligation for those who became richer earlier than others. The reason for the obligation was in a 'tacit consent' of Deng's economic reform design. Those who became richer first were supposed to have signed a contract with the nation: They would become the most beneficial group from the economic reform and they would possess more wealth than others, so they had an obligation to assist with the nation to improve other people's livelihoods. This tacit contract did not refer to specific persons but offered a macro-environment for gathering wealth through personal efforts.

The *responsibility* therefore was an *obligation* for the first prosperous group to bring along others. The second step of economic reform therefore should shift from exclusive autonomy to a theory of obligation. The rich persons should have an obligation to assist the nation to achieve the purpose of common prosperity. Chinese theorists also tended to justify this interpretation. From the perspective of productive forces, the first step in Deng's theory emphasized the emancipation and development of productive forces. The second step of Deng's justification should focus on elimination of exploitation and polarization. Both the first and second steps should be understood as means. The end was always common prosperity.[28] Wealth possessed by few rich persons could not bring socialism. The economic

---

[26] See Deng's speech in meeting with a delegation including senior American entrepreneurs organized by Time Inc. on 23 October 1985. Deng Xiaoping. 2001. Selected Words of Deng Xiaoping 3: 142. Beijing: The People's Publishing House.

[27] See Deng's speech in his interview with Prime Minister David Lange of New Zealand on 28 March 1986. ibid.

[28] Mengqing Lin. 2009. A Study of Deng Xiaoping's Theory and the Practice of Common Prosperity. Academic Forum 3:5–8.

reform was not for some persons but 'the people', i.e., the whole population. Therefore, the wealth should be re-distributed between the rich and the poor to realize common prosperity.

From the perspective of social justice, the common prosperity should include both economic development and social justice.[29] Common prosperity in this perspective was not circumscribed as a purely economic concept. It should contain values of justice. In a humanistic point of view, Deng's purpose was people-oriented.[30] Injustice caused by extreme polarization was unacceptable. Common prosperity referred to the prosperity of the people rather than few rich persons. Economic inequality should not justify other kinds of inequality. If common prosperity were interpreted as an advanced equality in the end, economic polarization became a temporary stage and should be eliminated in the end.

The tacit consent to the economic reform and the lawmaking related practices therefore should subject to a condition: those who become richer should have an obligation of bringing along the others. However, we were uncertain of the particular persons who would become richer than others. Should the obligation of assisting the poor be determined? A moral philosopher may disagree with this legalizing (verrechilichung) of the moral obligation of assistance. In his perspective, 'help' should always be offered voluntarily to others. People (the rich in this case) should not be forced to do good to others. This was a concern of individual free will. Individual freedom and autonomy were good excuses for the rich to evade their responsibilities: as long as they did not harm others, they did not have to care about other people because it was not their legal obligations. 'Freedom' and 'autonomy' was employed to confirm the result of the economic reform (some people became rich earlier than others). They were, however, against the reason for the economic reform (common prosperity). If the rich refuse to comply with their duty of assistance of the poor people, the legitimation of the supposed contract (the economic reform) became problematic. The rich person's promise or tacit consent to the first contract (a contract for common prosperity) was broken. The first contract then was no longer in force. An 'individual-interest-oriented' contract (the second contract) substituted the first 'collective-interest-oriented' contract.

The second contract, however, was from the beginning an unjust and unfair contract, even in the name of individual freedom and autonomy. The rich had already accepted the conditions of the first contract, and obtained great profits because of the first contract. Their wealth did not come exclusively from their own efforts. The society and other people also offered the macro-environment to assist their success as well. The poor and the rich in the second contract had originally equal economic status when they sign the first contract. But they (especially the poor) probably would not sign the contract (i.e., let some became richer first) if the richer broke their promises. Without the support of the majority, the economic reform could not

[29] Chaohui Jiang. 2006. The Principle of Justice in A Socialistic Harmonious Society. Studies of Theories of Mao Zedong and Deng Xiaoping 3:41–46.

[30] Zhenhua Zhang. 2004. A Study of Deng Xiaoping's Theory. Journal of Xihua University 3:18–19.

be realized and legitimized at all. The common people's agreement of the first contract was the starting point of the legitimation of the economic reform. Therefore few rich persons should be abided by their commitment to the first contract: to assist the less rich persons to develop. The economic reform was not aiming at the wealth of few rich persons but prosperity of the whole people. The economic reform was not individual-oriented directly: It was driven by the intention to improve the poverty of the whole country in the beginning. It was designed to maximize the people-nation combined interests. Collective interests were prior to individuals, especially when they were in conflicts. The obligation of the rich to assist the collective in this tacit consent was therefore stricter than a moral obligation like 'help'.

'*If our policy results in polarization, our reform fails*', Deng said.[31] It is a prudent forsight. Unfortunately, however, the polarization started to take shape. Statistics showed the realistic polarization: According to the Boston Consulting Group (BCG)'s report on Chinese Wealth Markets 2005, in China the degree of wealth centralization was very high. Less than 0.5 % families possessed over 60 % of the whole nation's personal wealth. Within this rich group, 70 % of wealth was held by the few families with more than five million dollar assets. It meant that 99.95 % family held two fifth of the total wealth of the society. In addition, those rich Chinese families held large amounts of cash: 71 % of their wealth was held by cash. The amount was far much higher than the average global level (34.6 %).[32] Personal financial assets were also in the hands of very few persons.

In 2009, China Merchants Bank published a report with Bain & Company on Chinese personal wealth. This report showed that until the end of 2008, 300,000 persons had investment assets exceeded 10 million Yuan. The number exceeded 320,000 in the end of 2009 which was 6 % up over 2008. These few rich persons possessed over nine trillion (9,000,000,000,000) Yuan investment assets, which were almost half of the total deposits of the whole nation's urban and rural residents. 320,000 rich persons, however, was only 0.2 % of the whole population.[33] In 2010 April, Hurun Luxury Business Portal published new statistics about Chinese rich people's wealth. It showed that there were 875,000 multimillionaires (0.67 % of the whole population) and 55,000 billionaires (0.04 %).[34] The escalate polarization gave rise to a discussion of the further policies of the economic reform: Whether to insist on the present legal system which focused mainly on the economy, or make some changes in the macro-economic policy for the sake of social justice?

---

[31] Xiaoping Deng. 2001. Selected Words of Deng Xiaoping. 3:110–111. Beijing: the People's Publishing House.

[32] Statistics from Junhao Deng, Luesi Guo, and Deming Ou. 2005. Chinese Wealth Markets, on BCG official website: http://www.bcg.com.cn/cn/files/publications/reports_pdf/Wealth__Markets_China__Dec2005.pdf. Accessed 02 Feb 2012.

[33] Statistics from China Merchants Bank and Bain & Company. The Report on Chinese Personal Wealth 2009. http://live.cmbchina.com/webpages/pfr2009/WealthReport.pdf. Accessed 02 Feb 2012.

[34] Statistics from Hurun Luxury Business Portal report 2010. http://www.hurun.net/listreleasecn450.aspx. Accessed 02 Feb 2012.

Arguments for the present economic-oriented legal system differentiated 'wealth gap' with 'polarization'. Some scholars recognized the wealth gap among people but denied that it was the same thing as 'polarization'. Polarization in their concerns was a classification of classes, which was not about the absolute standard of different economic status.[35] Some scholars argued that the polarization was the result of capitalistic private ownership, which did not possibly exist in the public ownership system of China.[36] Recent research adjusted the argument and recognized socialistic private ownership. A new concept, 'virtuous polarization' appeared in lately discussion.[37] However, 'virtuous polarization' was still based on a simplified differentiation between capitalism and socialism. In their perspectives, 'vicious polarization' (rather than 'virtuous polarization') existed in capitalistic countries; a socialistic system only had 'virtuous polarization'.[38]

I disagreed with their comments on Chinese polarization. From the statistics I analyzed above, we could see that the polarization in China was vicious. Its negative effects should be noticed. If the polarization was ignored and over-indulgent, the majority's enthusiasm for production would be harmed. Social morality might corrupt because of 'the worship of money'. It would further influence the average consumption level and add burdens to maintain the social order. The polarization would make the purpose of economic reform meaningless and shake the Communist Party of China (*hereinafter* CCP)'s leadership to its foundations. The continual growth of Gini coefficient could illustrate the great disparity between the rich and poor.[39] From 1992 to 2007, the average Gini index was 0.415.[40] Since 1994 the Gini coefficient was continuously over 0.4 (which was the alert line). In less than 20 years development, China changed from an equal-income-distribution country (in 1970s) to an

[35] Anyi Li and Yingtian Li. 2006. Common Prosperity Is Not Only An Economic Concept: A Study of the Content and Realization of Common Prosperity. Theoretical Investigation 6:52–55.

[36] Chunjiao Qu. 1994. Xiaoping Deng's Arguments for Common Prosperity and against Polarization. Journal of China Youth University for Political Science 4:1–5.

[37] Peizhao Hu. 2003. Common Prosperity and Virtuous Polarization in Wealth. Theory Front 22: 27–29.

[38] Ibid.

[39] The Gini coefficient can range from 0 to 1; it is sometimes multiplied by 100 to range between 0 and 100. A low Gini coefficient indicates a more equal distribution, with 0 corresponding to complete equality, while higher Gini coefficients indicate more unequal distribution, with 1 corresponding to complete inequality. Chinese Gini coefficient was 0.160 in 1978, 0.288 in 1981, 0.297 in 1984, 0.349 in 1989, 0.282 in 1991, 0.407 in 1993, 0.415 in 1995, 0.456 in 1998, 0.457 in 1999, 0.458 in 2000, 0.473 in 2004, and 0.496 in 2006. Statistics in 1991, 1998, 1999 and 2000 are from Hu Peizhao. 2003. Common Prosperity and Virtuous Polarization in Wealth. Theory Front 22:27–29. Statistics in 1981,1984,1989,1995 are from Tao Chunhai. 2003. A Thought about Increasing Gini Coefficient in China. Jiangxi Social Sciences 3:183–185. Statistics in 2006 are from Zhang Kui and Wang Zuxia. 2009. Measurement and Control of Income Inequality and Polarization. Statistical Research 26:76–80. Statistics of 1993 and 2004 are from ADB (Asia Development Bank) report from http://xxhs2.mofcom.gov.cn/aarticle/commonnews/200708/20070804972531.html. Accessed 02 Feb 2012.

[40] Statistic refers to Human Development Report 2009 Gini index, http://hdrstats.undp.org/en/indicators/161.html. Accessed 02 Feb 2012.

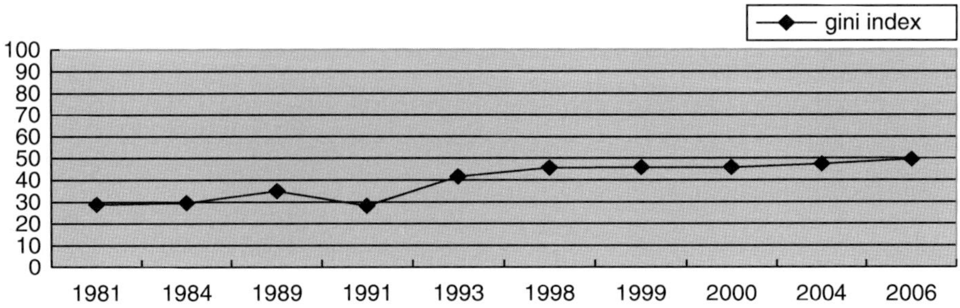

Fig. 2.4 Gini index from 1981 to 2006 in China

extreme unequal-distribution country (since late 1990s). Economic polarization in China was an irrefutable fact Fig. 2.4.

The amount of low-income citizens was increasing continuously. Since 1997 China started to institute the System of Minimum Living Standard Security of the Urban Residents (*hereinafter MLSUR*). At that time, less than two million urban residents were under the minimum living standard who needed the allowance. However, the amount had been rising continuously. In 1999, it was 2.8 million; in 2000, it raised to 4 million; in 2001, the amount was over 11.7 million; in 2002 it was again doubled to above 20.5 million; and the amount reached to 23.3 million in 2009.[41] The actual amount of the poor was more than the above official numbers because not all the poor were covered by the *MLSUR* system. In a research, the numbers of urban poor from 2000 to 2004 were at least 22.95 million, 28.83 million, 37.66 million, 39.12 million and 40.17 million.[42]

As a contrast, the rural population in poverty was decreasing in the recent 10 years, (the official numbers of the rural poor in 1993 was over 80 million; in 2002, it decreased to 28 million). However, the number of the poor in rural areas was still enormous. The minimum living standard (625 Yuan per person per year) of rural areas was much lesser than that of the cities of China. It did not reach to one fourth of the standard of developing countries (the standard of the World Bank was 1 dollar 1 day; that was 2,800 Yuan per person per year). According to the World Bank's standard, there were 126 million poor in the rural areas of China.[43] From China Foundation for Poverty Alleviation's statistics, the rural poor were about 90 million, which were 11 % of the whole population of the rural residents.

More than 145 million peasant-labors were not included in the official number of the rural population in poverty (nor were they included into the low-income citizens

[41] Statistics from Ministry of Civil Affairs of the People's Republic of China, http://www.mca.gov.cn/article/mxht/mtgz/200908/20090800034009.shtml; and http://dbs.mca.gov.cn/article/csdb/llyj/200711/20071100003469.shtml; Accessed 02 Feb 2012.

[42] Luo Zhuoyan. 2006. Re-estimate China's Urban Poor Population. Finance & Economics 9:82–89.

[43] Statistics from Global News, http://china.huanqiu.com/society/2007-12/37451.html, and the World Bank http://web.worldbank.org/WBSITE/EXTERNAL/COUNTRIES/EASTASIAPACIFICEXT/CHINAEXTN/0,,contentMDK:21639761~pagePK:141137~piPK:141127~theSitePK:318950,00.html. Accessed 02 Feb 2012.

since they were not citizens).[44] However, the peasant-labors living standard was far below the citizens and their income were at the bottom of the society, so they should be included into the category of people in poverty. If the numbers of the low-income citizens, rural populations in poverty and the peasant-labors were added together, the total impoverished population was around 150 million to 210 million, which was 11.54–16.15 % of the whole population. From the above analysis of statistics, we can see that the economic polarization was serious in China.

The economic polarization and poverty already caused social problems. In the beginning of the economic reform, people were in a relatively fair competition environment and were in a relatively equal starting point for gathering personal wealth. After 30 years reform, under the great disparity of rich and poor pattern, the approach to acquiring wealth through capital was much easier. But it was more difficult to earn money through labor. The social environment was more beneficial to the rich rather than the poor, which formed a Matthew Effect already. In 1980s, the 'rich standard' was 10,000 Yuan savings. Therefore the gap between the rich and poor was not too wide. A bidirectional transformation between the poor and rich was possible. Later on, however, the 'rich standard' became unattainable. The rich stratum held millions and billions of wealth so that the standard of becoming rich was extremely difficult. With the continuously widened gap of wealth, the temporary poor (for one generation) became diachronic poor (for several generations). The offspring of the poor and the rich had totally different opportunities for education, work, and distribution of wealth. And the poverty or prosperity easily transferred from one generation to another. The polarization and the social structure thus became stable and institutionalized. And a bidirectional transformation between the poor and the rich became impossible.

Apart from the above analyzed 0.5 % very rich families (who possessed more than 60 % wealth), and very impoverished population (which was 16.15 % of the whole population), the middle, the common people or the majority (83.35 %) had limited financial capability, especially facing with the high cost of medical treatment, education, and high price of living. The common people's life standard was just basic: in China, 80 % common rural people (the rural residents were 80 % of the whole population) could not get cleaned drinking water. From the official statistics of the National Bureau of Statistics, in the second national investigation of common rural people's living standard, 10.3 % people had difficulties in getting drinkable water; 48.6 % got pipe water; only 23.1 % got cleaned water; 41.8 % depended on deep well water; 27.8 % depended on shallow well water; 2.8 % directly used river water; 1.4 % used pond water; 1.4 % depended on rain; and 1.7 % through other resources.[45] 44.3 % of the common people had dry latrines; 42.9 % did not have toilets and have to use the outdoor toilets; only 12.8 % had flushing toilets.[46] The common rural residents' living

[44] Statistics from National Bureau of Statistics of China, 2009 Report on the Peasant-labors, http://www.stats.gov.cn/was40/gjtjj_detail.jsp?searchword=%C5%A9%C3%F1%B9%A4&channelid=6697&record=12. Accessed 02 Feb 2012.

[45] Statistics from http://www.stats.gov.cn/tjgb/nypcgb/qgnypcgb/t20080226_402464495.htm. Accessed 02 Feb 2012.

[46] Ibid.

standard was far behind that of urban residents. The per capita net income of rural people in 2009 was 5,000 Yuan. The per capital disposable income of urban residents was over 17,000, which were more than three times of that of the rural people's income, not to speak of the gap in the net income.

The common people in both of the rural and urban spent more than one third of the income for food. Engel coefficients (referring to the proportion of expenditures on food to the total consumption expenditures of households) of the rural and urban residents were 41.0 % and 36.5 %,[47] which also disclosed the fact that the common people's living standard in China was not comparable to that of the developed countries. Referring to my own experience of living at W city in China and E city in the U.K., the proportion on living costs to income had obvious difference: suppose a common people's income was 1,500 unit (1,500 RMB at W and 1,500 GBP at E), the proportion of expenses in most indexes of W was higher than E (Appendix 1). Since the common people's living standard was just on a subsistence level in China, and the proportion on living costs to income was so high, it was not reasonable to add legal obligation for this group to assist the poor. The law should not impose this obligation to them.

Then which group should be responsible to bring along the poor, the whole population in the rich region, the local governments' of the rich region, or the rich group exclusively? It certainly was not reasonable for the poor in the rich region to have such responsibility. In Deng's ideal, '*When some people and some regions get rich first, others will be brought along and through this process, common prosperity of the entire population will be gradually achieved…this is our policy. And it will be the responsibility for the first prosperous regions to bring along other less developed places.*'[48] From the first half of the expression, 'others will be brought along' seems to be a social prediction (the rich *will* help the poor) rather than a legal obligation (the rich *have an obligation* to help the poor). Some scholars also argued for this point and stated that the existence of the rich group per se benefited the poor because the rich provided more work opportunities for the poor. In this perspective, the rich should not be blamed.[49]

With special reference to the local finances this argument could be right, because rich entrepreneurs contributed to the main source of the local finances. According to statistics exposed by Sheng Huaren, the vice-chairmen of the National People's Congress, local governments' income from Real Estate industry was 50–80 % of the

---

[47] see Statistical Communique on the 2010 National Economic and Social Development Report of the National Bureau of Statistics, http://www.stats.gov.cn/tjgb/ndtjgb/qgndtjgb/t20100225_402622945.htm. Accessed 02 Feb 2012.

[48] See Deng's speech in his interview with Prime Minister David Lange of New Zealand on 28 March 1986. ibid.

[49] In 2007, a domestic famous economist Mao Yishi published an article 'Speak for the Rich; Serve for the Poor' and brought a national debate on the argument whether the poor benefit from the rich. See the original article at Mao's blog: http://blog.sina.com.cn/s/blog_49a3971d01000b48.html. Accessed 02 Feb 2012. In this argument, the rich was the main source of social wealth and should be more respected. Other well-know economist and scholars including Wu Jinglian and Jia Jinjing supported this argument; Xian Yan, Cao jianhai, Zhong Dajun, Yan Yu, Huang Zhong, Wang Congsheng, and Li Chunlin criticized this argument and pointed out that the rich were over-protected rather than over-looked. Zhang Xingshui and Zhang Ming stated that both of the rich and the poor should be protected equally from the legal perspective.

general property price; and the income from Land Grant Fee increased from 670 billion to 91,000 billion Yuan from 1998 to 2003; the Real Estate industry became a role of 'economic mainstay' of local governments.[50] When the common people, i.e., the majority, were concerned, however, the argument was not sound because this economic achievement was based on the exploitation of the majority especially the majority of the rural residents. Local governments got requisition lands from the rural residents in a low price, then sold them ten times of the requisition price, and invested in urban infrastructure or corruption. Since 1980s, the total amount of requisition lands was 98 million mu (1 mu = 0.067 ha). In a conservative estimate, if the peasants lose 50,000 Yuan for 1 mu, then the total loss since 1980 exceeded 5,000,000 million.[51] The peasant as the disadvantaged group lost more than they gain. Local governments and rich people should be responsible for paying compensation to the less favored group, and the latter was the majority of the population in this case. Even if they were not responsible for the wealth they gathered from exploitation of the less and least favored group, they should at least be responsible for future improvements of the living standards of the poor.

Local governments should have an obligation to improve people's lives and this responsibility was written in the legitimacy of governmental management. However, how to deal with the rich people's responsibility? Put this argument differently, even if the rich should be responsible, why should the responsibility a legal one rather than a moral one? Why could not we have some trust in their conscience? Some scholars criticized that a legal obligation was 'resentment of the rich': '*Chinese rich people are not that rich… the responsibility should be the nation's not the rich people's… rich people pay high tax so they already assist the improvement of other people's living conditions …in short, the society should not force the rich to donate*'.[52] This argument, as far as I was concerned, however, was not true. Chinese rich people were indeed very rich (possessed over nine trillion Yuan investment assets, which was almost half of the total deposits of the whole nation's urban and rural residents); the rich should also take the responsibility because they were the most beneficial group of the economic reform and should comply their duty of the 'social contract'.

From the statistics of Chinese taxation we could see that the rich individuals' tax were *not* the major source of individual income tax. On the contrary, the

---

[50] See Jian Yuan: the Real Estate Industry Kidnaps China, from scholars' Utopia net, http://www.wyzxsx.com/Article/Class4/200611/11472.html. Accessed 02 Feb 2012. Also see Shiwei Zhang. 2008. The Effects of the Public Policy Relating to the Recent Real Estate Fever. Social Sciences in Ningxia 1:13–15.

[51] Ibid.

[52] See Zhiqiang Ren. 2008. Taxation and Donation. Resources Inhabitant and Environment 15: 69–71. see also Ren Zhiqiang. 2008. The Society Should Not Force the Rich to Donate, http://bbs.soufun.com/1010253663~-1~10429/77934988_77934988.htm. Accessed 02 Feb 2012. Ren is a domestic famous representative of the rich, who is the president of Beijing Huayuan Real Estate Limited Company, the president of Huanyuan Group, a commissioner of Beijing Commercial Bank, and the director of Xinhua Life Insurance Agency. According to a 2010 investigation of the list of 10 persons that Chinese people want to beat, Ren was in top five, see http://news.wuxi.soufun.com/2010-05-06/3314113_5.html. Accessed 02 Feb 2012.

common wage earners were the principal source of it. According to the analysis of the Ministry of Finance, in 2009 the total individual income tax was 3,949, 270 million Yuan, in which the common-wage-earners contributed to 62.87 % (2,483,090 million).[53] According to statistics from State Administration Taxation, since 2002 the average common-wage-earners annual contribution was more than half of the total.[54] The very rich group who possessed more than 80 % social wealth contributed to less than 10 % of the individual income tax.[55] Since 2007, those whose annual income was higher than 120,000 Yuan should declare taxable income by themselves. However, only 1/6 of the high income group declared.[56] The proportion of payments that high income individuals evaded was 30 % of the total individual-tax.[57]

As referring to rich people's donations, the facts were more eloquent than arguments: there were over ten million registered industrial and commercial enterprises, but less than one tenth had the record of donations. 99 % enterprises had no record of donations. The fund of donations was only 0.1 % of GDP.[58] Statistics already showed that the rich did not fulfill their legal responsibility of tax, nor were they willing to donate. It was not what Mr. Ren Zhiqiang declared, that 'the society forced the rich to donate'. On the contrary, the rich did not take their legal and moral responsibilities.

In my point of view, the priority to efficiency in Chinese laws should change to the priority to justice.[59] The present legal system should provide practical institutions to narrow down the wealth gap between the rich and poor people and to improve the majority's livelihood. Chinese lawmaking should shift from economic-oriented to social-justice-oriented. The 30 years economic and legal reform was

---

[53] See the Structural Analysis of the Increase of Tax 2009 by the Ministry of Finance of the People's Republic of China, http://szs.mof.gov.cn/zhengwuxinxi/gongzuodongtai/201002/t20100211_270552.html. Accessed 02 Feb 2012.

[54] Statistics from the State Administration Taxation, http://202.108.90.130/n480462/n480513/n480934/2011979.html. see also http://www.chinanews.com.cn/cj/cj-plgd/news/2009/06-19/1741312.shtml. Accessed 02 Feb 2012.

[55] See http://www.zaobao.com/special/newspapers/2005/09/dayoo050912.html. Accessed 02 Feb 2012. See also Zheng Guozhong. 2002. The Chinese Rich People Evade to Taxation. Finance and Economy 9:9–10.

[56] Analysis is based on statistics in Feng Junxian. 2009. Suggestions on Intensifying Tax Collection and Management of the High Income Group. Chinese Enterprise Accounting of Villages and Towns 4: 66–67. See also http://news.cctv.com/20070425/106125.shtml, in this official report, the proportion is 1/4. Accessed 02 Feb 2012.

[57] Jingli Wu. 2008. A Study on the New Scheme of Individual Income Tax. Economics and Trade Update 15: 61.

[58] See the official of National Development and Reform Commission, Xinnian Chen's talk. 2005. Beijing Youth Daily. November 14. See also Xiaoming Liang. 2006. Maybe It is too Harsh to Force the Rich to Donate. Financial View 4:35. And see also Xi Muyu. 2006. Why the Chinese Rich People Are not Benevolent? Government Legality 13:21.

[59] See also the arguments of Quanrui Dong, Deming Tan, Xihou Zhang, Han Li, and Fan Yang. 2007. In Teng Peng's Research on the Recent Problems of Polarization of China. Journal of Lanzhou Commercial College 23:20–25.

worthy of a compliment because it achieved its first stage objective, i.e., let some people become rich. The economic reform, however, needed institutions to safeguard its second stage objective, i.e., let the rich bring along the poor for the sake of the ultimate goal of common prosperity. Chinese lawmaking should stress the legal responsibilities of both the government and the rich. Rich people obtained great profits from the economic reform already and were the prime beneficiaries of the reform. Individual autonomy, freedom and right should not become excuses for them to evade their legal and moral obligations to assist the poor. The economic reform could be seen as a social contract to which they had signed, so that they had to comply with their duties that regulated in the contract.

2.4 Efficient Lawmaking

According to *The Legislation Law of the People's Republic of China 2000 (hereinafter LLC2000)*, the formal law of lawmaking, the lawmaking authority belongs to the Chinese congress (National People's Congress of the People's Republic of China—*hereinafter NPC*) and its standing committee (*hereinafter SCNPC*), and is partly shared by the State Council after NPC or SCNPC's authorization.[60]

[60]The Legislation Law of the People's Republic of China 2000, section one, article 7: '…the National People's Congress and Standing Committee thereof shall exercise state legislative power.' The State Council can also share the legislative power authorized by the National People's Congress (NPC) and Standing Committee (SCNPC). see article 9:'In the event that no national law has been enacted in respect of a matter enumerated in Article 8 hereof, the National People's Congress and the Standing Committee thereof have the power to make a decision to enable the State Council to enact administrative regulations in respect of part of the matters concerned for the time being, except where the matter relates to crime and criminal sanctions, the deprivation of a citizen's political rights, compulsory measure and penalty restricting the personal freedom of a citizen, and the judicial system.' The necessary precondition for the authorization is that the former have not enacted laws for some less important issues. Matters relating to crime and criminal sanctions, the deprivation of a citizen's political rights, compulsory measure and penalty restricting the personal freedom of a citizen, and the judicial system, however, still require the former. The State Council can make law in the name of NPC or SCNPC's authorization. The enabled body may not re-delegate its authority to any other body. See *The Legislation Law of the People's Republic of China 2000*, section 1, article 9–11. The main contents of lawmaking by and only by the NPC and NPCSC are '(i) state sovereignty; (ii) the establishment, organization and authority of various people's congresses, people's governments, people's courts and people's procuratorates; (iii) autonomy system of ethnic regions, system of special administrative region, and system of autonomy at the grass-root level; (iv) crimes and criminal sanctions; (v) the deprivation of the political rights of a citizen, or compulsory measures and penalties involving restriction of personal freedom; (vi) expropriation of non-state assets;(vii) fundamental civil institutions; (viii) fundamental economic system and basic fiscal, tax, customs, financial and foreign trade systems; (ix) litigation and arbitration system; (x) other matters the regulation of which must be carried out through enactment of national law by the National People's Congress or the Standing Committee thereof.' See *The Legislation Law of the People's Republic of China 2000*, section 1, article 8. Those important political and legal issues can only be enacted as national law rather than administrative regulations or decrees.

The legislative process of the NPC (and SCNPC) includes: (1) Introduction of a bill[61]; (2) Deliberation[62]; and (3) Voting.[63]

Since 1978, comparing the Standing Committee of the National People's Congress (*SCNPC*) with the National People's Congress (*NPC*), the former played a dominant role in lawmaking, although according to the Constitution and *LLC2000*

[61] The institutions or organs that can introduce a bill to the National Congress and its Standing Committee are the presidium of the Congress or the Chairman's Committee of the Committee, or the State Council, the Central Military Committee, the Supreme People's Court, the Supreme People's Procuratorate, and the specific committees of the National Congress (the Legislation Law of the People's Republic of China 2000, article 12 and 24). To introduce a bill is the preliminary stage of creating a law. The right to introduce a bill therefore gives influence and power in the lawmaking process. In addition to the bill introducers mentioned above, another way to introduce a bill is to announce a bill by a delegation of the session or by delegates of at least 30 people acting jointly during the NPC, or by ten or more members of the SCNPC acting jointly in the Standing Committee. According to the introducers, it is naturally divided into three levels of introducing a bill. The first level is that the presidium of the NPC and the Chairman's Committee of the SCNPC; the bills introduced by them are spontaneously included into the agenda of the current session for deliberation (article 12, 24). The second level is that the State Council, the Central Military Committee, the Supreme People's Court, the Supreme People's Procuratorate, and the specific committees of the National Congress: whether bills introduced by them can be included into the agenda of the current session is a decision for the presidium of the congress or the chairman's committee (article 12, 24). The third level is the delegation or jointed delegates: the presidium of the congress or the chairman's committee decides whether such bills can be discussed in the current session, or whether to refer such bill to the relevant special committee for deliberation, with such special committee making a recommendation as to whether such bill shall be put onto the agenda of the current session (article 13, 25).

[62] After the bills being put on to the agenda of the current session of the Congress, the delegations and relevant special committee shall begin deliberation. After gathering their deliberation opinions, the Legislative Committee shall conduct a uniform deliberation, and afterwards shall deliver to the presidium a deliberation report and the amended draft law. Then after the presidium has deliberated and passed the deliberation report and the amended draft law, they shall be printed and circulated to the delegates attending the session. Following that, the amended draft law shall be further amended by the Legislative Committee based on the deliberating opinions of the delegations.

[63] Then the Legislative Committee shall present a voting version of the draft law to be submitted by the presidium to the plenary session for voting, and if it receives affirmative votes from more than half of all delegations, such version shall be adopted. Under the following circumstances a bill may fail to become a law. Firstly, the sponsor of a bill itself has the right to withdraw the bill which has been put onto the agenda of the session. If the bill sponsor withdraws the bill subjected to the consent by the presidium of the NPC or the Chairman's Committee of the NPCSC, the deliberation on the bill shall terminate (article 20, 37). Secondly, the voting on the bill may be postponed to be 'dead' if great different opinions exist on the major issues. If there are major disagreements on the major issues of the bill, further deliberation is needed. The NPC may authorize its Standing Committee to have further deliberation (article 21). If after three deliberations by the NPCSC session, a bill's major issues still require further study, voting on the bill may be postponed. When it has been postponed for 2 years, the deliberation on the bill shall terminate (article 39). Thirdly, if less than half of the affirmative votes of all delegates are received, the bill cannot be adopted as a law (article 22, 40). If a bill introduced to the NPC and NPCSC has been voted on the plenary session and fails to pass, the bill sponsor may re-introduce it in accordance with all legally prescribed procedures (article 50).

session	year	NPC		SCNPC				total
		Basic laws		Other laws	Interpretations and decisions	In all		
		no.	%	no.	no.	no.	%	
5th	1978-1982	28	38.36	22	23	45	61.64	73
6th	1983-1987	12	18.46	36	17	53	81.54	65
7th	1988-1992	27	30.68	38	23	61	69.32	88
8th	1993-1997	26	21.85	70	23	93	78.15	119
9th	1998-2002	13	11.40	72	29	101	88.60	114
10th	2003-2008	12	12.00	69	19	88	88.00	100
Total	1978-2008	118	21.11	307	134	441	78.89	559
Still Valid		39	16.88	192			83.11	231

Fig. 2.5 Laws passed by NPC and SCNPC from 1978 to 2008

the latter should take the dominant role.[64] As Fig. 2.5 showed, in the 9th session (1998–2002) SCNPC passed 72 laws. New laws, interpretations and decisions were 101 in total. The amount of laws passed by SCNPC was more than five times of NPC's legislations (NPC passed 13 laws). In the 10th session (2002–2008), NPC's legislations were still far less than SCNPC's. NPC passed 39 basic laws which were 17.03 % of the total laws. In contrast, SCNPC passed 190 laws which were 82.97 % of the total. Besides, SCNPC's legislations were also in a general rising trend since 1980s. Numbers of laws that made by SCNPC only dropped slightly in the 10th session (see Fig. 2.6).

From Fig. 2.7 we also see that in the 6th NPC, 37 laws were made and 5 laws were amended. They were 88.10 % and 11.90 % of the laws that passed in total.

[64] Statistics of this section are from the Legislative Affairs Work Committee of SCNPC ed. 2008. Statistics of Legislation of People's Republic of China. 490–570. Chinese Democracy and Rule of Law Publishing House.

See also Wu Bangguo's 'Report on the Work of the Government about Administrative Regulations and Local Decrees' made at the third session of the eleventh NPC. http://news.xinhuanet.com/politics/2010-03/09/content_13133496.htm.and;http://www.chinadaily.com.cn/zgzx/2009npc/2009-03/09/content_7556715.htm. Accessed 09 March 2010.

And Zhou Jing. 2009. Statistical Indicators of the Current Effective Nation Legislation. Journal of Comparative Law 5:147–160.

Fig. 2.6 Basic laws passed by NPC and SCNPC from 5th session to 10th session

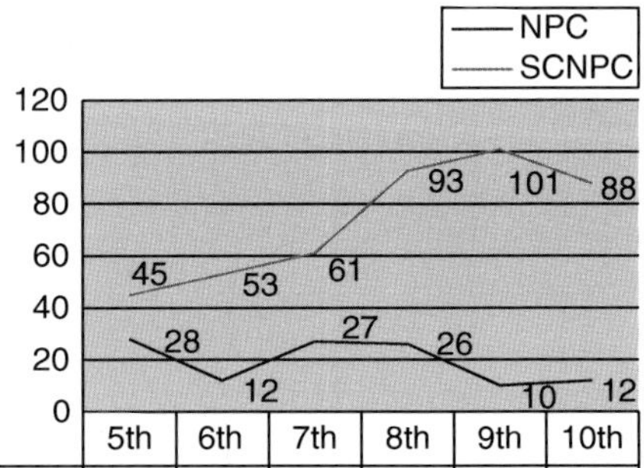

	5th	6th	7th	8th	9th	10th
NPC	28	12	27	26	10	12
SCNPC	45	53	61	93	101	88

session	year	constitution		law			Legislative interpretation	decision	total
		code	amendment	new	amend	total			
5th	1978-1982	1		33	4	37		28	66
6th	1983-1987			37	5	42		23	65
7th	1988-1992		1	44	5	49		38	88
8th	1993-1997		1	62	16	78	1	39	119
9th	1998-2002		1	35	40	75	8	30	114
10th	2003-2008		1	31	41	72	5	22	100
Total	1978-2008	1	4	242	111	353	14	180	552
now valid		1	4			228	14	87	330

Fig. 2.7 Laws amended since 5th to 10th session NPC

From 7th to 9th NPC, the new laws and amended laws were 88.90 % and 10.20 %; 79.49 % and 20.51 %; 46.67 and 53.33 %. In the 10th NPC, new laws were 43.06 % of the total passed laws; amended laws were 56.94 % of the total. From these statistics, we can see that from the 6th NPC to 8th NPC, the amount of new laws became less and in a downward tendency. In the 9th and 10th NPCs, the amounts of the amended laws were more than the new laws. From the 8th NPC, legislative interpretations appeared and increased. From 1983 (the 6th NPC) to 1997 (the 8th NPC), the total amount of laws was in an upward trend. It reached to the peak in the 8th NPC. Then it appeared a downward trend. After 2002, the number of NPC's law rose although that of SCNPC's fell.

In a statistical study of the speed of legislation, the average increase of laws was −3.29 % in the first 30 years (1949–1978). In the following 30 years (1979–2007), the average increase was 13.06 %. Total increase speed in these 60 years was 7.24 %.[65] Laws made in the first 30 years were mostly amended or abolished. And the average amount of the validity was 12.94 %. In the following 30 years, the laws were less amended or abolished, and the average amount of the validity rose to 41.36 %. The total amount of the validity was 37.18.[66] From these data, we can see that China entered into an era of high speed increase of legislation since 1979.

However, there was a theoretical conflict between the democratic representation system of NPC and the dominant legislative institution of SCNPC. Different from a unicameral system, both SCNPC and NPC shared the lawmaking power. Their positions were different from a bicameral system also, because they did not make laws together at the same conference. SCNPC's lawmaking power came from and was bound to NPC. During NPC's session, SCNPC could not make laws. SCNPC could make laws during the closed days of NPC. SCNPC and NPC were 'homologous' but different institutions.

From 1949 to 1982, the ultimate lawmaking power was held exclusively by the NPC. SCNPC was specially authorized to make laws in 1955 and 1959, and had the power to make regulations and to change and interpret laws during the closed days of the NPC gradually.[67] After the Constitution 1982 was promulgated, both SCNPC and NPC shared the legislative power.[68] The *LLC 2000* extended SCNPC's lawmaking power further to its special lawmaking sphere, legislative interpretation, adjudication of conflicts of laws and its opinions of controversial acts passing by the NPC.[69] SCNPC was thus called 'the Congress of the Congress' because of its expanding power and its dominant role in lawmaking.[70]

For the sake of efficiency, SCNPC was an appropriate institution to help NPC to deal with numerous and arduous lawmaking because SCNPC had more frequent sessions than NPC.[71] The NPC representatives were about 3,000 in every session since 1983. An average session was 15 days including two weekend days. So there were 13 working days per session. The working time of each session was about 6,240 min. So every representative had 2.08 min including the plenary report time to discuss a bill.[72] Every NPC representative had about 2 min in total to discuss,

[65] Jing Zhou. 2009. Statistical Indicators of the Current Effective Nation Legislation. Journal of Comparative Law 5:147–160.

[66] Ibid.

[67] Wangsheng Zhou. 2000. 50 Years Lawmaking History. Studies on Lawmaking 1, quoted from Yang Lijuan. 2004. The Relation of Legislative Competence Between National People's Congress and its Standing Committee. Journal of Guangxi Administrative Cadre Institute of Politics and Law 19:44.

[68] See the Constitution, article 62 and 67.

[69] See the LLC 2000, articles 8, 42, 85 and 21.

[70] Lijuan Yang. 2004. The Relation of Legislative Competence Between National People's Congress and its Standing Committee. Journal of Guangxi Administrative Cadre Institute of Politics and Law 19:43.

[71] NPC is held once in a year; while the SCNPC is normally held once in 2 months.

[72] See Number of Deputies to All the Previous National People's Congresses, China Statistical Yearbook 2010.

deliberate, question, debate and vote on a bill. Chinese NPC representatives had less time in a session than members of parliaments and congress in other countries.[73] SCNPC's frequent sessions can make up for the deficiency of working days for NPC's lawmaking.

However, SCNPC's lawmaking lacked democratic legitimacy because members of SCNPC (which were less than 200) were not chosen directly by the people. They were voted by representatives of NPC. Although lawmakers in most countries were the minority of the population, Chinese proportion of lawmakers to the population was too small: 0.23 % (NPC/whole); and 0.012 % (SCNPC/whole).[74] It was therefore a doubt about the lawmakers' representativeness. If the SCNPC did not gain the representative nature, the legitimacy of lawmaking was questionable. In practice, local electorate could hardly participate in the vote for the representatives of NPC, not to speak of SCNPC.[75]

The members of SCNPC did not communicate directly with the local electorate. They were not responsible to the local electorate but NPC, so it was problematic to take SCNPC decisions as the will of the people. People were not acquainted with SCNPC's work performance. So it was difficult for people to decide whether members of SCNPC were eligible for re-election. Actually, members of SCNPC were chosen from four indirect elections: The county-level representatives chose city-level representatives; the city-level representatives voted for the province-level; the province-level representatives elected the national-level; and finally the national representatives chose the members of SCNPC. Through these four indirect elections, distance between the will of the people and of the representatives became wider and wider.

If the NPC representatives could elect the SCNPC in an open democratic and free-will based fair procedure, the members of SCNPC could represent the will of the NPC, and in the end could arguable represent the people. However, NPC representatives could not nominate SCNPC candidates. The candidates were decided and introduced by the presidium of NPC exclusively. In the introduction of NPC presidium, information of the candidates' work performance was lacked. The candidates did not have to express a will of joining the SCNPC and plans for future work.

[73] International Centre for Parliamentary Documentation. 1986. Parliaments of the World: A Comparative Reference Compendium. 269–275. Gower Publishing Company Ltd. Especially table 8b, average number of plenary sittings. See also Lin Li. 2005. Insist to and Complete the Session System of the National People's Congress. Theoretical Trends 3:8–18.

[74] Chinese lawmaker/population is 3000/1,335,962,133; U.S: 535/306,221,000; Japan: 720/127,630,000; Germany: 667/82,062,200; France: 920/65,073,482; UK: 1378/61,612,300; Canada: 413/33,617,000. see data from World Population Prospects .http://www.un.org/esa/population/publications/WPP2004/WPP2004_Volume3.htm. and Inter-parliamentary Union. http://www.ipu.org/english/home.htm. Accessed 02 Feb 2012.

[75] For the author's own experience, she only had one chance to participate in one election of representatives of W district of W city of China since 1998–2010. At that election, she had the opportunity to choose one representative from two people who she never heard of. She was never informed of the political views of the two candidates, nor did she hear of the result of that election. The author had this opportunity because she was among the high educated group; other common urban residents were seldom involved in the elections.

Therefore NPC representatives were not offered sufficient information and solid standards to choose SCNPC representatives.[76] If were not nominated by the presidium, NPC representatives could not be recommended to join into SCNPC, even they were reliable and capable. The representativeness of the SCNPC was therefore problematic.

Another problem was: the members of SCNPC represented the collective and national interests rather than the multiple interests of different electoral districts. They were elected by the representatives of NPC, who were the national-level representatives. The Regulations of the Members of SCNPC clearly stipulated that the members of SCNPC should preserve the fundamental interests and common will of the whole nation.[77] They were therefore the representatives of a nationwide district rather than from different local districts. The disadvantage of such a nationwide district electoral mode was obvious: It was unfavorable to the common people to know, participate, choose and supervise their representatives. The representatives were responsible to 'the top' (the presidium of NPC) rather than to 'the down' (people). An effective supervision from both people and NPC representatives other than the presidium was difficult. In practice, direct communications among the members of SCNPC, common people and NPC representatives were rare. In a conservative estimate on the communications between common people and parliament members, less than 0.001 % local district elector met members of SCNPC. During the closed days of NPC, less than one fifth of the members of SCNPC communicated with the representatives of NPC.[78] The representativeness of the SCNPC was again problematic.

Apart from the representativeness of SCNPC, the conflicts in NPC lawmaking and SCNPC lawmaking were also difficult to solve. The following case could illustrate well about the conflicts in different lawmaking. On 27 January 2005, Jiahai Liu traveled out of the motorcycle lane and was thus fined 100 Yuan according to a summary procedure by a traffic police. Liu was unhappy with the results and he brought a suit against the traffic police on 18 March. He believed that according to Article 33 of the *Law of the People's Republic of China on Administrative Punishments 1996* (*hereinafter LAP1996*), the summary procedure should apply only to fines less than 50 Yuan and warning. Article 3 of LAP1996 claimed that all related administrative punishments should be regulated by this law. Liu claimed that the fine by the traffic police was an administrative violation.

The defendant (i.e., the police), however, argued that according to clause 1 of article 107 of the *Law of the People's Republic of China on Road Traffic Safety 2003* (*hereinafter LRTS2003*), and clause 2 of article 7 of the *Procedural Regulations on*

[76] According to Jingsong Jiang's study, the criteria of election were 'unwilling' choices because there lacked open and fair standards. Jiang Jingsong. 2004. Discussion of The Representativeness of the Standing Committee of the National People's Congress. Tribune of Political Science and Law 6:18–30.

[77] See article 2 of the Regulations of the Members of SCNPC 1993.

[78] Jingsong Jiang. 2004. Discussion of The Representativeness of the Standing Committee of the National People's Congress. Tribune of Political Science and Law 6:25.

Violation on Road Traffic Safety 2008 (*hereinafter Regulations 2008*), the fine was in accord with law. Plus LRTS2003 was promulgated later than LAP1996, the administrative practice was therefore in accord with the constitutional principles 'new laws are prior to old laws; special laws are prior to general laws'.

The court of first-instance supported the defendant's request and rejected the plaintiff (Mr. Liu)'s requests. Liu appealed to the court of second instance. His request was dismissed again. The court of second instance stated that this case was about the application of laws. It claimed that LRTS2003 made by SCNPC was not in conflict with LAP1996 made by NPC because the former was the special rules and the latter was the general rule. The court believed that SCNPC and NPC were not inferior-superior institutions but a same institution so that the laws they made were in a same level in the hierarchy of laws in LLC 2000. According to Article 83 of LLC2000, special rules were prior to general rules so the defendant did not break the law. The crux of the problem, as concerned by the court, was whether NPC and SCNPC were the same institutions, and whether laws of NPC and SCNPC were in the same level of validity. Disagreed with the court of second instance, Liu appealed for a retrial.[79]

I disagree with the courts' opinion because firstly LRTS2003 and LAP1996 had conflicting contents. It was a simple case, but the conflicts in the case were difficult to solve. The Constitution did not offer solutions to the conflicts between the two laws. According to the Constitution, NPC made 'basic laws' while SCNPC made 'other laws'. The contents of 'basic laws' and 'other laws', however, were not clarified. In LLC 2000, although the differentiation between basic and other laws were maintained, the classification criteria were still missing.[80] The basic laws and other laws were in a same level in the hierarchy of laws of LLC2000, so that when basic laws and other laws had conflicts, a superior law, i.e., the Constitution should be referred to judge their validity. In this case, however, the Constitution could not offer a clear standard for the validity LAP1996 and LRTS2003 so that both the plaintiff and the defendant had valid legal grounds.

Secondly, I disagree with the reasons offered by the second instance court because the constitutional principle 'new laws are prior to old laws; specific laws are prior to general laws' should be applied exclusively to the condition that the laws were made by a same institution. NPC and SCNPC, however, were different institutions. As analyzed in a previous section, they were homologous but independent institutions. The principle ('new laws prior to old laws; specific laws prior to general laws') was inapplicable here.

Thirdly, according to Article 85 of LLC2000, if there were conflicts between new general rules and old specific rules, the SCNPC could decide which rule was valid. However, in this case conflicts were between new specific rules and old general rules, the SCNPC therefore was not entitled to solve the problem.

[79] See Jiahai Liu vs. the 2nd group of Nanning traffic police Nanning, http://bbs.chinacourt.org/index.php?showtopic=242371&st=0. Accessed 02 Feb 2012.

[80] Xiaoyang Qiao. 2008. The Talks on The Legislative Law of People's Republic of China. 88. Beijing: China Democracy and Rule of Law Publishing House.

Fourthly, SCNPC's legislative interpretation could not apply in this case because according to *LLC2000*, when the contents of a law were ambiguous or the grounds of the law were uncertain, the court should apply the SCNPC's legislative interpretation. In this case, however, the contents of LRTS2003 and LAP1996 were clear and the administrative fine was made in accord with LRTS2003. Therefore we could not refer to SCNPC's legislative interpretation in this case.

Fifthly, according to the Constitution and LLC2000, NPC should change and annul inappropriate rules made by SCNPC. However, the Constitution and LLC2000 did not clarify which and in what degree a rule was inappropriate. In this case, the court and the police believed that the new law (LRTS2003) was appropriate. The plaintiff, however, believed that the old law (LAP1996) was appropriate. NPC as the representative institution of the people should investigate which opinion represented the people's interests indeed. In this solution, Mr. Liu should wait for nationwide discussion of the two laws, a decision of NPC afterwards, and then to appeal against the previous decisions made by the courts. It was not a satisfying solution to the plaintiff because it would cost him too much time waiting.

2.5 Bureaucratic Lawmaking

Chinese laws put too much emphasis on administrative power. Administrative laws became protective umbrellas of bureaucracy and the official monopoly. In this section I will discuss representative cases that highlight problems of bureaucratic lawmaking. The first example was about the freedom of assembly, procession and demonstration. After the *Law of the People's Republic of China on Assemblies, Processions and Demonstrations 1989* were made, local governments made related rules one after another. A Chinese local government regulated that processions should be prohibited in 15 streets of that city—but there were only 15 major streets in that city.[81] Therefore the rule made processions impossible. It did not protect the right or freedom of processions. Before the publication of this law, the lawmakers did not hold any legislative hearings to discuss the law with the public.

The second lawmaking example was about the conflict between a modern administrative order and a Chinese convention. On 12 October 1993, Beijing People's Congress Standing Committee passed the Prohibition of Fireworks. Other 200 Chinese cities made similar regulations in succession. The lawmakers, however, did not pay attention to the customs and conventions. The regulation faced difficulties in execution everywhere. In every spring festival, marriage and funeral ceremonies, and other important customary celebrations, people chose to break the law to let off fireworks. Local governments had to invest a large amount of budgets to reiterate the law. In 2004, Beijing municipal government published 53 notices of Prohibition of Fireworks; distributed 4,030,000 pieces of publicities; made 5,857 banners, 31,240

[81] Duanhong Chen. 1998. Democratic Legitimacy and Supremacy of Legislation – Critiques on Chinese Legislation. Peking University Law Journal 6:59–69.

slogans and 3,818 pieces of newsletters; sent 660 mobile loudspeakers; held 9,895 advertising activities; and sent 297,446 policemen during the spring festival.[82] These activities, however, had little effect. After 8 years of insistence, Beijing municipal government decided to change the rule in August 2005. In the legislative hearing of the regulation, absolute majority declared for the repeal of the regulation. Then 272 cities abolished the prohibition of firework one after another. In this example, the cost of lawmaking would be far less if the legislative hearing were held earlier.

Another example was about the conflicts between law and administrative rules. The case of Zhigang Sun initiated nationwide discussion on the legitimacy of the *Administrative Measures of Accept and Dismiss Vagrants and Beggars with No Means of Support in Cities 1982* (*hereinafter Measures 1982*). On the evening of 17th of March 2003, Sun was detained by Guangzhou police because he could not provide his residential permit and an identity card. He requested the police to ask his friend to send his identity card but his request was rejected. Three days later he was found dead in the house of detention. He was beaten to grievous bodily injury by the officers and was not treated until death. After his death, three famous domestic scholars Professor Jiang Yu, Professor Biao Teng and Professor Zhiyong Xu wrote a letter to SCNPC, and requested the SCNPC to review the constitutionality of Measures 1982. In this well-known letter, they wrote:

> *According to the Legislation Law of People's Republic of China 2000, Article 88 Clause 2, SCNPC has the authority to cancel any administrative regulations that violate the Constitution or national law. According to Article 90 Clause 2, where any state organ and social group, enterprise or non-enterprise institution or citizen deems that an administrative regulation, local decree, autonomous decree or special decree violates the Constitution or a national law, they may make a written proposal to the SCNPC for review. The operation office of SCNPC shall study such proposal, and where necessary, it shall distribute such proposal to the relevant special committees for review and comments. We as citizens of the People's Republic of China believe that the Administrative Measures of Accept and Dismiss Vagrants and Beggars with No Means of Support in Cities 1982 contravenes to the Constitution. We therefore request SCNPC to review the constitutionality of the Measures 1982...According to the Constitution article 37, freedom is inviolable. No citizen should be arrested without the approval of the People's Procuratorate or the decision of a People's Court. The Arrests must be implemented by the public security organs exclusively. Unlawful deprivation or restriction of citizens' freedom by detention or other means is prohibited by law. The unlawful search of the person is also prohibited. According to the Law of the People's Republic of China on Administrative Punishments, Article 9, administrative punishment that restrains personal liberty should be authorized by law. According to the Legislation Law of the People's Republic of China 2000, articles 8 and 9, the deprivation of the political rights of a citizen, or compulsory measures and penalties involving restriction of personal freedom should be enacted according to national law exclusively...we therefore believe that the State Council does not have the authority to make laws restricting citizen's freedom...and the part of restrictions on citizen's freedom in Measures 1982 violated the Constitution.*[83]

[82] Quan Tan and Xinning Zhang. 2004. The Possibility of Abolishing the Prohibition of Fireworks in Beijing. Engineering Blasting 3:86–89.

[83] See the original Chinese literature by Jiang Yu, Biao Teng and Zhiyong Xu. 2003. A Proposal on Constitutional Review of the Administrative Measures of Accept and Dismiss Vagrants and Beggars with No Means of Support in Cities 1982. Nanfang Daily. May 17. English here was translated by Peng He.

Professors Weifang He, Hong Sheng, Kui Shen, Han Xiao and Haibo He of Beijing University also wrote a proposal to SCNPC and requested SCNPC to establish a special committee to investigate Sun's case. Later on, Professor Anming Jiang and other four well-known domestic scholars were invited to discuss the Measures 1982 with the major officials of the State Council. Scholars stated that the Measures 1982 should be annulled immediately rather than to be amended. Law should protect and help common people, rather than restrict their freedom. The measures to accept and dismiss vagrants and beggars should help rather than force vagrants and beggars 'to be helped'. The institutions providing this service should respect human rights and should not charge vagrants and beggars any fee.[84] Three months after Sun's death, the State Council annulled the Measures 1982. New administrative measures put emphasis on providing services to the vagrants and beggars rather than keeping control of them.

Another example was about *The Regulation Governing Building Demolition and Resettlement 2001* (*hereinafter the Regulation 2001*), which was highly controversial in its execution. Some administrative institutions used the law to violate people's property rights. The local administrative institutions executed the policy of land expropriation in a brutal way that led to people's violent resistance to the law.[85]

According to LLC 2000, the validity of Regulation 2001 was inferior to the Constitution and the Property Law 2007. Regulation 2001 should not be in conflict with them. The legal executor, however, chose Regulation 2001 as the exclusive legal ground but ignored basic rights in Chinese basic laws. In fact, when the Property Law 2007 was made, Regulation 2001 should be void at the same time. Regulation 2001 should be supposed to aim at protecting people's rights of obtaining reasonable compensation from the government land expropriation, rather than a reason for mandatory control. In reality, however, Chinese legal executors emphasized the obligation to obey orders, but ignored governmental duties of compensation in wrong lawmaking events.

The law on land management stipulated that governments could expropriate collectively owned land for public interests. But there was no specific definition of 'public interests' in the law. It thus left space for governmental rent-seeking.[86] Jiyang Liang, a researcher of the Institute of Geographic Sciences and Natural Resources Research under the Chinese Academy of Sciences, stated that the term 'public interests' should be defined clearly to restrict the arbitrary land acquisition. Compensation for land acquisition should be paid in full. Other scholars believed that the public interests should refer to service for public transit, public health, disaster prevention

---

[84] See more details from Zhigang Sun. 2008. the Milestone of the History of Citizen's Rights. XiaoXiang Morning. December 19. see also http://www.xxcb.com.cn/show.asp?id=938509. Accessed 02 Feb 2012.

[85] See reports about Ms Tang's case: http://news.sohu.com/20091203/n268635575.shtml. Accessed 02 Feb 2012.

[86] See the Property Law 2007, article 42: 'for the purpose of satisfying the needs of public interests, it is allowed to requisition collectively-owned lands, premises owned by entities and individuals or other realities in accordance with the statutory power limit and procedures.'

and control, science, education and cultural diffusion, environmental protection, preservation of cultural and historical relics, protection of public water source and diversion and draining, protection of forests, and other public infrastructure and social services.[87] Regulation 2001 if violated the public interests should be void. It should write clearly about compensations for land acquisition.

Compensations should be paid in full in demolition cases. The price of land was many times the compensation the government paid for expropriation. The huge difference of prices lured some local governments to seek profits from the land. They transformed the arable land to commercial districts, and thus gained a high price from selling land to the real estate developer. A result was government corruption. Unrestricted land expropriation would harm the interests of the largest group in China, the peasants. The acreage of arable land in China was 121.8 million hectares, 0.09 ha per person, which was less than 40 % of world's average level, and decreased respectively 8.3 million and 0.11 ha from 1996.[88] According to Dr. Chunxia Gong's research on the farm land problems of China, excessive expropriation already led to the decrease of arable land. The result would be devastating: if 900 million peasants lost their land with no or very low compensation, it would lead to extreme poverty. The land expropriation already turned nearly 50 million farmers to a vulnerable group. It was prone to mass incidents and threatened social stability. Dr. Gong argued further that even when the peasants got compensation, since they lost their land they would become paupers in the end because they gained no skills for life other than farming.[89] The Property Law 2007 was a landmark of better protection of arable lands, which put strict restrictions on the 'land acquisition'. Regulation 2001 should not be the legal ground for the violent execution because it was in conflict with the Property Law 2007. When the Property Law 2007 was made, the lawmaker should announce the abolition of Regulation 2001.

Another case that disclosed lawmaking problems was a peasant-labor's fight for his compensation for industrial injuries. Haichao Zhang, a 28 year old peasant, worked for Zhendong Wear-resistant Materials Company of Xinmi City of Henan province during the slack farming season. He worked day and night and was surrounded by industrial dust, but the company did not provide any facilities to improve the work environment. In 2007, Zhang was diagnosed with pneumoconiosis, a lung disease caused by long-continuous inhalation of dusts, especially minerals or metallic dusts. Unfortunately, Zhengzhou Prevention and Treatment Institute of Occupational Disease (*hereinafter PTIOD*), the official appraisal institution, diagnosed Zhang's disease as tuberculosis. Zhang could not get any compensation because of this official appraisal.

On 22 June 2009, Zhang requested the Hospital of Henan University to open his chest and take pictures of his lungs. In this extreme way Zhang provided irrefutable evidence of serious pneumoconiosis. PTIOD had to change its previous decision and

[87] Qilin Fu. 1997. The Real Estate Law. Beijing: Law Press.

[88] Statistics from the report: Chinese Political Advisor Calls for Stricter Control in Land Expropriation. 2008. Xinhua News Agency. March 8.

[89] Chunxia Gong's 2010 PhD thesis. The Supply of the Rural Public Goods and the Choice of Farm Land System. Hua Zhong University of Science and Technology.

confirmed that Zhang was entitled to apply for the industrial injury compensation. However, the hospital that provided irrefutable evidence was criticized harshly by the Henan Health Department, the superior of the hospital. It criticized that the hospital did not gain the qualification to diagnose occupational diseases.[90] The criticism did not mention Zhang's right for compensation, but concentrated on the authority of PTIOD.

According to the *Report of Ministry of Health 2009*, 14,495 persons had pneumoconiosis, 748 died. Pneumoconiosis was the most serious occupational disease (which was 79.96 % of the total occupational disease).[91] The 16,000,000 enterprises caused occupational diseases directly because of bad working environment. 200 million people were affected and 140 million of them were peasant-labors.[92] It would cost too much for every peasant-labor to fight for compensation. Why was it so difficult for Zhang to get the official certification of pneumoconiosis? Why was the hospital blamed for the diagnosis? The underlying cause was that Zhang as a 'peasant' was not involved into the social security insurance system. Chinese medical insurance and subsistence allowances were not applicable to rural areas so that 900 million peasants had to pay for their own medical treatments. In the design of social security insurance system, the majority (90 % of the Chinese population) was unfortunately put into the least benefit situation. If, however, they could participate into the lawmaking system, the situation might be different.

Another example showed the flaws and blanks in hasty legislation. On 16 September 2008, the National Administration of Quality Supervision, Inspection and Quarantine published the Report on the Sampling Inspection on the Composition of Milk Products: In the inspection of 491 products of 109 enterprises, 69 products of 22 enterprises contained melamine, an industrial chemical used to produce plastic.[93] Before this investigation, the products of domestic well-known brands were 'national inspection-free products'. Illegal milk dealers knew those products did not need inspection, so they used melamine as a protein powder to boost false protein readings of the milk products.[94] Contaminated milk products killed more than six

---

[90] See Haichao Zhang (stated) and Hui Liu (wrote). 2009. The Truth of My Chest. Shangjie Chengxiang Zhifu 9:30–32. And Qiao Zheng. 2009. Expose the Inside Story of Official Appraisal for Occupational Diseases. Law and Life 19:35. see also http://news.sina.com.cn/s/2009-07-10/032718191682.shtml, http://news.sohu.com/20090729/n265556646.shtml, and http://news.xinhuanet.com/employment/2009-07/22/content_11753354.htm. Accessed 02 Feb 2012.

[91] See the Report of Ministry of Health 2009: http://www.moh.gov.cn/publicfiles/business/htmlfiles/mohwsjdj/s5854/201004/47129.htm. Accessed 02 Feb 2012.

[92] Hao Zhou, Nan Wang and Deqiang Wang. 2009. A Study of Peasant-Labors Occupational Diseases Reality and Legal Protections. Legal System and Social Society 10: 346–347.

[93] About the milk crisis see reports on http://news.sohu.com/20080917/n259590366.shtml. Accessed 02 Feb 2012.

[94] Yili Zhang. 2010. The Ignored Infants Affected by Sanlu Milk Crisis. People Digest 2:32–33. After this milk crisis the China Dairy Industry Association announced that 22 Chinese producers would provide one-time compensation payments to victims whose infants contracted kidney stones and urinary problems from milk. Victims of tainted milk-powder could receive up to 200,000 Yuan ($29,000) compensation from major dairy companies. Families of hospitalized babies would receive compensation around 30,000–50,000 Yuan.

babies and infected 294,000 infants; and the milk crisis started 2 years ago.[95] Food Safety Law of the People's Republic of China was made in 2009 after controversial debates on the food safety and public health. However, the law included no standards, no timeline, no budget, no procedure for obtaining the input of regulated parties and no clear way to resolve disputes. Like Mr. Steven M. Dickinson remarked, '*without…effective private sanctions, the standards imposed by the new food-safety law are unlikely to have any real effect*'.[96]

The above six examples were not isolated and marginal cases, but typical cases relating to the masses. From the above representative cases, we may catch a glimpse of the major problems of Chinese lawmaking: laws were made in a bureaucratic thinking mode; lawmaking lacked public participation; the majority's genuine requests and individual rights were less concerned; laws were made hastily to assuage popular indignation after the crisis. Realizing those problems, the public started to influence legislation. Common people's rights were more stressed and valued in new legislations including the Property Law of the People s Republic of China 2007, the Law of the People's Republic of China on Employment Contracts 2007, the Food Safety Law of the People's Republic of China 2009, and the Draft of the Social Insurance Law. These lawmaking activities showed a shift from the national-economy-centered to the people's-livelihood-centered. Law became more than 'a rubber stamp' or something symbolic. It should not be the rulers' mechanism for social control exclusively. It could contribute to the improvements of people's livelihoods also.

2.6 Conclusion

In this chapter, I disclosed the major characteristics of Chinese lawmaking. In the Chinese legal system, administrative and economic laws were the main body of the system. They were more than four times of the civil and commercial laws. I interpreted the priority of economic and administrative laws that were designed to rectify mistakes of egalitarianism which appeared in the movement of People's Communes in late 1950s. After discussing the background theory, Deng Xiaoping's theory of the economic and legal reform, I pointed out that the reform had obvious

[95] Since December 2007, Sanlu Group co., ltd, the milk company which was first disclosed of adding melamine to milk power, had received several consumers'complaints about infants adverse reactions of the Sanlu milk power. Sanlu Company did not pay much attention to their complaints until April 2008 when the complaints continually rising. In mid May Sanlu Company had already tested their products and was aware that abnormal compositions existed but not until July did they send their products to the official quarantine organs for inspection. When they were told by the official quarantine organ that 15 of the 16 product samples contained melamine, they did not warn the public and recall their products; they did not stop selling their products. See serious reports on http://news.sohu.com/20090101/n261527075.shtml. Accessed 02 Feb 2012.

[96] Steven M. Dickinson. 2009. Food Fumble. The Wall Street Journal Asia. March 3. http://online.wsj.com/article/SB123601731642111527.html. Accessed 02 Feb 2012.

achievements. It was worthy of compliments in the justification of the first stage that illustrated in the theory, i.e., letting some people become richer than others. The economic reform, however, did not accomplish its second and third stages, i.e., letting the rich to assist the others to reach common prosperity. The government as well as the rich should take ‘the responsibility of assistance’ as a legal obligation in the Chinese context because this obligation was a pre-supposed condition of the economic reform. And the rich should be abided by this social contract (the economic reform in the Chinese context) to which they ‘signed’. Wide gaps between the rich and poor, however, showed the fact that the rich took benefits from the social contract but refuse to comply with their duties. After pointing out the problems existed in the Chinese lawmaking mode, I believed that the purpose of lawmaking should shift from the economic-centered to social justice-centered.

I discussed the legitimate problem in Chinese lawmaking system. In my research I disclosed that SCNPC as the representative of the elite was the dominant institution of lawmaking. Laws made by SCNPC were more than that made by the National Congress, NPC, or, the representative of the people. The legitimacy of representativeness of SCNPC thus needed to be justified further. Conflicts in laws made by NPC and SCNPC also led to difficulties in the application of law. Besides, conflicts in macro-economic policies and common people’s livelihoods; efficient lawmaking and democratic representation system; and bureaucratic lawmaking and individual rights added difficulties to lawmaking and the application of law. It became a dilemma of Chinese lawmaking: Which is more important, to promote the development of the state or that of the individual? The official justifications put more emphasis on the state than on the individual. This problem was caused by the top-down and irreversible and non-interactive lawmaking mode. After discussing and criticising the problems of the reality, I will turn to the background theses of the non-communicative lawmaking in the next two chapters.

Chapter 3
The Legitimation of Chinese Lawmaking (I)

—子曰: "为政以德,譬如北辰居其所而众星拱之。"

—子曰:"道之以政,齐之以刑,民免而无耻。道之以德,齐之以礼,有耻且格。"

The Master said, 'He who rules by means of his virtue is like the north polar star, which remains in its place and all the other stars turn towards it.' 'If the people are guided by law, and kept in order by punishment, they may try to avoid crime, but have no sense of shame. If they are guided by virtue, and kept in order by the rules of propriety, they will have a sense of shame, and moreover will come to be good.' Confucius. 2004. The Analects of Confucius. II. 8–10. Trans. Zheng Wei. Fuen Pan and Shaoxia Wen. Shandong: Qi Lu Press.

3.1 Introduction

From the previous chapter we can see that the Chinese lawmaking mode is not much communicative. The most important lawmakers, representatives of SCNPC, are nominated exclusively by the presidium of NPC. And NPC as the top legislature are constituted by less than 0.23‰ of the whole population from four indirect elections. The structure of the legislature is a top-down mode. Since the legal reform 1997, Chinese society is a typical pyramid structure also. The few rich persons have more privileges in society and have more 'power of discourse'. What is the background ideology of this top-down lawmaking mode? In this chapter I will discuss the background themes of Chinese lawmaking.

I will start from the traditional Chinese philosophy Confucianism, to disclose Chinese ideology of 'order'. Then I will go to contemporary dominant ideology, Chinese Marxism, to analyze the logic of legitimation thesis in Chinese lawmaking.

Chapter note: Part of this chapter was published with SSRN eLibrary, http://ssrn.com/abstract=1635112 in July 2010.

P. He, *Chinese Lawmaking: From Non-communicative to Communicative*, Understanding China, DOI 10.1007/978-3-642-39507-9_3, © Springer-Verlag Berlin Heidelberg 2014

I will also introduce and analyze a legal conception with Chinese characteristics, the hidden rule (*Qian Gui Ze*), which represents Chinese social recognition of law. From these three ideologies we can see that the supporting value of Chinese lawmaking were 'order' and 'submission'.

3.2 Confucian Lawmaking

Confucianism established a humanistic concept of 'order' which confirmed the rationality of differences of people in relation to their different status. 'Order of different status' (*Cha Xu Ge Ju*) was one of the most important themes of Confucianism. This recognition of 'order' supported a top-down mode lawmaking.

In traditional China, orders from *Tian* (sky), *Di* (land), *Jun* (emperor), *Qin* (patriarch), and *Shi* (teacher) were five legitimated authorities.[1] People should be subordinate to these five powers. Orders from these five authorities were absolute commands and people should obey them strictly. *Tian* and *Di* regulated natural rules. *Jun* regulated political and legal rules. *Qin* was in charge of the social order that was constituted by families. *Shi* was about the education, which could also be seen as the procedure of learning and obeying the rules. The meaning of 'order of different status' here means a person's different status when confronting these five authorities: one is a *Cang Sheng* (creature) to *Tian* and *Di*, *Chen Ming* (subject) to *Jun*, *Wan Bei* (successor) to *Qin*, and *Di Zi* (student) to *Shi*. In these five relationships, one is always in a status of submission.

In Confucianism, people should obey to the natural rules and live a harmonious life. Confucius was a sage and founder of Chinese culture. He became 'the secular lawmaker' in his seventies.[2] Through editing chronicle *Chun Qiu* (Spring and Autumn Annals), making collation of ancient literatures *Li, Yue, Shi, Shu* (礼乐诗书 rites, music, poetry and other official literatures), and teaching his theory of virtue, politics and knowledge, Confucius introduced and established a set of normative discourse to the whole society. In his summary of his life, Confucius made a well-known statement, which was also the ideal life mode for every Chinese:

> *(The Master said, 'At fifteen I set my heart on learning. At thirty I could stand firm. At forty I had no doubts. At fifty I knew the Tian Ming (the natural rules). At sixty I was already obedient (to these rules). At seventy I could follow the desires of my heart without overstepping the boundaries (of natural rules).'*[3]

In the above quote, *Tian Ming* (the natural rules, the order of *Tian*) was translated as Decree of Heaven in Pan Fuen and Wen Shaoxia's edition of the Analects of

[1] Zi Xu. 2006. Tian Di Jun Qin Shi Yuan Liu Kao (A study of the origins of the Sky, the Earth, the Emperor, the Parents and the Teacher in Chinese Culture). Journal of Beijing Normal University 2:34.

[2] Zhong Yu. 2009. Free Confucius and Un-free Socrates. 12. Beijing: China Renmin University Press.

[3] Confucius. 2004. Wei Zheng. The Analects of Confucius. II. Shandong: Qi Lu Press.

Confucius. But we should notice that *Tian Ming* was different from the will of God in Western philosophy. *Tian Ming* was Confucius' positivistic observation and interpretation of natural rules. It was the ultimate source of his ideal morality. *Tian* literately referred to sky in Chinese. In Confucianism *Tian* was not a religious concept or a transcendental realm, but referred to the objective existence of natural rules. In a question of the rule of *Tian*, the Master said, '*Does Heaven speak? The four seasons run their courses, and all things are continually being produced. Does Heaven speak*?' *Tian He Yan Zai? Si Shi Xing Yan, Bai Wu Sheng Yan, Tian He Yan Zai*?[4] In such a question and his answer, he supposed that *Tian* spoke in the natural rules: four seasons and all creatures spoke for *Tian*. He in another dialogue with a scholar stated that no one could deceive *Tian*, or disobey the natural rule. '*Wu Qi Shei? Qi Tian Hu?'* (…whom do I deceive? Do I deceive Heaven?)[5]

Ming literally means destiny in *Ming Yun* or decree in *Ming Ling*. In Confucianism *Ming* also referred to natural rules. A friend of Confucius was dying, Confucius was very sad and referred the result of death as *Ming*: '*Wang Zhi, Ming Yi Fu!'* (Death is *Ming,* which is a natural rule).[6] Different from Western ideals of eternally and revival of life, Confucianism represented an empirical observation of life. Every creature experiences birth, old age, sickness and death. These experiences were *Ming* (the destiny and the natural rule) of human beings.

Confucius knew *Tian Ming* after 35 years learning and observing the nature and the society. He learnt to obey *Tian Ming* since then and found freedom in his late years. He could follow the desires of his heart without overstepping the boundaries of natural rules. In Confucian freedom, natural rules (as the external limits) and desires of the heart (as the internal limits) should be respected and obeyed. When he knew and accepted these boundaries or limits of life, he found freedom. The Confucian summary of the natural rules and morality was also accepted and respected by his students, who popularized his theory in China. *Tian Ming* was not exclusive external rules. Everyone followed *Tian Ming*, and everyone experienced *Tian Ming*. For example, one should put more clothes on in winter is following *Tian Ming*; one should rest in his sickness and old age is following *Tian Ming*. Following *Tian Ming* one could be more free, and going against it one would suffer.

From the discussion of *Tian Ming* we can see that in Confucianism one is not free because of *Tian Ming*. But one can be freer when he recognizes, accepts and obeys it. Confucius as 'the secular lawmaker' advised us to submit to rules for freedom. *Tian Ming* disclosed the relationship between man and the nature. Confucianism also provided a normative system based on the observation of the interpersonal

---

[4]Confucius. 2004. Yang Huo. The Analects of Confucius. XVII. Shandong: Qi Lu Press.

[5]Confucius. 2004. Zi Han. The Analects of Confucius. VIIII. Shandong: Qi Lu Press. (When the Master was very ill, Zilu had some discilies to act as retainers to prepare for funeral affairs. During a better spell the Master said, 'Long has the conduct of Zhong You been deceitful! By pretending to have retainers when I have done, whom do I deceive? Do I deceive Heaven? Moreover, is it not better to die in the hands of you disciples than to die in the hands of retainers? And if I may not have a grand burial, shall I die by the roadside?').

[6]Confucius. 2004. Yong Ye. The Analects of Confucius. VI. Shandong: Qi Lu Press.

relationship, which was stated in a hierarchical order. In Confucian system, one's rights and duties were decided according to his family and social status. The status was not absolute therefore his rights and duties were relative. One in a family can enjoy his patriarchy powers but he at the same time may be the son of his father, and therefore he should submit to another one's patriarchy powers. The Confucian hierarchical order was provided to put the complex relationships into an ordered system.

'Order of different status' (*Cha Xu Ge Ju*) emphasized the values 'order' (*Xu*) and 'difference' (*Bie*). Apart from the five 'natural' relations (of a person with *Tian, Di, Jun, Qin, Shi*) that discussed previously, Confucian law expanded around five basic human relations, that between the ruler and the ruled (*Jun Chen*), that between parents and children (*Fu Zi*), that between siblings (*Xiong Di*), that between husband and wife (*Fu Fu*), and that between friends (*Peng You*). The order emphasized that the juniors should respect and obey the elders, and the elders should love and take care of the juniors; that there should be differences between men and women, and women should obey men; that the ruled should be loyal and the ruler should be benevolent; and that friends should keep faith.[7] If people obeyed this order, then the ruler was the (real) ruler (*Jun Jun*), and the ruled was the (real) ruled (*Chen Chen*). Otherwise, if they disobeyed the order, the ruler was not the ideal ruler (*Jun Bu Jun*), and the ruled was no longer the ideal ruled (*Chen Bu Chen*).

'Order of different status' in Confucianism emphasized submission (*Cong*) and love (*Ai*) also. The respected person (the ruler, parents, husband, elder) should love the humble person (the ruled, children, wife, junior); the humble should submit to the respected. People were firstly differentiated from each other (*Bie*), and then put in a hierarchical order (*Xu*). In this order, the people at the top of the hierarchy should love (*Ai*) people of a lower grade, and 'the lower' should submit to (*Cong*) 'the higher'. In this Chinese traditional ethics, love (*Ai*), difference (*Bie*) and submission (*Cong*) constituted the order (*Xu*).

In this 'order of different status', love (*Ai*) was a core value. It softened the other three values: difference, submission and order. Without love, the 'order of different status' would lead to plain inequality, exploitation and oppression. Love (*Ai*) was also known as humanity (*Ren*).[8] *Ren,* 'to love people', started from one's close blood relationships, especially from loving one's father and brother. In an interpretation of *Ren*, '*Xiao Di Ye Zhe, Qi Wei Ren Zhi Yu Yi*', filial piety and brotherhood were seen as the root of *Ren*.[9] Love in Confucianism was differentiated by different status in one's relationships with others. *Ren* (humanity) was interpreted by second-order values further, including *Xiao* (filial piety)、*Di* (brotherhood)、*Zhong* (loyalty)、*Shu* (forbearance)、*Li* (courtesy)、*Zhi* (wisdom)、*Yong* (braveness)、*Gong* (respect)、*Kuan* (tolerance)、*Xin* (faithfulness)、*Ming* (agility)、and *Hui*

[7] Mencius, Teng Wen Gong I."

[8] Zhongxin Fan. 2001. The Basic Spirit of the Tradition of Chinese Law. 404. Shandong: Shandong Renmin Publishing House.

[9] Confucius. 2004. Xue Er. The Analects of Confucius. I. Shandong: Qi Lu Press.

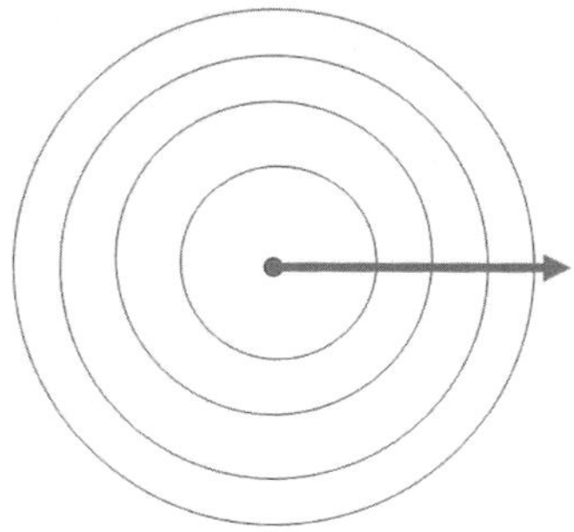

Fig. 3.1 A water-wave structure

(kindness).[10] Those second-order values were all related to one's multiple relationships with other persons, especially their family members. Confucian laws were to protect different status in these relationships and to punish disobedience.

Loving people (*Ai Ren*) or humanism in Confucianism were different from Western humanism. Western humanism valued individuals' freedom and personality, especially the natural inborn individual rights. In Chinese literatures, Western humanism was translated as *Ren Wen Zhu Yi,Ren Dao Zhu Yi,*or *Ren Quan Zhu Yi.*[11] Chinese humanism was *Ren Ben Zhu Yi*. In Western humanism, *Ren* in *Ren Quan Zhu Yi* referred to independent isolated individuals. In Chinese humanism, *Ren* in *Ren Ben Zhu Yi* referred to social beings. In Chinese humanism, a person was born and lived in relationships and was never isolated from the society. A person's responsibilities to the relationship that he belonged were more important than his personal desires.

Another characteristic of Chinese humanism was that its practical route was from the inside to the outside in a structure of 'concentric circles', or a 'water wave' structure (Fig. 3.1): firstly, Confucianism emphasized *Wei Ren You Ji*, which means 'virtue comes from yourself to the outside, not from the outside to you'.[12] And secondly, the closer the relationships, the more rights and responsibilities one had. In Confucianism, relationships are classified by one's status to another in the 'hierarchical order of different status'. Accordingly, the law regulated that the closer the relationship, the respected persons (the ruler, parents, husband, elder of a family) had lighter punishments, while the humble persons (the ruled, children, wife, junior) had more severe punishments.[13] As a contrast, in the well-known metaphor of Western humanism, 'you shall love your neighbor as yourself', we see a parallel structure of love, or love on the basis of equality. This parallel structure implied an

[10] Hegao Yang. 2000. History of Chinese Legal Thoughts. 51. Beijing: Beijing University.

[11] Zhongxin Fan. 2001. The Basic Spirit of the Tradition of Chinese Law. 20. Shandong: Shandong Renmin Publishing House.

[12] Confucius. 2004. Yan Yuan. The Analects of Confucius. I. Shandong: Qi Lu Press.

[13] The according punishment system was also known as *Zhun Wu Fu Yi Zhi Zui*. Regulated since *Laws of Jin Dynasty* (267 A.D.). Chinese system of kinship concealment, *Qin Shu Rong Ying* also reflected this 'water-wave' structure of practicing humanism.

equal treatment to others and a dichotomous classification between the self (or the inside) and the others (the outside).

Transcendental values in Western philosophies were from the outside (the will of God did not exist in ignorant people in Socrates' argument). Chinese humanism emphasized 'to put oneself in another's position' (*Tui Ji Ji Ren*), which was a 'deduction' from the inside to the outside. By comparing Confucius with Socrates, interesting contrasts between Chinese and Western philosophies appeared. Socrates was put into prison in his seventies when Confucius became 'the secular lawmaker' at the same age. As a messenger of God, Socrates faced difficulties with other people's acceptance of his theory because Socrates supposed that the will of God did not exist in people but him. Socrates believed that he had a responsibility to enlighten others. However, he supposed that the belief of others was the antithesis of his. Therefore he had to impose his belief on others and wake up others because to him others were 'in their sleep' and ignorant. The result was that he faced attacks from those 'ignorant' people and was punished to death. The Socrates' dilemma existed in the difficult choice between freedom and virtue: He chose to be abided by the command of God and to practice virtue. However, he attempted to persuade others to give up their free will (freedom in a conceptual sense):

> *Men of Athens, I honour and love you; but I shall obey God rather than you, and while I have life and strength I shall never cease from the practice and teaching of philosophy, exhorting any one whom I meet and saying to him after my manner: You, my friend,--a citizen of the great and mighty and wise city of Athens,--are you not ashamed of heaping up the greatest amount of money and honour and reputation, and caring so little about wisdom and truth and the greatest improvement of the soul, which you never regard or heed at all? And if the person with whom I am arguing, says: Yes, but I do care; then I do not leave him or let him go at once; but I proceed to interrogate and examine and cross-examine him, and if I think that he has no virtue in him, but only says that he has, I reproach him with undervaluing the greater, and overvaluing the less. And I shall repeat the same words to every one whom I meet, young and old, citizen and alien, but especially to the citizens, inasmuch as they are my brethren. For know that this is the command of God; and I believe that no greater good has ever happened in the state than my service to the God.*[14]

The Socrates' argument was widely accepted in Western philosophy. 'Wisdom' was believed better than 'ignorance' in Western philosophy. We see such famous words from John Stuart Mill: '*It is better to be a human being dissatisfied than a pig satisfied. Better to be Socrates dissatisfied than a fool satisfied. And if the fool or the pig is of a different opinion, it is because they only know their side of the question*'.[15] When wisdom was accepted, those ignorant people in Socrates judgment should give up their own insistence of desires. The freedom of being ignorant was thus criticized and abandoned.

The Socrates' argument was different from Confucian way of persuasion. Confucius made distinctions in teaching different students. He developed a teaching principle: teaching students according to their abilities. He never forced others to

[14] Plato. Apology. Trans. Benjamin Jowett. Online text from http://www.gongfa.com/apology.txt. Accessed 02 Feb 2012.

[15] Mill, John Stuart. 1906. Utilitarianism. 260. Chicago, IL: University of Chicago Press.

accept his standard and knowledge so that Confucius relationships with people and the ruler were not so tense as Socrates' with the ignorant. In a reply to a criticism, Confucius showed his humorous: A man of Daxiang said, '*Great indeed is the Master Kong (Confucius)! His learning is extensive, and yet he has no speciality to render his name famous.*'[16] The man implied that Confucius knew lots of things but could do nothing to make a living. Indeed, Confucius and other Chinese scholars did not know how to cultivate the land, or raise live stocks, or do business, or fight as a soldier. When the Master heard this he said to his disciples, '*What shall I take up? Shall I take up chariot-driving? Or shall I take up archery? I think I will take up chariort-driving.*'[17] Confucius did not blame the man. He thought the man was right and he thought he could learn chariot-driving to support his life. He absorbed advices from the man rather than retorted upon him. Confucius' students thus summarized four characteristics of Confucius: '*From four things the Master was entirely free. He made no arbitrary conjectures. He was never stubborn, obstinate, and egotistic.*'[18] A high minister asked why Confucius had various abilities. Confucius replied that when he was young he was in humble circumstances, so he learnt many things including humility.[19] Different from Socrates who worried that other people did not know the truth (that only Socrates knew), Confucius worried that he did not know (the truth of) other people.[20] Western philosophies represented by Socrates discussed external limitations imposed to a subject (from the outside to the inside). Chinese philosophies represented by Confucius stressed an individual recognition of the world (from the inside to the outside).

In this section I discussed Confucian 'hierarchical order of different status' and 'water-wave' structure of humanism. I believe that they supported Chinese traditional top-down lawmaking ideology because both the Confucian order and the structure of Chinese humanism emphasized the submission from the humble persons to the respected in social relationships. Although *Ren* (love) in Confucianism stressed the benevolence of the persons of higher status, it did not alter the top-down structure of the order.

3.3 Chinese Marxism

Confucianism, however, was no longer the dominant philosophy of China since the New Culture Movement in 1919. The legitimation of authority was justified by Chinese Marxism officially since then. Legitimate lawmaking was no longer justified by status or virtue that emphasized in Confucianism. The 'different love' in

[16] Confucius. 2004. Zi Han. The Analects of Confucius. VIIII. Shandong: Qi Lu Press.

[17] Ibid.

[18] Ibid.

[19] Ibid.

[20] Confucius. 2004. Xue Er. The Analects of Confucius. I. Shandong:Qi Lu Press.

Confucianism was substituted by equality in Chinese Marxism. In this section I will discuss Chinese Marxism.

A direct cause of choosing Marxism as the theoretic support for Chinese modern construction of the state was the disappointment of the result of the Paris Peace Conference. In January 1919, the Paris Peace Conference (*hereinafter PPC*) was held to set the peace terms for Germany and other defeated nations. China was a victorious nation and she sent a delegation led by Lu Zhengxiang, to attend the conference. Instead of rewarding China for its contribution to the Allies' victory, the conference passed the Versailles Treaty of April 1919, and transferred German colonial privileges in Shangdong Province to Japan. The Chinese delegation required that Shandong province should be returned to China. It called for an end to colonial institutions including extraterritoriality, legation guards, and foreign leaseholds. These requests were refused by the conference. The Chinese delegation was the only one that did not sign the Treaty of Versailles at the signing ceremony.

'Might overcome right' was the lesson that Chinese learnt from the conference. Chinese territory was carved up by the powerful states. Even when China was a victorious nation of the World War I, the powerful states still refused to listen to China's rightful requests. This conference was unfair to China, and it directly caused the May Fourth Movement (Wu Si Yun Dong), which was also named as the New Culture Movement (Xin Wen Hua Yun Dong). Chinese scholars realized that the Western concepts of the right and peace were not applied universally to all states. They were slogans for the imperialistic states to carve up the world. Chinese scholars started to pay attention to the Russian Revolution of 1917 and its supporting philosophy, Marxism. After the Great October Socialist Revolution, many articles of Marxism appeared in Chinese journals.[21] The earliest leaders and founders of the Communist Party of China, including Dazhao Li, Duxiu Chen, and Qiubai Qu, all published articles about the Russian Revolution, Socialism and Marxism in that era.[22] Marxism was used to justify the revolution against imperialism, bureaucrat-capitalism and feudalism in China. It was also used to legitimate the leadership of the working class. At that time, Marxism-Leninism was the source of thoughts to guide the Chinese revolution.

From 1949 to 1980s, Chinese research of Marxism tended toward 'fundamentalism'. And the topics discussed were about productivity, relations of production, the economic base and superstructure, contradiction, the identity of opposites, the struggle of opposites, objectivity and subjective capability.[23] Criticisms of fundamentalism appeared in 1980s. Discussion at that time re-discovered the practical materialism in Marxism. In 1978, a national debate on 'the standards of examining truth' became

[21] Yuanpei Cai. 1985. The Political Works of Cai Yuanpei. 197. Hebei: Hebei Remin Publishing House.

[22] Yuan Liu. 2008. The Enlightenment of Marxism in China. Journal of Ideological and Theoretical Education 3:36. see also Liqun Zhang. 2008. The Cultural Self-realization of Marxists in May Fourth Era. Journal of Shengli College China University of Petroleum 1:30–32.

[23] Xinyan Wang. 2008. The Paradigm for Research on Marxist Philosophy in Contemporary China. 9. Beijing: Social Sciences in China.

the focus of the criticism of the fundamentalism Marxism in China. The criticism re-emphasized the importance of testing a theory through social practice rather than through ideological allegiance.[24] Since then, Chinese Marxism concerned specific and realistic social problems more. 'Problem consciousness' appeared in this period.[25] The color of the socialistic political ideology was relatively blurred. Western theories (or the capitalistic ideology in some literatures) and multi-cultural elements were absorbed in China.[26] Western Marxism or Neo-Marxism and Postmodern Marxism were also introduced and absorbed into Chinese Marxism since then. Works of Lukács, Korsch, Gramsci, Sartre, Lefebvre, Adorno, Marcuse, Della Volpe, Colletti, Althusser, Habermas, Derrida, Barry; Bourdieu, Mann, Runciman; Stiglitz, Sen, Dasgupta were introduced widely in China. They were also the theoretical resources of Chinese Marxism.[27] Topics of humanism and human dissimilation, modernity and postmodernity, multiple values and win-win negotiations were all inspired by the development of Marxism.

A widely accepted interpretation of Chinese Marxism was that it was the Chinese practice of Marxism, or an integration of Marxism and the Chinese practice.[28] The representative Chinese Marxism theories were Thoughts of Mao Zedong, Theories of Deng Xiaoping and the Three-represent (*San Ge Dai Biao Li Lun*) Theory. The core of Chinese Marxism was stated as 'the scientific concept of development' (*Ke Xue Fa Zhan Guan*).[29] Chinese Marxism valued practical and realistic attitude. It proposed seeking truth from facts.[30] The facts referred to the historical and traditional roots of Chinese culture as well as the realistic problems of contemporary China. Chinese Marxism aimed to disclose and examine truth relying on legacy and reality.[31]

---

[24] The national discourse was caused by an article by Hu Funing. 1978. Practice is the Sole Criterion for Testing Truth. Guangming Daily. May 11. This famous event is also named as a favorable turn in Chinese modern history.

[25] Zhengli Sun.2005. Studies on Contemporary Chinese Marxism. Journal of Henan University (Social Science) 4:6–8.

[26] Zhen Li. 2009. A Study of Contemporary Chinese Marxism CPC Ideology. Journal of Xue Xiao Dang Jian Yu Si Xiang Jiao Yu 9:14–26.

[27] Xiaomei Huang and Zelin Lei. 2008. Issues of Chinese Marxism Philosophy since Thirty Years of Enforcing the Opening and Reform. Journal of Zhongnan University of Economics and Law Yanjiusheng 3:91–92. See also Yuepeng Ren. 2009. Introduction of Western Marxism, in Habeimasi: Law as Communication. 1–15. Heilongjiang: Heilongjiang University Press.

[28] Laigui Feng. 2008. From the Localization of Marxism in China to Chinese Marxism—the Transformation of the Research Visual Angle and the Transfer of the Focal Point of Research. Journal of Shangrao Normal College 4:1.

[29] The Speech of Hu Jingtao on 28 July 2003 at the 17th CPC national congress. http://news.xinhuanet.com/newscenter/2007-10/24/content_6938568_2.htm. Accessed 02 Feb 2012.

[30] Xiaoping Deng. 1993. Works of Xiaoping Deng 2. 278. Beijing: People's Publishing House.

[31] Zedong Mao. 1991. Works of Zedong Mao 2. 533–534. Beijing: People's Publishing House. also see Xinyan Wang. 2008. The Paradigm for Research on Marxist Philosophy in Contemporary China. 5. Beijing: Social Sciences in China.

3.4 The Hidden Rule of Lawmaking

In this section I will discuss 'the hidden rule of lawmaking', which interprets the legitimacy of lawmaking from another route. There was a Chinese concept that referred to common persons' recognition of law: *Qian Gui Ze* (潜规则 the hidden rules). 'The hidden rule of lawmaking' in China refers to the people's moral judgment on the power and procedure of lawmaking. It is not about the recognition of plain powers and the factual publication of laws. It means a shift from the focus on the official law to the people's recognition of the law. The question of the legitimacy of law was no longer exclusively about the existence of the official rules. People's recognition of the law could be different from the official law although their judgments were often influenced by the latter. As I will explain later in this section that the existence of hidden rules disclosed that we distorted the meaning of the Rule-of-law: We saw it as a plain fact of control by legal forces since interactive elements were lacked in Chinese lawmaking.

Qian Gui Ze, the hidden rules, although literally means 'lurking' or 'underneath' rules, were apparent and obvious rules indeed in China. A hidden rule in the Chinese context was *not* a rule underneath or simply imbedded in a formal rule. It was the opposite of the official rule. It was recognized and chosen by the people. Hidden rules were formed from custom and conventions. The term 'hidden rules' in the Chinese context had a derogatory meaning. It implied a negation of the legality. The efficacy of hidden rules was uncertain: some of them were illegal from the beginning, some of them were in the grey zone of the law. Different recognition of rules led to diverse behavior patterns: People holding the recognition of the official rules behaved lawfully. Those who chose hidden rules, however, broke the law or acted in a grey zone.

The Rio Tinto case illustrated well about a debate on a hidden rule. On 12 August 2009 Chinese official media, China Daily and Xinhuanet reported the news that China's Supreme People's Procuratorate had announced the arrest of four employees of the Anglo-Australian mining giant Rio Tinto. The four were detained on July 5 on charges of stealing commercial secrets and bribery. At a press conference, Vice Minister of Commerce Fu Ziying said '*…this is an isolated judicial case…China is ruled by law and the judicial decision on the case would undoubtedly be fair*'.[32] The Australian government and Rio Tinto spokesmen disagreed with the Chinese 'rule by law' approach. Rio Tinto called the allegations surprising and denied their awareness of any evidence to support an investigation.[33] It became important to ascertain whether the Chinese judicial jurisdiction was exclusive and whether bribery was

---

[32] See Rio-Tinto case reports on China Daily and BBC: http://www.chinadaily.com.cn/cndy/2009-08/12/content_8558038.htm; and http://www.bbc.co.uk/worldservice/learningenglish/language/wordsinthenews/2009/07/090710_witn_iron_page.shtml. Accessed 02 Feb 2012.

[33] See reports from The Australian and CNN:
http://www.theaustralian.news.com.au/business/story/0,,25754321-36418,00.html. And
http://edition.cnn.com/2009/WORLD/asiapcf/08/11/china.riotinto/index.html?iref=newssearch. Accessed 02 Feb 2012.

illegal in the present commercial environment, or on the contrary was assumed as a well-known hidden rule by which most companies abide. The answer to the first question was certain: China had exclusive judicial jurisdiction in this case. The second question was controversial.

In the *Criminal Law of People's Republic of China 1979*, commercial bribery was a crime. In reality, however, commercial bribery was adopted by traders in China including Rio Tinto and thus became a trade hidden rule. This contradiction was exemplified well in the Rio Tinto case. In this case there was a written legal norm which regulated that bribery in commercial activities should be punishable. Yet the hidden rule was that commercial bribery was 'ok'. The legal norm regulated that traders should not bribe, otherwise they should be punished by law. But the hidden rule was opposite: the bribe was the 'guild regulation'. Through the Rio Tinto case, Chinese government expressed the attitude of rectifying the hidden rule of commercial bribery. Chinese authorities also stressed in the recent legislations and interpretations that those inglorious hidden rules such as public official corruption, sexual bribery, official appointment by favoritism, should all be abolished by law.[34]

Another kind of hidden rules, however, was in the gray zone of the law and some of the rules were morally neutral. They were less serious than the criminal offences that stated above, but related to individuals' recognition of the law. These hidden rules were not regulated by law directly. A no-passing-permitted sign beside the East Lake scenic spot of the W city of China, pointed out, ironically, a free short-cut to the park. When people saw such a sign they recognized a fact that some people entered the park for free previously. Then they had a choice: whether to follow the hidden rule (free entrance) discovered by other people; or to obey the rule (no entrance). They took a risk of being caught (and fined) by the park keeper, if they entered from the short-cut. But they also knew that, more often than not, they might go there free from charge. In this case, when most people were following the hidden rule, the formal normative rule became *nominal*. If the park keeper dedicated to eliminate the hidden rule, he could either add a charge spot or add inspectors to stop the free entrance practically. In this case, the sign of 'no entrance' of the public park, however, should not be referred to as the legal cause to punish 'trespasser', because according to *the Law of Land Administration of the People's Republic of China 1999*, the socialist public ownership of the land was the ownership by the whole people. And thus all people had the right to enter the public land freely. Therefore in this case, the hidden rule was not against the basic law. The official sign of 'no entrance' was, however, illegal (although it was consistent with other laws relating to public property management, such as *the Regulation of Management of Scenic Spots 2006,* we should notice that regulations was inferior to basic laws according to *LLC2000*. So the official sign was against Chinese basic laws and should be changed).

[34] Since 2005, the Chinese legislature has been working on legislations on anti-corruption. In July 8 2007, the supreme court and supreme procuratorate published an official interpretation on official bribery and regulated specified bribery crimes with 'people with special relationships with the officers'.

A well-known 'hidden rule' about legislation in Chinese legal practice was: '*law is less useful than its judicial interpretation; judicial interpretation is less useful than the Party's forum note; a forum note is less useful than a red-headline-document; a red-headline document is less useful than (the Communist Party of China, hereinafter CPC) leaders' instructions*'.[35] This hidden rule was in conflicts with the normative rules regulated in the *Legislation Law 2000. LLC2000* established the hierarchy of the validity of legal rules. It put the national law above decrees and other local rules.[36] The hidden rule of legislation that stated above, however, put orders of CPC above law. If the hidden rule represented the reality, and the legal rule referred to the normative order, then there existed a gap between the reality and the formal law: When people chose to obey the hidden rule, their behavior deconstructed the legitimacy and validity of official laws. A paradoxical phenomenon appeared: this hidden rule was the 'real' rule but people who followed the hidden rule were disobedient to the official formal law. The legitimacy of the official lawmaking was questionable.

The above hidden rule of lawmaking influenced legal practice greatly. This hidden rule was not in the gray zone of the law because it was not against the spirit of *the Constitution of the People's Republic of China 1982* (*hereinafter the Constitution*) necessarily. In the 7th paragraph of the preamble, the basic task of the nation was '*to concentrate its effort on socialist modernization. Under the leadership of the Communist Party of China and the guidance of Marxism-Leninism and Mao Zedong thought, the Chinese people of all nationalities will continue to adhere to the people's democratic dictatorship and the socialist road...*'[37] The hidden rule of lawmaking emphasized the CPC's authority and legitimacy, and put the validity of law under the CPC's instruction. Therefore the hidden rule of lawmaking was consistent with Chinese Constitution. But apparently it was opposite to the *LLC2000*: in *LLC 2000*, the law rather than orders of any party was in the highest level of the hierarchy of rules. If the hidden rule of lawmaking was legal, the legality of *LLC2000* was questionable. The relationship between Chinese Constitution and the constitutionality of *LLC2000* needed to be clarified.

[35] 'Red-headline documents' refer to the official documents of the Chinese Communist Party because their titles are always written in red. Translated by Peng He. See the original Chinese literature of Tao Yang. 2008. New Lawyers Law and the Hidden Rules. Xinjing News. June 02. Also see Zhibo Hai. 2008. Why is Law Less Useful Than Documents? Procuratorial Daily. June 11.

[36] 'The Constitution has the highest legal authority, and no national law, administrative regulation, local decree, autonomous decree and special decree, or administrative or local rule may contravene the Constitution.'; 'National law has higher legal authority than administrative regulations, local decrees and administrative or local rules. Administrative regulations have higher legal authority than local decrees and administrative or local rules.'; 'A local decree has higher legal authority than local rules issued by governments at the same level and lower level. Local rules enacted by the People's Government of a province or autonomous region have higher legal authority than local rules enacted by the People's Government of a major city located in its jurisdiction.' (LLC2000, articles 78, 79, and 80).

[37] The Constitution of the People's Republic of China 1982.

Ironically, however, even if the hidden rule lacked legality, the constitutionality of *LLC2000* was still problematic. The clauses about the CPC's leadership and the democratic dictatorship principle that were regulated in the Chinese Constitution were excluded by *LLC2000*. When the hidden rule's legitimacy was confirmed, the constitutionality of *LLC2000* was problematic. Thus a normative theory was especially necessary for the affirmance of the legitimacy of lawmaking. An interpretation of the constitutionality of *LLC 2000* could clarify further the obscure provisions about the ultimate authority of both CPC and law in the Chinese Constitution. A question was: which was the ultimate 'rule of recognition' in Chinese lawmaking: the CPC's instructions, or the legislature's formal law, or the Chinese Constitution?

Theoretically, Chinese constitution should have a peerless status in the Chinese legal system. '*No laws or administrative or local rules and regulations may contravene the Constitution. All state organs, the armed forces, all political parties and public organizations and all enterprises and institutions must abide by the Constitution and law.*'[38] *LLC2000* re-affirmed this principle also.[39] However, in the Chinese Constitution, the CPC's leadership had a supreme status: According to the Chinese Constitution, CPC should be abided by the constitution and law also; but the constitution did not admit that the law should have an authority independent to CPC's leadership. Under such logic, the rule of recognition in the Chinese context was simplified as: formal rules under the CPC's leadership. Therefore, in extreme cases, CPC's instruction was the ultimate rule of recognition. In normal situations, the legislature's laws represented the authority. If, however, the ultimate rule of recognition in the Chinese legal system was the CPC's instruction, then the hidden rule of lawmaking was consistent with this 'rule of recognition'. This hidden rule confirmed that the leaders' instructions were the ultimate authority of the Chinese legal system and the origin of legitimacy. If this argument was tenable, then the four justifications of lawmaking stated previously in this chapter could be consistent with the justification of the hidden rule. The validity of this hidden rule of lawmaking could contribute to the legitimation of Chinese lawmaking. However, was this hidden rule right?

To answer this question, we need to differentiate further between the hidden rule and the sincere requests of people. Although hidden rules were different from official rules, they were not necessarily genuine requests from the people. In my previous analysis of Chinese lawmaking I concluded that common people's right of discourse was not equal: there were differences between rural peasants and citizens;

[38] See Article 5 of the Constitution.

[39] See Article 78,79, and 80 of LLC2000: 'The Constitution has the highest legal authority, and no national law, administrative regulation, local decree, autonomous decree and special decree, or administrative or local rule may contravene the Constitution.'; 'National law has higher legal authority than administrative regulations, local decrees and administrative or local rules. Administrative regulations have higher legal authority than local decrees and administrative or local rules.'; 'A local decree has higher legal authority than local rules issued by governments at the same level and lower level. Local rules enacted by the People's Government of a province or autonomous region have higher legal authority than local rules enacted by the People's Government of a major city located in its jurisdiction.'

poor and rich; common people and successive persons. People accepted the hidden rule of lawmaking because it could be compatible with the actual official legitimacy of lawmaking. And it was more direct and practicable. If we ignored the fact that there lacked discourse between the people and the lawmakers, we mistook the hidden rule for the real request of the people.

Here I would like to refer to the meaning of 'living lawfully' again in Professor Bankowski's argument on the relationship between following law and breaking law, to support my argument of absorbing some 'hidden rules' into lawmaking. As argued in *Living Lawfully*, '*to live lawfully means living a life where the law is constantly interrogated and renewed, it is broken but from within and not from outside.*'[40] Living lawfully was not the literal sense of just following the law but both following and breaking the law as appropriate. In circumstances where people obeyed 'hidden rules' rather than 'formal rules' in China, the problem of 'hidden rule' seemed to slide into a problem of anarchism, although some of the 'hidden rules' could be moral and represented the will of the people. The trust of 'hidden rule' rather than 'legal rule' would lead to a sort of 'legal nihilism'. From this perspective, 'hidden rule' was 'bad' and should be removed from the Chinese legal system. But from another perspective, where hidden rules as the opposite of formal rules can renew the latter, the 'hidden rules' could be deemed as a part of the law also.

The existence of hidden rules and the recognition of them could contribute to a discourse between lawmakers and common people. But it would cause difficulties in respect of the application of law for Chinese lawyers and judges because hidden rules were not the official rules but the common people's creative discovery of principles behind laws. Such creativity was at the same time 'risky' since it always open to the outside of the law. In order to stick to the rules, we have to make the boundary of discretion. The problem was how to apply hidden rules and formal rules separately. When shall we follow the formal rules? When shall we ignore the formal rules but apply the hidden rules? In Professor Bankowski's argument, the way to maintain in the rigid limits of the law without losing the 'outside' justice, was to 'pay attention' to the outside. Law and love were not the two opposing contradictories and it was better stay 'in the middle'.[41] Now the picture might be clearer if we look at people's own choice, the hidden rules in China, as the outside rules; as in contrast to the formal law, the inside rules. We need both of them but we should respect the inside rules in the beginning. However, we should pay attention to the outside rules also because they renew the law. People following the hidden rules seemed to break the law, the inside system. At the same time, they were creating the law, from absorbing elements of the outside system to the inside. In this perspective, there were reasons to keep the hidden rules. What we need to do was to 'pay attention' to their application rather than reject them exclusively.

---

[40] Zenon Bankowski. 2001. Living Lawfully-Love in Law and Law in Love. 186. Dordrecht: Kluwer.

[41] Ibid.

3.5 Conclusion

In the beginning of this chapter I discussed Confucian lawmaking and concluded that the Confucian hierarchical order supported a top-down lawmaking ideology. Although it also stressed humanity, the principle of love, it did not alter the unequal structure of lawmaking and law-application. It emphasized the internal restrictions of desires of a self, but this conception of freedom based on different status of social communication, in which the social being was emphasized but the autonomy of an individual was not so much stressed. Confucianism was substituted by Chinese Marxism since 1919. I also interpreted Chinese legitimacy thesis from another route, i.e., from the people's active acceptance of the power and procedure of lawmaking instead of a passive recognition of the law. I analyzed a special Chinese concept of the legal phenomenon, 'hidden rules', which was ignored in Chinese academic research. In my research, the hidden rule of lawmaking, i.e., the CPC's ultimate and peerless authority and legitimacy, instead of the four justifications, were the ultimate justification. The problem was how to introduce 'hidden rules' into 'formal rules'. I employed Bankowski's paradigm of 'bringing outside in' to solve this problem. My conclusion was that the recognition of hidden rules could contribute to the constitution of an open legal system. The Chinese legal system should absorb rather than exclude 'hidden rules'.

In the next chapter, I will focus on Chinese legalism, the opposite theory of Confucianism. It was another legitimation route of Chinese lawmaking. Chinese legalism as an ancient school of philosophy influenced the major characteristics of Chinese law greatly.

Chapter 4
The Legitimation of Chinese Lawmaking (II): Chinese Legalism

—古者未有君臣上下之时,民乱而不治。是以圣人别贵贱,制爵位,立名号,以别君臣上下之义。地广,民众,万物多,故分五官而守之。民众而奸邪生,故立法制为度量以禁之…明王之治天下也,缘法而治,按功而赏。

Shang Yang (B.C.390–B.C.338), Shang Jun Shu, Prince and Minster, see online texts: http://chinese.dsturgeon.net/text.pl?node=47249&if=en&remap=gb. Accessed 02 Feb 2012.
(In the days of antiquity, before the time when there were princes and ministers, superiors and inferiors, the people were disorderly and were not well administered, and so the sages made a division between the noble and the humble; they regulated rank and position, and established names and appellations, in order to distinguish the ideas of prince and minister, of superior and inferior. As the territory was extensive, the people numerous and all things many, they made a division of five kinds of officials, and maintained it; as the people were numerous, wickedness and depravity originated, so they established laws and regulations and created weights and measures, in order to prohibit them, and in consequence there were the idea of prince and minister, the distinctions between the five kinds of officials, … The way in which an intelligent prince administers the empire is to do so according to the law, and to reward according to merit.)

4.1 Introduction

In this chapter I will discuss Chinese legalism. I will summarize and analyze the origin of Chinese legalism, its major propositions and its characteristics. This chapter compares the difference between Chinese legalism and other Chinese philosophies including Confucianism, Taoism and Mohism. It also discloses the difference between

Chapter note: Part of this chapter was published with Higher Education Press and Springer-Verlag. 2011. Frontiers of Law in China 6:645–669.

P. He, *Chinese Lawmaking: From Non-communicative to Communicative*, Understanding China, DOI 10.1007/978-3-642-39507-9_4, © Springer-Verlag Berlin Heidelberg 2014

Chinese legalism and Western legalism in their concerns with morality. Western legalism defended the Rule-of-Law but argued against the morality of law. In contrast, Chinese legalism, especially in the early Pre-Qin era, did not separate morality from law. However, the fidelity to law in Chinese legalism was interpreted as the fidelity to the monarch, and was thus different from the Western Rule-of-Law.

Chinese legalism (Fa Jia Si Xiang) argued for the legitimacy of political relationships. It claimed that law was more important than ethical morality.[1] In Western theories, analytic positivism, and positivism in general, have a close connection with legalism.[2] Professor Bankowski explained from a Western perspective that Chinese legalism belonged to legal formalism.[3] In this perspective, a distinction between law and morality was quite clear-cut. Chinese legalism, however, was different from Western legalism in its historical background. Chinese legalism had close ties with Confucianism, Taoism and Mohism in its origin. As will be discussed later in this chapter, Chinese legalism did not exclude morality in its early form.

4.2 Chinese Legalism

Chinese legalism was one Pre-Qin school of thoughts in Chinese history. It originated and developed from the period 475 B.C. to 221 B.C., the Warring States Period.[4] During that time, three other Pre-Qin schools of thoughts (Confucianism, Mohism and Taoism) were also significant. These four major schools held different propositions and political suggestions. Confucianism claimed that the state was better to be governed by virtue rather than by coercive laws.[5] Mohism advertised ‘impartial care’ and ‘universal love’ and was thus object to wars among states.[6] The

[1] See Zhongxin Fan. 2001. The Basic Spirit of the Tradition of Chinese Law. 143. Shandong: Shandong Renmin Publishing House.

[2] Zenon Bankowski. 2001. Living Lawfully-Love in Law and Law in Love. 49. Dordrecht: Kluwer.

[3] We had discussion of Chinese legalism and formalism and I disagree with this equation. But our interesting debates inspired this comparative study of Western legalism and Chinese legalism.

[4] See Honglie Yang. 2004. History of Chinese Legal Ideology. 51. Beijing: China University of Political Science and Law Press. The period was named after wars among the states in China at that time. Plato, Aristotle, Kyng Alisaunder and Maurya Dynasty existed around the same period in other places of the world.

[5] The Master said, ‘if the people are guided by law, and kept in order by punishment, they may try to avoid crime, but have no sense of shame. If they are guided by virtue, and kept in order by the rules of propriety, they will have a sense of shame, and moreover will come to be good.’ Confucius. 2004. The Analects of Confucius. II. Wei Zheng. 11. Shandong: Qi Lu Press.

[6] The Master said, ‘if every one in the world will love universally; states not attacking one another; houses not disturbing one another; thieves and robbers becoming extinct; emperor and ministers, fathers and sons, all being affectionate and filial—if all this comes to pass the world will be orderly. Therefore, how can the wise man who has charge of governing the empire fail to restrain hate and encourage love? So, when there is universal love in the world it will be orderly, and when there is mutual hate in the world it will be disorderly. This is why Mozi insisted on persuading people to love others.’ Mohism. Book IV Universal Love. Chinese Text Project, http://chinese.dsturgeon.net/text.pl?node=1069&if=en&remap=gb. Accessed 02 Feb 2012.

key concept of Taoism was about 'men-cosmos correspondence', which was in a way similar to the natural law in Western legal theory.[7]

Chinese Legalism, however, focused on strengthening the political power of the ruler. Different from the other three schools, Chinese legalism emphasized that the function of law was to control the society. It argued for a society ruled by law. It valued legal rules (Fa), art of control (Shu) and force of control (Shi) as three 'trumps' of the ruler.[8] Liu Shao in *Ren Wu Zhi Liu Ye Pian* said that 'legalists (Fa Jia) were those who attempted to establish laws and a legal system to make the state strong and rich.'[9] Si Matan in his introduction of six Pre-Qin major schools stated that 'Legalists were strict and were not mercy'; '[They] clarified, established and strengthened the difference between the emperor and his ministers, *i.e.*, their superior and subordinate relationship'; '[They] treated persons of close and distant relationship equally, regardless of their noble or humble social status; they treated all according to the law.'[10] Liang Qichao, a scholar of the Republic of China (1912–1949) defined Chinese legalism as

> *[A thought] started from materialism. It noticed social and economic circumstances. It believed the all-powerful government and denied the sanctity of human nature. [Chinese legalists] argued for strict interferences from the government and objective criterion (law). Under the law people had [relative] freedom and equality.*[11]

The representative Chinese legalists were Guan Zhong, Zi Chan, Deng Xi, Li Kui, Wu Qi, Shen Buhai, Shang Yang, Shen Dao, Han Fei and Li Si. Most of them had literatures handed down from ancient times, including *Guan Zi*, *Fa Jing*, *Shen Zi*, *Shang Jun Shu*, *Shen Zi*, *Han Fei Zi*. Those legalists could be classified further as Qi legalists and Jin legalists. Qi legalists, who led the legal reform in state Qi (Qi was named after an ancient state of China; was referred to the area also), stressed the law but did not abandon morality exclusively. Jin legalists (legalists of the Jin area; or Jin state), however, argued for absolute monarchy and believed that morality should be substituted by legal norms. Jin legalists even believed that law was the [only] textbook and the [legal] official were the [only] teacher.[12] A contemporary scholar, Zhang Dainian concluded that Jin legalists were too strict and were against humanity. Qi legalists' statesmanship was better than Jin legalists in their inclusiveness of

[7] The Master said, 'man takes his law from the Earth; the Earth takes its law from the Heaven; the Heaven takes its law from the Tao; the law of the Tao is its being what it is.' Tao Te Ching, chapter 25. Chinese Text Project, http://chinese.dsturgeon.net/text.pl?node=11591&if=en&remap=gb. Accessed 02 Feb 2012.

[8] Classical Chinese Literature:Han Fei. Han Fei Zi. Ding Fa. Jian Jie Shi Chen. Nan Shi. Nan Mian at Chinese Text Project, http://ctext.org/hanfeizi/ens. Accessed 02 Feb 2012.

[9] Liu Shao. 1989. Ren Wu Zhi . Si Bu Cong Kan. Shanghai: Shanghai Book Store Publishing 74:12.

[10] Si Matan. Liu Jia Yao Zhi. In Si Maqian. 2008. Historical Records. Wang Bojun ed. 560. Liaoning: Volumes Publishing Company.

[11] Qichao Liang. 2003. Political Ideology of Pre-Qin Period. 79. Tianjing: Tianjing Ancient Books Publishing House.

[12] Lin Yang. 2005. A Comparative Study of Pre-Qin Legalism. 1–2. PhD dissertation of Zhe Jiang University.

morality.[13] Legalists of early Pre-Qin did not exclusively deny the role of morality (Guan Zhong was the representative). In early legalism, law was referred to an alternative conception: the 'force' or 'art of control' (Shen Dao and Shen Buhai were the representative defenders). Legalists of late Pre-Qin represented by Han Fei made a comprehensive expression of law: Law should be supported by force as well as the art of control.

4.3 Connections with Other Pre-Qin Schools

The rose of Chinese legalism was no later than the other Pre-Qin schools. Legalists Guan Zhong and Zi Chan were earlier than Confucius (the founder of Confucianism). Deng Xi and Confucius were at the same period. Li Kui, Wu Qi and Shen Buhai were earlier than Mencius (another representative of Confucianism). Shang Yang was earlier than Zhou Zhuang (the founder of Daoism). Their thoughts were more or less influenced by the other schools. Shen Buhai, Shen Dao and Shang Yang studied Daoism (Taoism) before legalism, while Han Fei and Li Si studied from a Confucian, Xun Zi (a representative of Confucianism).[14] Han Fei was especially named as the Master of Confucianism, Mohism, Daoism, Yangism, and Shenism.[15]

Legalism was related to Confucianism. Guan Zhong, a representative early legalist valued livelihood of the commons and righteousness of the liege. Unlike later legalists who focused on law exclusively, Guan Zhong regarded morality and education as the positive methods besides law. Many legalists even studied from Confucians directly. Li Kui studied from Zi Xia, Shang Yang studied from Shi Jiao, and Han Fei studied from Xun Kuang. Zi Xia valued talents (and merits) over favoritism. He also classified the external form and the internal spirit of rites. Those thoughts were absorbed by legalism. Shi Jiao like Confucius stressed the importance of 'name' ('name' means the concept or reason in Chinese), but he further connected 'name' (concept) with rewards and punishments. The proper 'name' of an action therefore came from proper rewards and punishments. Shang Yang studied from Shi Jiao and inherited his thoughts on the relationship between the 'name', rewards and punishments. Han Fei also developed the theory of 'establishing the name by rites' in Confucius into a theory of "using law to establish the 'name' and to resolve disputes".[16]

[13] Jiacong Hu. 1995. Guan Zi Xin Tan. 2–3. Beijing: China Social Science Press.

[14] Si Maqian. 2008. Historical Records. Liaoning: Volumes Publishing Company. See records of each legalist.

[15] Long Chuan Zheng Ci Lang. History of Chinese Legal Thoughts. quoted from Yang Honglie. 2004. History of Chinese Legal Ideology. 76. Beijing: China University of Political Science and Law Press.

[16] About the relations of legalists and their teachers, see Si Maqian. 2008. Historical Records. Liaoning: Volumes Publishing Company. See records of each legalist.

Legalism had similarities with Mohism and Daoism also. On the argument of equality and the sole standard of law, legalists were influenced by Mohists.[17] Legalists inherited Mohists' theory of autocracy and pragmatism.[18] Theses of Shang Tong (arguing for conformity), Shang Xian (arguing for virtuous and talented persons), Fei Ming (arguing against unchanging mandates from heaven), and the positivistic attitude of Mohism were more or less absorbed by legalists. In Daoism, no-intervention was better than the positive interference from the ruler. Legalism, however, stressed the active interference from the ruler. From the surface, Daoism and Legalism were absolutely different. However, Daoism developed into two different Daoism. Lao Zi and Zhuang Zi represented an 'exclusive' Daoism which focused on metaphysics and argued for detachment from the society. Tian Pian, Shen Dao and Yin Wen, represented the other Daoism, or an 'inclusive' Daoism which argued for governance through less intervention (but they argued against detachment from the society). Inclusive Daoism was believed to be one of the earliest origins of legalism.[19] In Guan Zi, three significant articles, Fa Fa, Ren Fa and Ming Fa were believed to connect legalism with Daoism.[20] Legalist Shen Dao argued for legislation according to the nature and less interference from the ruler. Han Fei's legal thoughts were also partly originated from Daoism.[21]

Nevertheless, Chinese legalism differed from other Pre-Qin schools in the following aspects: Law was employed to approach Chinese legalists' purpose of constructing a mighty state, together with (political) trickery and (military) force in Chinese legalism.[22] As a contrast, Confucianism required (and attempted to justify) the ruler's morality. Mohism argued against wars . Taoism believed that ruling without rules was the best way to strengthen a state. Legalism, however, proposed that a state should be ruled by strict and severe rules. Unlike the other three schools of thoughts, Chinese legalism put an emphasis on the function of law as an effective social control mechanism. Different from *Li Zhi* (rule by rites) in Confucianism, legalists argued against the order based on patriarchal relations. They argued for political subordination; and using political relations to substitute patriarchal relations. They suggested sever punishments instead of morality and education. Punishments were supposed to guide individuals' behaviors. In Chinese legalism, law means punishments and rewards; and they came exclusively from the official (Guan Zi Fa Jing). Law was created by the official and publicated to the common people (Han Fei Zi Nan San). Law was written by the authorities (Han Fei Zi Ding Fa).

---

[17] Yang Honglie. 2004. History of Chinese Legal Ideology. 70. Beijing: China University of Political Science and Law Press.

[18] Lin Yang. 2005. A Comparative Study of Pre-Qin Legalism. 25–28. PhD dissertation of Zhe Jiang University.

[19] Bozan Jian. 1999. History of Qin and Han Dynasties. 88. Beijing: Beijing University Press.

[20] See Moruo Guo, Dejian Jin, Jiacong Hu and Yuanming Ding's arguments in Zhang Guye. 2006. Criticisms on the Three Arcitles of Guan Zi. Social Science Front 5.

[21] Si Maqian. 2008. Historical Records. 295–298. Liaoning: Volumes Publishing Company.

[22] See Han Fei. Han Fei Zi. Ding Fa. http://chinese.dsturgeon.net/text.pl?node=2601&if=en&remap=gb. Accessed 02 Feb 2012.

Therefore law was the official mandates from the emperor and governors, which were separated from social morality or the natural law.

Fa (Law) in Chinese legalism was thus different from *Li* (which includes social conventions) in Confucianism, *Dao* (Chinese natural law) in Daoism, and *Tian Zhi* (Chinese natural law) in Mohism. Legalists specified the concept of law and standardized the recognition of law (law as official orders). They also drove the movement of codification of Pre-Qin era and attempted to make laws clear and certain. Law was applied as the manipulative and coercive measurement so that law could make all behaviors and movements in order ('*Qi Tian Xia Zhi Dong*').[23] Law became 'the formula of the world and the instrument of everything' ('*Tian Xia Zhi Cheng Shi, Wan Shi Zhi Yi Biao*').[24]

4.4 A Review of Lord Shang's Reform

Lord Shang Yang's reform disclosed the legalists' argument against the other Pre-Qin schools.[25] Old aristocrats of Qin resisted Shang Yang's reform. They claimed that it was necessary to obey ancient laws and it was just to follow old observances, *Li*..

> *Unless the advantage be a hundredfold, one should not reform the law; unless the benefit be tenfold, one should not alter an instrument…in taking antiquity as an example, one makes no mistakes, and in following the established rites one commits no offence.*[26]

A Western scholar Joseph Needham recognized *Li* (courtesy) as the Chinese natural law [147].[27] However, *Li* should not be simplified as natural law; and the differentiation between *Li* and *Fa* (law) should not be simplified as the Western division of the natural law and positive law. The Western natural law theory and its

[23] Shen Zi. Shen Zi Yi Wen. http://ctext.org/shenzi/ens. Accessed 02 Feb 2012.

[24] Guan Zi. Guan Zi Ming Fa Jie. http://ctext.org/guanzi/ming-fa-jie/ens. Accessed 02 Feb 2012.

[25] Shang Yang, A representative legalist of Chinese legalism, was a retainer of the prime minister of Wei state. Before the prime minister's death, the minister told his king that Shang Yang was a very talent man. The king could use him as the succeed prime minister, or kill him just in case he would bring troubles to the state of Wei. The king, however, did not listen to the minister's words. He neither employed nor killed Shang Yang. Another king, the king of Qin state, appreciated Shang Yang's talents and invited him to serve for Qin. Later on, Shang Yang led the legal reform of Qin and assisted Qin to become the most powerful state in the Warring State period. Qin eliminated other states, unified China, and in the end built the first empire in Chinese history—All these historic achievements should owe to Shang Yang's successful legal reform, according to Si Maqian's records and comments. Book of Lord Shang. Reform of the Law. Chinese Text Project, http://chinese.dsturgeon.net/text.pl?node=47113&if=en&remap=gb. Accessed 02 Feb 2012. See also Si Maqian. 2008. Historical Records. 312–315. Liaoning: Volumes Publishing Company.

[26] Book of Lord Shang, Reform of the Law, Chinese Text Project, http://chinese.dsturgeon.net/text.pl?node=47113&if=en&remap=gb. Accessed 02 Feb 2012.

[27] See J. Needham. 1980. Science and Civilization in China. History of Scientific Thought 2. 521, 532, 539, 544. Cambridge: the Syndics of the Cambridge University Press.

background religious and cultural sources were entirely different from the Chinese tradition. In Chinese ancient literatures, discussion of 'natural law' in the sense of Western natural theory could hardly be found.[28] In Chinese traditional legal culture, *Li* was a set of rules centered on the order of the clan system. The content of *Li* was more than the official [legal] rules. *Li* was also a set of positive rules and abstract principles above the positive rules, or legal principles (like obedience to the ethical relations *Jun Chen Fu Zi*). *Li* did not gain its authority from God but from positive and natural blood relationships.[29] Confucianism focused on the relationship among people. At first *Li* and *Xing* (criminal law; penalty) were opposite concepts: *Li Bu Shang Shu Ren, Xing Bu Shang Da* Fu .[30] *Li* and *Xing* were supposed to cover all the norms: *Li Zhi Suo Qu, Xing Zhi Suo Qu, Shi Li Ze Ru Xing, Xiang Wei Biao Li.*. It meant *Xing* should be used in situations where *Li* could not be used. *Xing* and *Li* were interdependent.[31] *Li* was social rules based on the patriarchal culture. To a certain extent, both *Li* and *Xing* were legal norms. But from the above old aristocrats' argument we could see that *Li* akin to natural law stressed the (relative) permanency and unchangeable character of 'old' norms: People should always abide by *Li* made by former sages. But Shang Yang argued against this unchanging law conception in Confucianism:

> *Former generations did not follow the same doctrines, so what antiquity should one imitate? The emperors and kings did not copy one another, so what rites should one follow? Fu Xi and Shen Nong taught but did not punish; Huang Di, Yao and Shun punished but were not angry; Wen Wang and Wu Wang both established laws in accordance with what was opportune and regulated rites according to practical requirements; as rites and laws were fixed in accordance with what was opportune, regulations and orders were all expedient, and weapons, armour, implements and equipment were all practical. Therefore... there is more than one way to govern the world and there is no necessity to imitate antiquity, in order to take appropriate measures for the state. Tang and Wu succeeded in attaining supremacy without following antiquity, and as for the downfall of Yin and Xia – they were ruined without rites having been altered. Consequently, those who acted counter to antiquity do not necessarily deserve blame, nor do those who followed the established rites merit much praise.*[32]

Lord Shang thus criticized the old aristocrats' static law idea and argued for a dynamic conception of law. This argument was a preparation for the implementation of his later reform. In historical records, Qin's agricultural production, economic and military forces were greatly enhanced because of Shang Yang's reform.[33]

[28] Zhiping Liang. 1997. Searching for the Harmony of the Natural Order: Studies on Traditional Chinese Legal Culture. 326. Beijing: China University of Political Science and Law Press.

[29] As a contrast, Chinese philosophy Taoism concentrated on the harmonious relationship between the nature and the human world. Dao De Jin (or Tao Te Ching), 1. See English translation: http://acc6.its.brooklyn.cuny.edu/~phalsall/texts/taote-v3.html. Accessed 02 Feb 2012.

[30] Ruan Yuan ed. 1980. Li Ji. Shi San Jing Zhu Shu. 1249. Beijing: Zhonghua Book Company.

[31] Ban Gu. 1962. The Bibliography of Chen Chong. Chronicles of the Han Dynasty. 1554. Beijing: Zhonghua Book Company Press. (first published around 79–105 A.D.).

[32] Ibid.

[33] Han Feizi. 1996. He Shi, and Jian Jie Shi Chen. 119. Literatures of Historical Chinese Legal Thoughts. Law Press.

Shang Yang's reform illustrated a story of a legalist who made efforts to persuade people to believe in and accept new legal reform. More than 2000 years ago, Shang Yang realized that if people lost their fidelity to law, law would fail in practical effects. Shang Yang believed that if the law was credible and just, people would obey it, and the society would be better. Thus an important proposition of Chinese legalism was stated like this: It was not about people but the law. If the law were credible, people could have more faith in it.

I would like to interpret this proposition further. It started from the first premise: human nature was amoral (even worse, some legalists held that human nature was evil or corrupted). In Chinese legalism, all people in nature were utilitarian: They tended to pursue interests and advantages, and at the same time aimed to avoid danger and disadvantages. The relationships between people, the monarch and the officials, were all maintained through interests:

> *[H]uman beings don't have feathers. Without clothes they would catch cold. Human beings need to eat; otherwise they will starve to death. All of those are natural rules. Human beings' selfishness is also a natural thing. Doctors' work is to cure disease. They suck the blood of the wounded part not because they like to, but because of the benefit they will get from the patients. Craftsmen who make vehicles look forward to wealthy customers; craftsmen who make coffins are expecting customers who have a dead relative. We cannot say that the vehicle-maker have a higher standard of morality than the coffins-maker. The vehicle-producer wishes people wealthy because otherwise his vehicles cannot be sold; the coffin-maker wishes people dead because otherwise his coffins cannot be sold. It is hard to conclude that the former love people or the latter hate people. Both of them love the benefits behind their business.*[34]

From the above quote we can see that human beings' selfishness nature in Chinese legalism was seemed as a fact, or a rule of nature. This rule was seen as existed everywhere: The relationship between the monarch and the subject was seen as a 'buyer-seller' relationship. Between the ruler and the ruled, 'the ruler sells nobility and salary; the ruled sell their intelligence and strength'.[35] Neither morality nor law was necessary for ancient societies because people in the very ancient time did not have to fight against each other for the plenteous resources.[36] Later on, law became necessary for maintaining an orderly society because of the lack of resources.[37]

Then Chinese legalism provided the second proposition: Law was the result of a corrupt society.[38] From Chinese legalists' point of view, morality was not the necessary condition of law. The idea of benevolent law held by Confucianism was unrealistic to legalism. Law was believed amoral in nature. Amoral facts in Chinese legalism referred to the existence of law. Holding this epistemology of human

[34] Han Fei. Han Fei Zi. Bei Nei. http://chinese.dsturgeon.net/text.pl?node=1967&if=en&remap=gb. Accessed 02 Feb 2012.

[35] Ibid.

[36] Ibid.

[37] Han Fei. Han Fei Zi. Wu Du. http://chinese.dsturgeon.net/text.pl?node=2660&if=en&remap=gb. Accessed 02 Feb 2012.

[38] Ibid.

nature and law, Chinese legalists developed a strict duty-first philosophy: Law was not for the protection of rights but for submission to orders. It led to the third proposition: The disobedience to law was immoral.

In Shang Yang's era corporal punishments were applied to trifling misbehaviors like throwing dust onto the road.[39] The reason of establishing severe punishments for unimportant matters, in Chinese legalism, was that people would be afraid of breaking law, so that there would be no crimes in the end.[40] Critics might question the effect of those severe punishments. From historical literatures we saw examples of strict obedience to law influenced by severe laws: The reformer Shang Yang himself swallowed the result of his law—after the death of his king, the king's successor ordered to arrest Shang Yang because the new King was previously punished by Shang Yang's law. Lord Shang run to a small inn near the border and asked for temporary lodging. The innkeeper, however, told Lord Shang that he could not serve him because according to the latter's law, anyone who served the escapee would be punished.[41]

The innkeeper's reply was unfortunate news for Lord Shang. But it showed an honorable result for his legal reform. The fact of Qin's rapid growth seemed to also prove legalists hypothesis: Severe laws would benefit a state's rapid growth.[42] Chinese legalists Shang Yang, Han Fei, and Li Si assisted the state Qin's development. Qin strengthened in force in decades. In history, Qin unified the other strong states and established the first empire of China. Later on, the political institutions and the structures of Qin's legal system were carried forward for more than 2000 years. Confucianism, Taoism and Mohism were all well-known philosophies, but Chinese legalism was more than a school of philosophical thoughts; it was practiced and succeeded indeed in the history.

Relying on the above three propositions, Chinese legalism reached to its conclusion and the fundamental premise of the argument of the fidelity to law: People should obey law because law was credible. Now we may understand the profound meaning of Lord Shang's well-known experiment before his promulgation of the new laws in 359 B.C. Shang Yang firstly sent an officer to erect a 30 ft high wood at the south gate of the capital city, and declared that whoever moves the wood to the north gate would be rewarded 10 gold coins. It was a great fortune at that time so the news spread over quickly. The masses gathered at the south gate and discussed about this decree. People could not believe that such an easy work would worth so much. They wondered whether it was a joke made by the government. No one tried to move the wood and all were waiting for the government's reaction. Shang Yang raised the reward to 50 gold coins then. The crowd was more curious. Finally a man

[39] Han Fei Zi. Nei Chu Shuo (shang) 33 http://chinese.dsturgeon.net/text.pl?node=2141&if=en&remap=gb. Accessed 02 Feb 2012.

[40] Ibid.

[41] Si Maqian. 2008. Wang Bojun ed. Shang Jun Lie Zhuan. Historical Records.312–315. Liaoning: Volumes Publishing Company.

[42] Han Feizi. 1996. He Shi and Jian Jie Shi Chen. 119. Literatures of Historical Chinese Legal Thoughts. Beijing: Law Press.

came out and carried the wood from the south to the north gate. Shang Yang paid him the reward as promised. This story spread over the whole state immediately and people were all aware of the credit of Shang Yang's law. They started to believe that Shang Yang's law would be enforced strictly.

Nevertheless, the Great Qin Empire also collapsed because of its severe laws. The peasant uprising peasant leaders, Cheng Sheng and Wu Guang, were rule-followers (they were low rank officers) at the beginning. They were ordered to guard the border. On their way to their destiny they encountered heavy rains so as to postpone their march. According to a law of Qin, deferring the march would face the death penalty. Sheng and Guang had no other ways to save their lives but led the peasants' revolt against Qin. Their revolution spread over the whole country and overthrew the empire Qin.[43] Severe laws assisted Qin's growth but also ruined the empire. The successors, however, still employed legalism as an effective social control ideology, although they start to pay attention to soften legalism by combining Confucianism with it. They even established the priority of Confucianism and the secondary of Legalism.[44]

Confucianism, in contrast to Chinese legalism, did not necessarily support the argument of the fidelity to law. In Confucianism the ruler and lawman would be blamed if they did not practice law properly. However, it was about the nature of the ruler rather than people's fidelity to law. In Confucianism, human nature was good.[45] According to *Li*, the legitimacy of law came from legitimate ruler (in a patriarchal pedigree), the morality of law therefore referred to a justification of legitimacy of the supreme authority.

If we compared the first and second presuppositions of Confucianism and Legalism, we discovered that they were contrary to each other. In Chinese legalism, the nature of human beings was corruptive and should be guided by sever coercive norms; while in Confucianism, human nature was good and could be moralized through *Li*. In Chinese legalism, the fidelity to law was rather a legal obligation than morality; while in Confucianism, the fidelity to the legitimate ruler was a content of morality. We thus see different solutions that Confucianism and Legalism offered. To Confucians, people should learn *Li*, rules of proprieties; legalists, however, emphasized that people should learn *Fa*, law, rules of the ruler.

Thus Confucianism and Legalism showed different attitudes on the morality of law and human beings. Confucianism had more optimistic judgments on human nature, and had more faith in the morality of law. Chinese legalism, as a contrast, had pessimistic opinions on human nature, and doubted the morality of law. Anarchists, legal nihilists, the skeptic and radical reformers also held a pessimistic

[43] Si Maqian. 2008. Chen She Shi Jia. Historical Records. 249–253. Liaoning: Volumes Publishing Company.

[44] Fan Zhongxin. 2001. The Spirit of Chinese Legal Traditions. 340–354. Shandong: Shandong People's Publishing House. see also Yu Ronggen ed. 2000. History of Chinese Legal Thoughts. 345–347. Beijing: Law Press.

[45] Meng Zi. Gao Zi I. Gong Sun Chou I. Teng Wen Gong I. http://ctext.org/mengzi/gong-sun-chou-i/ens. Accessed 02 Feb 2012.

view of law, but they abandoned law. Chinese legalists although did not claim law as moral rules, put emphasis on law as the effective social control mechanism. Law in Chinese legalism was thus empirical and amoral.

Confucian would argue that those who practiced law should take the responsibility because law was lifeless—to rely on something lifeless was unrealistic. Confucians would further claim that in every legal system, if there were 'bad' laws, ultimately it was the person who made, executed and practiced 'bad' law. Those who refused to follow 'bad' laws were not necessarily disobedience to *Li* (the ultimate law in Confucianism). Legalists could hardly deny the fact of injustice of 'some' law. The essential difference between Confucians and legalists, however, was that the former had more faith in human's goodness. Confucians expected a morally good governor to manage the society and emphasized benevolent love especially the governor's love of the ruled. Legalists, on the contrary, disclosed the selfish nature of all people *including* the governor. Legalists based their theory on the awareness of human's badness. Human being's selfishness, rather than their morality was seen by legalists as the *necessary* pre-condition of establishing the authority of law.

4.5 Characteristics and Propositions of Chinese Legalism

In Shang Yang's legal reform, people were praised for military exploit and agricultural work.[46] The obedience to officers' orders in the army and the rules of agriculture therefore constructed the essential content of people's behavior paradigm: submission to rules. Law in Chinese legalism therefore meant submission; and was recognized as an obligation and was applied (exclusively) to the subject. In Chinese legalism, before conquering an empire, the emperor should conquer his subjects first.[47] The best tool to assist him was the law. An emperor's attitude to his people was similar to facing enemies in wars. The relation between law and the subject in this perspective was therefore antagonistic. In Shang Yang's work, the reason of establishing the authority of law was described as the requirement of the conquest:

> *Of old, the one who could regulate the empire was he, who regarded as his first task the regulating of his own people; the one who could conquer a strong enemy was he, who regarded as his first task the conquering of his own people. For the way in which the conquering of the people is based upon the regulating of the people is like the effect of smelting in regard to metal or the work of the potter in regard to clay; if the basis is not solid, then people are like flying birds or like animals. Who can regulate these? The basis of the people is the law. Therefore, a good ruler obstructed the people by means of the law, and so his reputation and his territory flourished.*[48]

[46] Si Maqian. 2008. Wang Bojun ed. Shang Jun Lie Zhuan. Historical Records. 312–315. Liaoning: Volumes Publishing Company.

[47] Shang Yang, Book of Lord Shang. Policies. http://chinese.dsturgeon.net/text.pl?node=47226&if=en&remap=gb. Accessed 02 Feb 2012.

[48] Ibid.

The way of making law effective in this perspective was to put severe punishments to minor offences. Legalists believed that severe punishments would establish the authority of law because people were forced to obey it; and that it would also benefit for the ruler's control of the ruled.[49] In Chinese ancient literatures, there were records of tattooing in the face of the people who threw dust on the street:

If a person threw dust on the street, it might irritate other persons and caused quarrels and fights among them. According to the law, those who had fights on the street may be punished to death, and his relatives would be punished associated. Comparing with the cruel results, it would be better to punish the dust-throwing behavior at the beginning.[50]

This was a severe and insulting corporal punishment. Legalists attempted to justify such severe punishment on minor offences: they used a hypothetical premise (the person who threw dust might cause quarrels with others) to justify an established rule (people should be punished severely). Such a deduction was inconsequent because the person who threw the dust should not necessarily have fights with other people in reality! The reasons for putting sever punishments on a minor offence was to establish people's dread of law. Shang Yang argued that:

If there are severe penalties that extend to the whole family, people will not dare to try (how far they can go), and as they dare not try, no punishments will be necessary. The former kings, in making their interdicts, did not put to death, or cut off people's feet, or brand people's faces, because they sought to harm those people, but with the object of prohibiting wickedness and stopping crime; for there is no better means of prohibiting wickedness and stopping crime than by making punishments heavy. If punishments are heavy and rigorously applied, then people will not dare to try (how far they can go), with the result that, in the state, there will be no people punished. Because there are no people punished in the state, I say that if one understands punishments, there is no capital punishment.[51]

The legalist believed that establishing severe punishments could prevent crimes in the end, and thus nobody would be punished. It was a theory of prevention of crime. Related topics were proposed including: the objectivity, fairness and publicity of law; the equal application of law; law should not have retrospective effects; a legal system should be stable; and what law requires should be possible.

Firstly, about the objectivity of law: Chinese Legalists looked law as the objective and the just criterion of judging and normalizing people's behaviors. In *Guan Zi*, law was compared to measurement: '*law is the measurement of people's behaviors...(law) is the compass for everything and every procedure*.'[52] Shen Dao also used this metaphor to state that law could measure behaviors just like a scale could

[49] See works of Shang Yang, Han Fei, Li Si and Lü Buwei, in Si Maqian. 2008. Historical Records. 312–315. 295–298. 386–393. 378–380. Liaoning: Volumes Publishing Company. See also Chen Yanqing. 2001. A Comparative Study of the Aristotelian Rule-of-Law Idea and Chinese Legalism. Journal of Gansu Social Science 3:19–22.

[50] Han Fei Zi. Nei Chu Shuo. http://chinese.dsturgeon.net/text.pl?node=2141&if=en&remap=gb. Accessed 02 Feb 2012.

[51] Shang Jun Shu. Rewards and Punishments. http://chinese.dsturgeon.net/text.pl?node=47220&if=en&remap=gb. Accessed 02 Feb 2012.

[52] Guan Zi. Qi Fa. http://chinese.dsturgeon.net/text.pl?node=48238&if=en&remap=gb. Accessed 02 Feb 2012.

weigh heavy and light.[53] Shang Yang described law as the scale of the state.[54] Han Fei employed this metaphor as well. He proposed that law was the scale for judging behaviors and also the mechanism to normalize behaviors.[55] Those legalists emphasized the objectivity of law to persuade the ruler to employ law, and the ruled to believe in the fairness of law.

Secondly, about the fairness of law: The fairness was embodied in the division of public and private affairs. In Chinese legalism, law represented the public. Han Fei stated that law was used to prevent selfish motives (of the ruler).[56] Chinese legalists further proposed their famous statement that everything and everyone should be judged by law, based on the fairness of law.[57] This was totally different from Confucians' ethical philosophy that differentiated a person's rights and duties according to his status in his family and in the society. The fairness of law in Chinese legalism meant that law should be equally applied to everyone.

Thirdly, for the equal application of law: Legalists argued against inequality order held by Confucians. Confucianism argued that 'rules of the ceremony do not go down to the common people. The penal statutes do not go up to great officers.' [58] In the order of *Li* (rules of propriety) in Confucianism, rules should:

> *[Rules should] furnish the means of determining (the observances towards) relatives, as near and remote; of settling points which may cause suspicion or doubt; of distinguishing where there should be agreement, and where difference; and of making clear what is right and what is wrong.*[59]

> *The course (of duty), virtue, benevolence, and righteousness cannot be fully carried out without the rules of propriety; nor are training and oral lessons for the rectification of manners complete; nor can the clearing up of quarrels and discriminating in disputes be accomplished; nor can (the duties between) ruler and minister, high and low, father and son, elder brother and younger, be determined; nor can students for office and (other) learners, in serving their masters, have an attachment for them; nor can majesty and dignity be shown in assigning the different places at court, in the government of the armies, and in discharging the duties of office so as to secure the operation of the laws; nor can there be the (proper) sincerity and gravity in presenting the offerings to spiritual beings on occasions of supplication, thanksgiving, and the various sacrifices. Therefore the superior*

---

[53] Shen Dao. Shen Zi. Yi Wen. http://chinese.dsturgeon.net/text.pl?node=47109&if=en&remap=gb . Accessed 02 Feb 2012.

[54] Shang Yang. Shang Jun Shu. Xiuquan. http://chinese.dsturgeon.net/text.pl?node=47207&if=en&remap=gb. Accessed 02 Feb 2012.

[55] Han Fei. Han Fei Zi. Wai chu shuo you xia. http://chinese.dsturgeon.net/text.pl?node=2479&if=en&remap=gb. . Accessed 02 Feb 2012.

[56] Han Fei. Han Fei Zi. Gui Shi. http://chinese.dsturgeon.net/text.pl?node=2616&if=en&remap=gb. Accessed 02 Feb 2012

[57] Si Maqian. Historical Records. Zixu. http://chinese.dsturgeon.net/text.pl?node=9270&if=en&remap=gb. Accessed 02 Feb 2012.

[58] Ibid.

[59] Li Ji. Qu Li I. http://chinese.dsturgeon.net/text.pl?node=9480&if=en&remap=gb. Accessed 02 Feb 2012.

man is respectful and reverent, assiduous in his duties and not going beyond them, retiring and yielding – thus illustrating (the principle of) propriety.[60]

Therefore in Confucianism rules should *not* be applied equally but should be applied differently to the commons and the noble. Chinese legalists argued against this differential treatment and defended the equality of law. Han Fei, Guan Zhong, and other legalists criticized Confucianism and stated that punishments and rewards should be applied equally to the commons and the noble.[61] In *Shang Jun Shu (Book of Shang Yang)*, Lord Shang stated that

What I mean by the unification of punishments is that punishments should know no degree or grade, but that from ministers of state and generals down to great officers and ordinary folk, whosoever does not obey the king's commands, violates the interdicts of the state, or rebels against the statutes fixed by the ruler, should be guilty of death and should not be pardoned. Merit acquired in the past should not cause a decrease in the punishment for demerit later, nor should good behaviour in the past cause any derogation of the law for wrong (that was) done later. If loyal ministers and filial sons do wrong, they should be judged according to the full measure of their guilt, and if amongst the officials who have to maintain the law and to uphold an office, there are those who do not carry out the king's law, they are guilty of death and should not be pardoned, but their punishment should be extended to their family for three generations. Colleagues who, knowing their offence, inform their superiors will themselves escape punishment. In neither high nor low offices should there be an automatic hereditary succession to the office, rank, lands or emoluments of officials.[62].

Fourthly, about the publicity of law: Since law should be applied equally to everyone, it should be known by everyone. Legalists argued that the law should be proclaimed publicly. Early in the Spring and Autumn Period, there were discussions about whether laws should be written and published among famous scholars.[63] A milestone in Chinese legal history was the penal-code-casting event in 536 B.C. in the Zheng Kingdom and 513 B.C. in the Jin Kingdom. A legalist, Zichan, had a famous debate with Confucius and Shuxiang about whether the penal code should be cast on the vessel, the entity that symbolized the supreme authority.

Confucius believed that a country should be ruled by morality rather than law; and that the publication of law would nourish disputes about justice and would demolish the harmonious relationships among people. Zichan's response was that he did not have the wisdom (as Confucius had), and he did not cast the penal code for himself or for the future generation, but rather as a way to save their era. Zichan

---

[60] Ibid.

[61] See Han Fei. Han Fei Zi. You Du. http://chinese.dsturgeon.net/text.pl?node=1905&if=en&remap=gb. Accessed 02 Feb 2012. Same conclusions see also Zheng Liangshu.1989. Shang Yang and His School. Shanghai: Shanghai Ancient Books Publishing House. Wu Shuchen and Li Li. 1998. Chinese Legalism and its Spirits. Beijing: China Radio and Television Publishing House. Su Nan. 2000. Aspects of the Chinese Culture of Legalism. Shandong: Qilu Book Press. Su Fengge. 2008. Pre-Qin Chinese Legalism and Its Influences to Posterity. Journal of XinXiang University 22:21–24.

[62] Shang Jun Shu. Rewards and Punishments. http://chinese.dsturgeon.net/text.pl?node=47220&if=en&remap=gb. Accessed 02 Feb 2012.

[63] The Spring and Autumn Period:722 B.C.–481 B.C.

then published the law by casting it on the vessel.[64] Han Fei stated that law should be published so that people could know how to conduct, and officials would dare to bend the law for personal gain.[65] Shang Yang also argued that

> *Indeed, subtle and mysterious words, which have to be pondered over, cause difficulty even to men of superior knowledge. There may be one case in ten millions, where the directing guidance of the law is not needed and yet it is correct in everything. Therefore, a sage governs the empire for the ten million cases. For, indeed, one should not make laws so that only the intelligent can understand them, for the people are not all intelligent; and one should not make laws so that only the men of talent can understand them, for the people are not all talented. Therefore did the sages, in creating laws, make them clear and easy to understand, and the terminology correct, so that stupid and wise without exception could understand them; and by setting up law officers, and officers presiding over the law, to be authoritative in the empire, prevented the people from falling into dangerous pitfalls. So the fact that when the sages established the empire there were no victims of capital punishment, was not because capital punishment did not exist, but because the laws which were applied were clear and easy to understand. They set up law officers and government officials to be the authority, in order to guide them; and they knew that if the ten thousands of people all knew what to avoid and what to strive for, they would avoid misfortune and strive for happiness, and so restrain themselves. Therefore, an intelligent prince follows the existing conditions of order and so makes the order complete, with the result that the empire will enjoy great order.*[66]

Law should be known to the common people. It was an argument against Confucian's idea of mysterious law. Chinese legalists believed that although the purpose of having law was to control the subjects, the subjects should at least know what they were required to do by law; otherwise it was unjust to use mysterious laws to punish them afterwards. Therefore law should be published, clear in content and easy to understand.

Fifthly, about the retrospective effects: Relating to the publicity of law, Chinese legalists proposed that law should not have retrospective effects. In Chinese legalists' point of view, the function of law was to lead people living lawfully and punish the offender; law therefore should not have retrospective effects. Guan Zi stated that if law were not publicized but people got rewards or punishments, the ruler rather than the people should be responsible for the results.[67] This proposal was similar to Confucius prospective law conception:

> *To put the people to death without having instructed them – this is called cruelty. To require from them, suddenly, the full tale of work, without having given them warning – this is*

---

[64] Honglie Yang. 2004. History of Chinese Legal Ideology. 51. Beijing: Chinese University of Political Science and Law Press.

[65] Han Fei. Han Fei Zi. Nan San. http://chinese.dsturgeon.net/text.pl?node=2562&if=en&remap=gb. Accessed 02 Feb 2012.

[66] Shang Yang. Shang Jun Shu. Ding Fen. http://chinese.dsturgeon.net/text.pl?node=47260&if=en&remap=gb. Accessed 02 Feb 2012.

[67] Guan Zhong. Guan Zi. Fa Fa. http://chinese.dsturgeon.net/text.pl?node=48351&if=en&remap=gb. Accessed 02 Feb 2012.

called oppression. To issue orders as if without urgency, at first, and, when the time comes, to insist on them with severity – this is called injury.[68]

Both Confucians and Chinese legalists argued for the non-retrospective rules. The difference between them was that Confucians put emphasis on the education and generalizing *Li* (rules of propriety); legalists, however, focused on the general knowledge of *Fa* (law).[69]

Sixthly, about the stability of a legal system: Chinese legalists argued against the statistic conception of law that defended in Confucianism. Chinese legalists argued that law should be changed according to the spirit of the age. This was the statement Shang Yang proposed before his legal reform. Nevertheless, Chinese legalists also stated that law should be stable: they compared law to measurement and stressed its objective and its stable characteristics. Guan Zhong concluded that if the law were made but then changed all of a sudden, people would not follow the law even if the rewards were generous; and people would not be afraid of the law even if the punishments were severe.[70] Han Fei also agreed that 'law should be unified and stable; then people could know law'.[71] Otherwise, 'if laws were changed frequently, people would suffer from the result'.[72] They proposed that if laws were paradox, or the law was changed too frequently, people could not comprehend law; neither could they make appropriate judgments on the legal results of their behaviors.

Seventhly, what law requires should be possible. Chinese legalists illustrated the objectivity of stable law to increase the credibility of law. They also realized that if the law's requirements were impossible, people would not obey law. As stated in *Guan Zi*,

A wise ruler would consider the ability of his subjects. He would not require them to achieve impossible tasks. His orders should be in the range of their capabilities so that his laws could be applied. If a ruler required his subjects obey laws which were impossible to obey, his law would be inefficacious. So a wise ruler would never force his subjects obey impossible rules.[73]

The above seven propositions were the major topics of law argued in Chinese legalism.[74] As a legal thought, it presupposed human beings' corrupted nature, and

---

[68] The Analects. Yao Yue. http://chinese.dsturgeon.net/text.pl?node=1101&if=en&remap=gb. Accessed 02 Feb 2012.

[69] Hegao Yang. 2000. History of Chinese Legal Thoughts. 39–84. 125–183. Beijing: Beijing University Press.

[70] Guan Zhong. Guan Zi. Fa Fa. http://chinese.dsturgeon.net/text.pl?node=48351&if=en&remap=gb. Accessed 02 Feb 2012.

[71] Han Fei. Han Fei Zi. Wu Du. http://chinese.dsturgeon.net/text.pl?node=2660&if=en&remap=gb. Accessed 02 Feb 2012.

[72] Han Fei Zi. Jie Lao. http://chinese.dsturgeon.net/text.pl?node=1981&if=en&remap=gb. Accessed 02 Feb 2012.

[73] Guan Zi. Xing Shi Jie. http://chinese.dsturgeon.net/text.pl?node=48731&if=en&remap=gb. Accessed 02 Feb 2012.

[74] See also about Hongyi Chen's 12 major topics of Chinese Legalism in Hongyi Chen. 2002. Introspect of Legalists' (Fajia) Thoughts. China and Western Legal Traditions 2:108–135.

proposed a duty-centered philosophy. It put emphasis on the coercive nature of law and was thus different from Confucians' moral propositions. In its debates with the other three major thoughts in Pre-Qin era of China, legalism became a unique and significant ideology because of the successful legal reforms led by Chinese legalists in the Warring State period.[75] Chinese legalism efficiently supported the rapid growth of the state Qin, assisted it to unify the whole country and to build the first great empire in the history of China.

4.6 Chinese Legalism and Western Legalism

In history, Chinese legalism as a philosophy had a formidable adversary, Confucianism, because of their divergence of opinions on law and ethics. At present, Chinese legalism faced another antithesis, The Western Rule of Law ideology. Western theorists might misunderstand Chinese legalism. They might use the concept of Western legalism to cover Chinese legalism incorrectly because of the English translation. If relying simply on the definition *per genus et differentiam* Chinese legalism could be (but was incorrectly) interpreted as a branch of legalism: Chinese legalism in this approach was understood as a kind of legalism.[76] However, Chinese legalism differed from Western legalism not only in its geographic origin and historical development, but also their theoretic grounds. Chinese legalism developed originally from its debate with Confucianism about the functions of coercive norms from the state and the government; Western legalism was rather a modern ideology about the justification of rule-following.

Western legalism was described as the legalistic attitude, and normative behavior to be a matter of rule-following. In legalism, law merely was a heteronomous system of rules.[77] It was not only 'an ideology internal to the legal profession as a social whole' or 'the operative ideology of lawyers' and of those who have a 'rule-oriented thinking', but also a background theory of law, which implied a rule-based way of looking at things and a tendency to treat law as just 'there' and separated of

[75] About the debates of Legalism with Confucianism, Taoism, Mohism see Liangshu Zheng. 1989. Shang Yang and His School. Shanghai: Shanghai Ancient Books Publishing House. Shuchen Wu and Li Li. 1998. Chinese Legalism and its Spirits. Beijing: China Radio and Television Publishing House. Nan Su. 2000. Aspects of the Chinese Culture of Legalism. Shandong: Qilu Book Press. Honglie Yang. 2004. History of Chinese Legal Ideology. Beijing: China University of Political Science and Law Press.

[76] According to *Definition per genus et differentiam*: definition = a genus + species; in this way of definition, Chinese Legalism = Legalism + Chinese (characteristic). It is, however, not a correct definition.

[77] Zenon Bankowski. 2001. Living Lawfully—Love in Law and Law in Love. 43. Dordrecht: Kluwer.

non-law.[78] Professor Bankowski described this attitude as 'it is the rules that are important, not how they are arrived at'.[79]

> *For legalism the power of natural law would lie in the rules that it generates and not in the nature, God or practical reason that might be said to produce them.' and 'no matter where the rules come from, the effect of legalism is to make them appear objective and unchangeable.*[80]

The 'thereness' of law entailed that within a legalistic form of thinking, there was no need for a theory about rules, since the only thing that was to be taken into account is the rule. Legalism in this definition was a *rule-centered* attitude, which focused on the legitimacy of rule-following rather than the source of law and its content.

Different from the Rule of Law principle that developed from the Western legal tradition, Chinese legalism focused on the legitimacy of *the ruler's control*. Chinese legalism emphasized the source of law (from the legitimate political ruler) and its content (to strengthen the state). Chinese legalism was not only rule-centered, but most importantly, a *ruler-centered* philosophy. Apart from the authority and the dignity of law, Chinese legalists also stressed the authority of the emperor: the logic was that if the law were respected, the emperor's honorable status could be certain; if the law were belittled, the emperor's honorable status could not be ensured. And most importantly, if people were incredulous about the emperor's honorable status, the state would be unstable—therefore law should be valued![81] Law in this philosophy could ensure the honorable status of the emperor as well as the stability of the state. The emperor should therefore regard his first task as conquering his subjects through law.[82] The ultimate source of law in Chinese legalism was the emperor. The source of legalism was in contrast with *Dao* (the nature; the natural law) in Daoism, *Ren* (mercy) in Confucianism and *Ai* (love) in Mohism. The emperor was recognized as the ultimate creator and interpreter of law:

> *The tasks of creating law, practicing law and obeying law should be differentiated. The emperor is in charge of legislation; his officials are responsible for legal practices; his subjects should obey law.*[83]

---

[78] J.N. Shklar. 1986. Legalism, Law, Morals and Political Trials. vii-viii, ix-x. 2–3. p.5. 35. Cambridge, Mass.: Harvard University Press. See also Bankowski's introduction of Shklar's legalism in, Zenon Bankowski. 2001. Living Lawfully—Love in Law and Law in Love. 44. Dordrecht: Kluwer.

[79] Zenon Bankowski. 2001. Living Lawfully—Love in Law and Law in Love. 48. Dordrecht: Kluwer.

[80] Ibid. 59.

[81] Guan Zhong. Zhong Ling. Guan Zi. http://chinese.dsturgeon.net/text.pl?node=48343&if=en&remap=gb. Accessed 02 Feb 2012.

[82] Shang Yang. Hua Ce. Shang Jun Shu. http://chinese.dsturgeon.net/text.pl?node=47226&if=en&remap=gb. Accessed 02 Feb 2012.

[83] Guan Zhong. Ren Fa. Guan Zi. http://chinese.dsturgeon.net/text.pl?node=48580&if=en&remap=gb. Accessed 02 Feb 2012.

Thus the Chinese legalism implied a top-down and unidirectional lawmaking mode. In this irreversible dimensional mode, the ruler's major responsibility was to make law. Rule-following was the duty of his subjects including his officials. This top-down lawmaking model did not emphasize the lawmakers' responsibility of rule-following, and did not involve the possibilities of proposing new laws by people. In practice, people did not have such a lawmaking right indeed, because the privilege of lawmaking represented the authority of the ruler and should belong to the ruler exclusively.[84] The lawmaker, *i.e.*, the emperor was born in the highest status above all the law-accepters. His privileges of lawmaking were justified in this model.

In Western legal history, the sovereign's lawmaking privilege was similar to the above model in the early periods but different in its later development. As Thomas Hobbes described in *Leviathan* and Jean Bodin in *Six Books of the Commonwealth*, the most evident identification of the lawgiver in Western history was the sovereign, or the conqueror of a territory.[85] The sovereignty theory indicated that the sole-and-ultimate lawmaking power was one of the central powers of the sovereign, and that the sovereign in turn was self-explanatory 'lawmaker'. The question of 'who is the lawmaker' therefore transformed to 'who is the sovereign'. Lawmaker was the other name of the sovereign. In pre-modern societies, a controller or conqueror attached great importance to the announcement of his supreme lawmaking power. His legislation was called declaratory legislation.[86] A wholesale rule-setting, ordering and making of laws occur under the absolute power of a King or Emperor. So, '*no sovereign no law*'.[87] The power to make law was the most obvious expression of the supreme authority. The sovereign announced and confirmed its supreme status, power and its legitimacy through lawmaking. 'Lawmaker' was therefore the other name of the sovereign in history.

The sovereign's supreme status was also symbolized as the lawmaking power. However, the content of the 'sovereignty' in Western history changed.[88] It therefore increased difficulties in the recognition of the lawmaker. As a matter of fact, the unity of sovereign and (actual) lawmaker began to separate although countless ties between them could still be found. 'Parliamentary sovereignty', (in this sense, the sovereignty refers to the 'lawmaker's sovereignty' rather than the 'monarch's

---

[84] Deng Xi, a famous scholar in Pre-Qin era, also a legalist, was killed because he privately made Law. See Zuo Zhuan. Ding Going Jiu 2. Lü Shi Chun Qiu. Li Wei. 1996. Literatures of Historical Chinese Legal Thoughts. 56. Beijing: Law Press.

[85] Hobbes T. 2002. Leviathan. Toronto: Broadview Press. J. Bodin and J.H. Franklin. 1992. On Sovereignty: Four Chapters From the Six Books of the Commonwealth. Cambridge: Cambridge University Press.

[86] Pound R. 1959. Jurisprudence. III .579–584. St Paul: West Publishing co.

[87] Ingram A. 1994. A Political Theory of Rights 203. Oxford: Oxford University Press.

[88] In history, the British parliamentary sovereignty included the structure of the King-in-Parliament, which meant the King and the rest of the Parliament shared the sovereignty together from the sixteenth century to the Glorious Revolution. After the Glorious Revolution, however, the Parliament (or in a strict illustration, the Commons of the House) was the only substantive sovereignty.

sovereignty') appeared in English legal history during the time when the monarch had less power, and the actual lawmaker was no longer the monarch.[89]

The concept 'parliamentary sovereignty' was made to cover the fact that the actual lawmaker and the sovereign began to separate in England. Parliamentary sovereignty established the supreme status of a collective organization, the legislature (Parliament). The role of the Parliament was different from that of the sovereign in history. The classical theory on 'legislative sovereignty' represented by Dicey differentiated the theoretical uppermost power with the actual limited power of parliament. Sovereignty was accordingly divided into two kinds: the 'legislative sovereignty' and the 'political sovereignty'.[90] Parliamentary sovereignty meant the parliament had the unrestricted power of lawmaking. It should, however, obey the will of the people, which meant that the electorates were the political sovereignty. Therefore, parliamentary sovereignty was regarded as a legislative sovereignty in theory, but was like the 'popular sovereignty' in politics. In this sense, although the parliamentary lawmaking power was exclusive and should not be restricted, it should be under the control of 'the people'.

Thus the theoretical backgrounds of Chinese legalism and Western legalism were different. When legalism developed in Western societies after the seventeenth century, laws and theories about laws were already there. Laws were relatively mature. Chinese legalism was proposed in a unique historical and cultural background during 475–221 B.C., when law was not recognized necessary for social control before that era. Ethical norms supported by Confucianism were the official and mainstream norms to manage the society.[91] Legalism in Western contexts was an ideology *lacking of awareness* for the justification of rule-following behaviors because 'law is simply there'. Chinese legalism as a practical philosophy, however, was from the beginning proposed to construct (rather than to justify) the fidelity to (rulers') law.

Is the difference between 'rule-centerd' (of the Western Legalism) and 'ruler-centered' (of Chinese Legalism) a real difference? Professor Bankowski pointed out that in *the Politics of Jurisprudence* Cotterrell defended Austin saying that his theory of law was also based on a top down authoritarian society. In Luc J. Wintgens'

[89] Parliamentary sovereignty meant that Parliament (rather than the monarch) was the supreme legal authority in the UK. According to A.V. Dicey (Law of the Constitution. 1885), 'in theory Parliament had total power. It was sovereign.' Dicey's view of parliamentary sovereignty consisted of four factors: (1) Parliament was competent to pass laws on any subject; (2) Parliament's laws could regulate the activities of anyone, anywhere; (3) Parliament could not bind its successors as to the content, manner and form of subsequent legislation; and (4) Laws passed by Parliament could not be challenged by the courts. However, Parliament might in practice limit its own sovereignty. Two examples were: (1) The European Communities Act 1972; (2) The Human Rights Act 1998.

[90] A. V. Dicey. 2005. Introduction to the Study of the Law of the Constitution. 34. Boston, MA: Adament Media Corporation.

[91] Ronggen Yu. 2000. History of Chinese Legal Thoughts. 2–4; 9–17. Beijing: Law Press. see also Yang Hegao. 2000. History of Chinese Legal Thoughts. 6–15. Beijing: Beijing University Press. And Fan Zhongxin. 2001. The Spirit of Chinese Legal Traditions. 120–134; 210–225; 384–389. Shandong: Shandong People's Publishing House.

Legislation in Context and Legisprudence, (Western) strict legalism was also criticized. So what is the real difference between 'rule-centered' of a top-down authoritarian society and 'ruler-centered' in ancient China?

To answer this question, we should better recall theories of Bentham and Austin, which were the foundation of the ancient Western top-down authoritarian legal system. Bentham's theory was to justify utilitarianism, *i.e.*, to promote the greatest good for the greatest number. Therefore it was *not necessarily* 'ruler-centered' but the result-centered. Austin also stressed the coercive nature of law from a consequentialist moral reasoning, so that the coercive nature of law was *not necessarily* 'ruler-centered' but force-centered. Although Austin's theory was apparently referred to a top down authoritarian society, we do not need to justify the status of the ruler from a consequentialist moral reasoning, but the force behind the status as the reasoning for others' obedience to the law.

Ruler-centered in Chinese Legalism, however, was not merely a consequentialist philosophy. It also put an emphasis on the legitimate status of the ruler, rather than the recognition of the force of the ruler. In a well-known Chinese classic, *Romance of Three Kingdoms*, the reason that Lord Liu Bei should be the legitimate King was that he had a blood relation with the previous emperor. He did not have force in the beginning. The other two comparative Lords, Sun Quan and Cao Cao, although had the force, were not recognized to have legitimated status to be the King. The other two Lords therefore were not recognized as legitimate rulers.[92] Fidelity to Liu's law led to just behaviors while the laws of the other two Lords were coercion norms that people 'had to' obey. The *legitimacy* of a ruler was different from the *force* of the ruler. Chinese legalism stressed the necessity to strengthen the ruler's force. It also defended that the ruler's status should be legitimate. It therefore differed from Western legalism in which coercion rather than legitimacy was the necessary premise of law. In Western legal history, as stated previously, the sovereign's status was much stressed *before* rather than after the growth of the ideology of legalism after the seventeenth century. Such a transformation (from status to contract) was stated clearly in Maine *Ancient Law*: '*The movement of the progressive societies has hitherto been a movement from status to contract*'.[93] Chinese legalism as an ancient philosophy did not go through this transformation.

4.7 Conclusion

As an important ancient legal thought, Chinese legalism emphasized the ruler's authority and the subjects' obedience to law. It aimed at a pursuit for the order and security of the society. It differed from the other Pre-Qin schools of thoughts. In

[92] Guanzhong Luo. 2008. Romance of Three Kingdoms. 266. Beijing: Remin Publishing House.

[93] Henry Maine. 1861. Ancient Law. 165. The last paragraph of Ancient Law chapter 5, see texts from http://en.wikisource.org/wiki/Ancient_Law#Chapter_5_Primitive_Society_and_Ancient_Law. Accessed 02 Feb 2012.

Confucianism rights and duties of the family were analogously applied onto the society as well as the nation.[94] Chinese legalism, as a contrast, distinguished the rules of the nation and the society. It focused on the function of law in controlling the nation. It did not deny the ethical morality but stressed that ethical norms and morality should remain in the realm of family and private fields.[95] It, however, denied the morality of law of the nation indeed—law and nation in Chinese legalism were in nature something bad, although they could lead to something good. Taoism and Mohism also held this classification: they claimed that *Dao* (rules of the nature) and *Ai*(love)should be applied universally to everyone; rules of the nation although should be harmonious with *Dao* or *Ai*,were different norms.[96]

Indeed, Confucianism, Legalism and Daoism (with Mohism) had argued for diverse norms of different fields: Confucianism—the norms in private interaction; Legalism—norms of the nation; and Daoism—norms of the nature (universal norms or transnational norms). Focusing on the norms of the nation, Chinese legalism excluded the other two kinds of norms, *i.e.*, norms of the private interaction and of the nature, and provided a formalistic and coercive concept of law: Rule-by-Law.

Chinese contemporary scholars had a debate on the Rule-by-Law concept in Chinese legalism. Shuchen Wu in his reply to Shiqun Yang's criticisms on Chinese legalism argued that the differentiation between *Li* (礼, rules of propriety) and *Fa* (法, law) in Pre-Qin era represented by Confucianism and Legalism, represented two different social controlling models: rule by the sage or rule by law. 'Chinese Rule-of-Law' in his perspective originated from Pre-Qin era and was connected with the power of the sovereign from the beginning. 'Chinese Rule-of-Law' was natural and conformed to the trend of the times. Comparing to the Aristotelian Rule-of-Law tradition, Chinese Rule-of-Law was not based on the value of freedom or the check and balance of powers, but emphasized other basic values including equality and equal application, order and obedience to law.[97] Shiqun Yang, Ronggen Yu, Zhiping Liang and Zhongqiu Zhang argued that the rule-by-Law in Chinese legalism was totally different from the Western Rule-of-Law idea. Professor Liang wrote that '*in ancient China, there did not exist or have the possibility of an existence of the Rule-of-Law*'.[98] Professor Zhang Zhongqiu also held that '*in ancient China there never existed the Rule-of-Law*'.[99] Professor Yang Shiqun stated that rule-by-Law was indeed rule-by-the emperor. Although it was different from Confucian rule by the

[94] Ibid.

[95] Hairen He. 2007. The Enemy of the Legalists in Pre-Qin Era: The Normative Theory on Ruling the Country through the Law. Tribune of Political Science and Law 25:36–50.

[96] Ronggen Yu. 2000. History of Chinese Legal Thoughts. 67–79. Beijing: Law Press. See also Hegao Yang. 2000. History of Chinese Legal Thoughts. 84–125. Beijing: Beijing University Press.

[97] Shuchen Wu. 1998. Discussion on Rule-of-law in Chinese Legalism: A Reply to Shiqun Yang. Journal of the East China University of Politics and Law 1:54–63.

[98] Zhiping Liang. 1991. Searching for the Harmony of the Natural Order: Studies on Traditional Chinese Legal Culture. 60. 83. Shanghai: Shanghai People's Publishing House.

[99] Zhongqiu Zhang. 1991. A Comparative Study on Western and Chinese Legal Cultures. 278. 290. Nanjing: Nanjing University Press.

sage, it was still Rule-of-Man.[100] In a comparative study on Aristotelian Rule-of-Law and Chinese legalism, the differences between the two conceptions were concluded as: diverse recognitions of the relationship between morality and law; different treatments of law (law as public norms or as the emperor's controlling instrument); emphasis on the right or the duty of the commons; balanced powers or concentration of powers; and whether they aimed at a governance of virtue.[101] Their different comments on Chinese legalism reflected different attitudes on modern legislative construction. Other scholars held an apprehensive attitude of understanding the traditional legal culture. They criticized the trend of separation present and past.[102] Some scholars believed that Chinese legalism could contribute to the modern legislative construction in present China.[103] Others, however, held a rather radical attitude and denied any values in Chinese legalism.[104]

As discussed previously in this chapter, I believe that the Chinese Rule-by-Law concept contained topics akin to Western ideas of Rule-of-Law. They both defended the objectivity of law, fair treatment and equal application, non-retrospective law, a stable legal system and 'the possible law'. Those seven propositions were similar to Lon L. Fuller's principles of legality.[105] However, Chinese legalism and Western legalism had fundamental distinctions from their historical backgrounds, theoretical hypotheses, their starting points and their ultimate purpose.

Chinese legalism was the major 'competitive' of Confucianism. Western legalism was the opposite of the natural law theory. Major concerns of Chinese legalism were to break the authority of hierarchical patriarchal system that defended by Confucianism. Western legalism argued against the morality of law that defended by the natural law theories. In Chinese legalism, the morality of law was not a necessary premise of law, but morality was not exclusively denied, especially in the early Pre-Qin legalism. And in general, unlike Western legalism, Chinese legalism did not make the classification of morality and law a *necessary* premise of law. However, in Western legalism, especially 'strict' or 'hard' legalism, the morality

---

[100] Shiqun Yang. 1999. Further Discussion on Rule-by-law in Chinese Legalism: A Reply to Shuchen Wu. Journal of the East China University of Politics and Law 2:50–54.

[101] Yanqing Chen. 2001. On Similarities and Differences between Aristotelian Rule-of-law and Rule-by-law in Chinese Legalism. Gansu Social Science 3:19–21.

[102] From Professor Chen Jingliang's lecture notes (1999–2005) at Zhongnan University of Economics and Law.

[103] Zhouya Li. 2003. The Legal Theory of the Legalists in Ancient China and its Influential Significance in Modern Times. 36–39. Modern Law Science 25.

[104] Shiqun Yang. 1999. Further Discussion on Rule-by-law in Chinese Legalism: A Reply to Shuchen Wu. Journal of the East China University of Politics and Law 2:50–54.

[105] See my previous discussion on the seventh major propositions of Chinese Legalism. In Fuller's The Morality of Law, eight principles of legality, or, 'eight routes of failure for any legal system' were stated as: (1) the lack of rules or law, which leads to ad-hoc and inconsistent adjudication; (2) failure to publicize or make known the rules of law; (3) unclear or obscure legislation that is impossible to understand; (4) retroactive legislation; (5) contradictions in the law; (6) demands that are beyond the power of the subjects and the ruled. (7) unstable legislation (ex. Daily revisions of laws). (8) divergence between adjudication/administration and legislation. Lon. Fuller. 1996. The Morality of Law.33–94. Princeton: Yale University Press.

and law were exclusively uncompetitive. The starting point and the ultimate purpose of Chinese legalism were for the strengthening of the authority of the ruler and the state. Western legalism was for the authority of the law (therefore the authority of the ruler was another topic). Although both theories emphasized the fidelity of law, in Chinese legalism the topic was transformed to the fidelity of ruler, while in Western legalism it referred to the promise to the social contract (Wintgens), the rule of recognition (Hart), the creative chain of norms (Kelsen), or the authority of social norms (Raz).

Therefore, we should be very cautious in constructing a modern legal system for the recognition of Chinese legalism. I disagree with the argument that Chinese legalism was a kind of legalism in Western perspective. Neither Chinese legalism nor Western legalism could be the sole reference for Chinese legal system. In my opinion, we should recognize the Chinese native legal contexts formed by Chinese legalism and other Chinese philosophies, and rebuild Chinese legal culture by absorbing positive elements of Western law. In the next chapter, I will turn to Western jurisprudence of lawmaking.

Chapter 5
Lawmaking in Jurisprudence (I)

—Act always so that you treat humanity whether in your person or in that of another always as an end, but never as a means only. (Kant)

—The end of the law is peace. The means to that end is war... The life of the law is a struggle, —a struggle of nations, of the state power, of classes, of individuals. (Jhering)

5.1 Introduction

In previous chapters I discussed Chinese theories of legislative legitimation including Confucianism, Chinese Marxism and Chinese Legalism. None of those theories emphasized on communication. In this chapter I will turn to Western theories about lawmaking. Lawmaking was a marginal topic in Western jurisprudence. Classic materials on this topic such as Bentham's *Theory of legislation* and Maitland's study on the early history of institutions were written centuries ago.[1] *The Science of Law and Law Making* was published over 100 years ago also.[2] Other works explored the historical evolution of law.[3] But those literatures referred to a specific branch of law exclusively.[4] Comparative studies attempted to interpret the relationship between

---

[1] Bentham was seen as the father of the theory of legislation. His Science of Legislation was major expressed through his three books: Bentham. 1864. The Theory of Legislation. London: Trübner. Bentham. 1891. A Fragment on Government. F.C. Montague ed. Oxford: Clarendon Press. And Bentham. 1948. An Introduction to the Principles of Morals and Legislation. New York: Hafner Publishing Co. The Theory of Legislation was written 200 years ago. F. W. Maitland and F. C. Montague. 1915. A Sketch of English Legal History. New York: G.P.Putnam's sons. was written a 100 years ago.

[2] Floyd C. R. 1898. The Science of Law and Law Making. New York:Macmillan.

[3] Such as Anderson J.S. 1992. Lawyers and the making of English Land Law 1832–1940. Oxford: Oxford University Press.

[4] Such as Buergenthal T. 1969. Law–making in the International Civil Aviation Organization. Syracuse, N.Y.: Syracuse University Press.

P. He, *Chinese Lawmaking: From Non-communicative to Communicative*, Understanding China, DOI 10.1007/978-3-642-39507-9_5, © Springer-Verlag Berlin Heidelberg 2014

law and politics.[5] Communicative lawmaking although existed in Western legislative practice, lacked jurisprudential debate.

In this and the next chapters I chose four representative Western theories of lawmaking. I attempted to analyze Western theories of lawmaking from a Chinese perspective. To me, theories of Bentham, Hayek, Waldron and Wintgens offered four different paradigms in the research of lawmaking. The four different theories showed the width and depth of Western theories on lawmaking. Bentham and Hayek represented a classical debate on the nature of law and legislation, i.e., a utilitarian lawmaking in contrast to liberalistic lawmaking. Waldron and Wintgens offered solutions for the crisis of contemporary legitimation of lawmaking. Waldron studied lawmaking from the structure and procedures of legislatures, while Wintgens discussed the values behind the legitimacy of lawmaking.

5.2 Benthamnism and Chinese Utilitarianism

Let us see such expressions: If a policy could promote economic development, it was good; if law could promote GDP, it was good; if the sacrifice of the minority could promote the welfare of the majority, it was good. These were particular expressions of the consequentialist moral reasoning. As disclosed in previous chapters, most Chinese lawmaking theories were justifications for consequentialism in the legitimacy of lawmaking. Therefore it was natural for us to think of a representative classical and positivistic theory of law and lawmaking, Bentham's theory of legislation, which was famous for its consequentialist moral reasoning. The principle of utility in Bentham's philosophy of law was used widely to justify modern legislations. Chinese scholars were influenced by Bentham's theory deeply during late 1902, the modern legal reform era of China, when Liang Qichao introduced Bentham to Chinese for the first time.[6]

Except for the rather late translation of four works of Bentham including *A Fragment on Government* (1995), *An Introduction to the Principle of Morals and Legislation* (2000), *The Theory of Legislation* (2004) and *Of Laws in General* (2008), other works of Bentham has not been translated and introduced to Chinese yet including *An Essay on Political Tactics* and *Deontology or Science of Morality*. In my research of the recent 10 years theses on Bentham in China, I did not find any doctoral theses on Bentham's theory. Only 3 of 14 master theses on Bentham were about his legislative ethics.[7] The highest level

---

[5] Such as Miller M. C. and Barnes J. 2004. Making Policy, Making Law—an interbranch perspective. Washington DC: Georgetown University Press.

[6] See Zhongxin Fan and Peng He. 2009. The Contributions and Characteristics of the Legal Works of Liang Qichao. Journal for Legal History Studies16:329–357. see also Qichao Liang. 1902. The Father of Utilitarianism Bentham and his Theory. Xin Min Cong Kan 15:11–25.

[7] My search was from the PhD and Master theses data base of Wanfang Data and CNKI Data. Accessed 02 Feb 2012.

of Chinese academic articles about Bentham was still represented by Liang Qichao in the beginning of 20th century.[8]

However, Bentham's principle of utility has been known and accepted widely by Chinese lawmakers and scholars. Ideas of common prosperity, collective interests and the principle that the sovereignty belongs to the people in Chinese legitimation of lawmaking were all similar to Bentham's theory of lawmaking. Comparing with other Western theories, Bentham's theory was closer to Chinese contemporary understanding of law: law was legislation; and legislation was law. Law in both theories was positivistic and man-made order.

The principle of utility was considered to be the foundation of law and morality in Bentham's theory. The principle of utility was proposed to answer questions such as: (a) what was law? (b) Why was law necessary? (c) What should be law? Utilitarianism answered these three questions like this: (a) law was a coercive rule. '*Every law when complete is either a coercive or un-coercive nature. A coercive law is a command. An un-coercive, or rather a dis-coercive law, is the revocation in whole or in part of a coercive law.*'[9] Law was used to punish the disobedient, and it operated by imposing a psychological dread on potential wrongdoers.[10] (b) Law was necessary because it enabled the members of a community to be happier than they could be without it: '*the greater part of men is neither of sufficient strength of mind nor sufficient moral sensibility to place their honesty above the aid of the law. The legislator must supply the feebleness of this natural interest by adding to it an artificial interest steadier and more easily perceived*'.[11] Law could contribute to the happiness of a community by reinforcing moral and religious sanctions against harming other people as well as by creating institutions which were compatible to utility.[12] (c) Only if the evil that it prevented was greater than it created, should a rule be law.[13]

Bentham mentioned concepts of un-coercive law or dis-coercive law. Those concepts, however, were '*the revocation in whole or in part of a coercive law*'.[14] Therefore the primary criterion to differentiate law from non-law was its imperative nature. The imperativalist acknowledged that legal systems contained provisions that were not

[8] About Qichao Liang's contribution, see Zhongxin Fan and Peng He. 2009. The Contributions and Characteristics of the Legal Works of Liang Qichao. Journal for Legal History Studies 16:329–357.

[9] J. Bentham. 1948. An Introduction to the Principles of Morals and Legislation. 302. New York: Hafner Publishing Co.

[10] A.J.M. Milne. 1973. Bentham and Legal Theory. Bentham's Principle of Utility and Legal Philosophy. Northern Ireland Legal Quarterly:14–15.

[11] Bentham. 1864. The Theory of Legislation. 64. London:Trübner.

[12] Two examples he gave were (1) legislation protects private property; (2) legislation resists other morally wrong acts as the offences against the state. Bentham's theory therefore does not totally exclude morality from a positive theory of law. See Bentham. 1948. An Introduction to the Principles of Morals and Legislation. 292. New York: Hafner Publishing Co.

[13] Otherwise '*the evil of the punishment [by law] would be greater than the evil of the offence*', see Bentham. 1864. The Theory of Legislation. 60. London:Trübner.

[14] Bentham. 1864. The Theory of Legislation. 64. London:Trübner. And see also Bentham. 1948. An Introduction to the Principles of Morals and Legislation. 302. New York: Hafner Publishing Co.

imperatives, for example, permissions and definitions; but these were regarded as part of the non-legal material that was necessary for, and part of every legal system.

The legitimacy of a legal system was examined from its purpose, i.e., the happiness of the community. To justify the legality of law from the existence of law was insufficient; law should also achieve its purpose, public welfare for example. Bentham was therefore distinct from other positivists such as Austin, Kelsen and Hart—he did not exclude morality entirely from a legal study as those positivists did.[15] There was an implicative proposition, however: law was regarded as a fruit of evil rather than a result of natural justice, which denied the moral dimension of positive law. If the evil that law prevented was greater than it created, i.e., when law was conformable to utility, a legal punishment could be justified. Therefore the principle of utility although connected with morality, did not change the nature of positive law, i.e., amoral law. The purpose of lawmaking in Bentham's theory should be understood as creating law conformable to utility. Bentham was thus different from natural law theorists: to him, law was not something 'good' by nature but justified evil. Thus, lawmaking was only a mechanism to prevent and punish something even worse. To Bentham, law was a reasonable choice which could promote morality in the end, but was not necessarily something desirable.

The theory of legislation was constructed according to both the substance and the shape of law. Utility was the ruling principle of legislation, and related to the substance of law. To Bentham, the form of law was also important. He believed that law was imperfect until expressed in the form of a code.[16] Codification was therefore the key in his concept of legal reform. His ideal codification should achieve four conditions: integrity, universality, logicality and synonymy. Integrity required any given body of law should be complete before they could form a code. In other words, '*it must set forth the whole of the law with such fullness as to need no supplement in the form of commentaries or of reported cases*'.[17] Universality demanded law to consist of rules stated with the utmost generality attainable in each instance, or of the fewest possible rules in which the whole of the law could be expressed. Logicality meant rules must be enunciated in a rigorously logical order. Synonymy must be achieved through the enunciation of rules using a rigorously uniform terminology, '*affording one and only one term accurately defined for everything which there is occasion to name in the course of the work*'.[18] The advantages of

[15] A connection between law and morality is admitted: law is to promote the greatest happiness of the greatest number. Law and morality are therefore connected by the principle of utility. About the relationship between utilitarianism and morality, see R.B. Brandt.1992. Morality, Utilitarianism and Rights. Cambridge: Cambridge University Press. And R.E. Goodin. 1983. Political Theory and Public Policy. Political Science: 104. see also L. P. Nucci. 2001. The Nature of Morality and the Development of Social Values. 7. Cambridge: Cambridge University Press.

[16] J. Bentham, P. Schofield, and J. Harris. 1998. Legislator of the World: Writings on Codification, Law and Education. 1. Oxford: Clarendon Press. Also see Bentham. 1891. A Fragment on Government. F.C. Montague ed. 49. Oxford: Clarendon Press.

[17] Ibid.

[18] Ibid.

codification were considerable: it assisted the public in knowing the law as well as the legal professionals who apply law. A code might remedy the defects of fragmentary legislation by '*extracting the real law from the mass of doubtful or antiquated matter in which it lies buried*',[19] and '*by stating this real law in a terse, clear and connected form*'.[20] Lawyers could at once grasp the law as a whole and referred to a particular rule by using a specifically advanced code. Codification should never be regarded as precluding the development of law that was promoted by commentaries, judicial decisions or further legislation also. According to Bentham, '*only a code intended to be unalterable and worshipped with superstitious veneration can really paralyze the growth of law.*'[21] Thus a code should pay more attention to principles rather than details and needs periodical revision by legislative authority.

The formula of happiness in Bentham's theory was difficult to substantiate because there was a 'hard' concept, 'happiness', which was incompatible with 'the greatest number'. It was unclear whether happiness was an individual's physical or physiological state, or one's reason or motivation for a conduct. In my view, happiness should always refer to a specific person. 'The greatest number', however, referred to the collective. Hence it was impossible to measure and calculate the collective's happiness. Bentham himself realized this conflict and in his later work he ceased referring happiness to the greatest number. The formula was explained in an abstract way, that '*the greatest amount of happiness might take the form of an intense happiness enjoyed by a smaller as opposed to a diffused happiness enjoyed by a great number*'.[22] Thus pleasures and pains were calculated basing on an abstract form. The calculation took account solely of the quantity rather than quality of pleasures and pains. In this way, he made a compromise between 'happiness' and 'the greatest number'. The calculation of happiness, however, was fruitless as long as happiness was a subjective judgment. Mediating principles including security and equality were proposed to substantiate utility: by maintaining security and by favoring equality, the legislator could ensure happiness.[23] '*The root of the trouble, [however], lies in the psychological part of the principle: that is, in psychological hedonism*'.[24] The formula referred all human action to the effect of only two causes: desire for pleasure and aversion from pain. Such a reductive proposition failed in distinguishing reasons from causes of action.[25] Psychological hedonism, i.e., the

---

[19] Ibid. 53.

[20] Ibid.

[21] Ibid. 54.

[22] Bentham. 1891. A Fragment on Government. F.C. Montague ed. 34. Oxford: Clarendon Press.

[23] Bentham believes that if the claims of security conflict with the claims of equality, the former should always be preferred because security is to Bentham the first, the all-important condition of human happiness. The first object of the legislator is to preserve and strengthen the feeling of security, but in so far as is consistent with security; their second object is to further equality. Ibid.

[24] M.H. James. 1973. Bentham and Legal Theory. Northern Ireland Legal Quarterly:19.

[25] Utilitarianism was the doctrine that focuses on the outcome—the rightness of acts is to be judged by their consequences. J.J.C. Smart. 1973. Extreme and Restricted Utilitarianism. Northern Ireland Legal Quarterly:27.

cause of action, could not justify the reason of action. The motivation of an action should also be separate from the outcome, and in this sense utilitarianism as a consequence-oriented doctrine was not the sole foundation of law.

Apart from the problem of psychological hedonism, another insufficiency of the principle of utility existed in a circular reasoning (see Fig. 5.1 below): lawmaking was to promote the greatest happiness of the greatest number; happiness, the psychological hedonism in turn was the cause for lawmaking. It was therefore argued in a cyclical pattern: why were laws made?—because people were happy to make law—why were they happy?—because law promoted happiness!

Such a circular argument was caused by confusing an ontological thesis with a teleological thesis. Law per se should be different from its purposes or results but the circular argument mixed them up. 'Rule utilitarianism' emphases that '*the rightness or wrongness of a particular action is a function of the correctness of the rule of which it is an instance*', and that '*it is rules not individual acts that are to be judged by their consequences*'.[26] Rule utilitarianism attempted to avoid circular arguments by excluding psychological hedonism from reasons for an action. It was still, however, misleading because it again focused solely on the consequences—the goals, purposes, or achievements of law. We should notice that '*Law can be unjust in themselves, quite apart from their consequences: for instance, laws upholding slavery, or enforcing racial religious or sex discriminations. A principle*

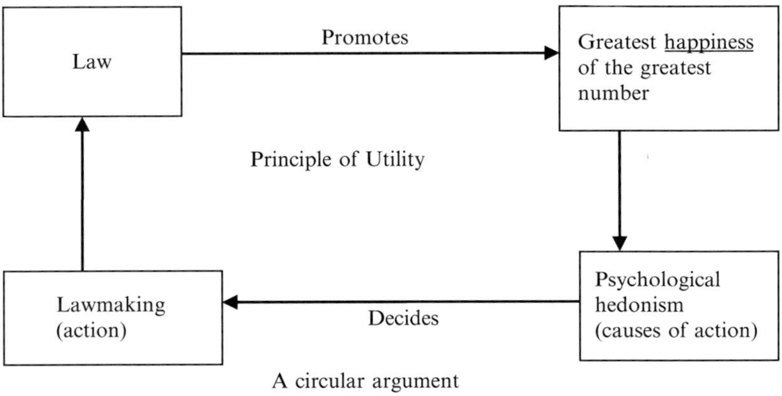

Fig. 5.1 A circular argument

[26] B. Parekh. 1993. Jeremy Bentham: Critical Assessments. 30. London and New York: Routledge. About rule utilitarianism, see R.T. Garner and B. Rosen. 1967. Moral Philosophy: A Systematic Introduction to Normative Ethics and Meta-ethics. 70. New York: Macmillan. Rule utilitarianism was also called restricted or indirect utilitarianism. In stead of looking at the consequences of a particular act, rule-utilitarianism determines the rightness of an act by finding the value of the consequences of following a particular rule. The rule the following of which has the best overall consequences is the best rule. Early proponents were J. Austin (*The Province of Jurisprudence*) and J.S. Mill (*Utilitarianism*), see T. Mautner ed. The Penguin Dictionary of Philosophy http://www.utilitarianism.com/ruleutil.htm. Accessed 02 Feb 2012.

which fails to take account of this possibility is surely not a good guide to the legislator.'[27] In utilitarianism the ontological thesis of law, i.e., law as justified evil, was mixed up with its teleological thesis, i.e., the purpose of law as a mechanism to promote utility.

Utilitarianism developed by Bentham had a great influence on lawmaking. It was used to justify the legitimacy of governance.[28] The reason for democratic decision-making was often described as 'by the people and for the people'. The concept of 'the people' implied the principle of utility: the greatest interests of the greatest number—a new utilitarianism.[29] The principle of utility was to justify the purpose of law. Law aimed at punishing the disobedient, and it operated by imposing a psychological dread on potential wrongdoers.[30] Law was necessary because it enabled the members of a community to be happier than they could be without it.[31] Law contributed to the happiness of a community by reinforcing moral and religious sanctions against harming other people, and by creating institutions which were compatible to utility.

I found that utilitarianism and consequentialism dominated Chinese lawmaking. When the purpose was for the good of the collective (the people and the nation), the law was justified. If the result of lawmaking could contribute to the GDP, the economic development, lawmaking was justified. The result of lawmaking was more important than the procedure per se. Law made by the procedure was not necessarily moral in Chinese philosophy. But if it could bring good effects (including social control, security, and order) it was tolerable.[32] In Chinese perspective, law was not something 'good'; but rather justified evil. Lawmaking was a mechanism to prevent

---

[27] M.H. James ed. 1973. Bentham and Legal Theory. Northern Ireland Legal Quarterly:37.

[28] The influence of the utilitarianism, see G. I. Molivas. 1997. The Influence of Utilitarianism on Natural Rights Doctrines. Utilitas 9:183–202; also see J. Rawls' criticism on utilitarianism: J. Rawls. 1971. A Theory of Justice. Cambridge, Mass.: Harvard University Press. And J. Rawls. 1993. The Law of Peoples. Critical Inquiry 20:363–368.

[29] J. Skorupski. 2006. Welfare and Self-governance. Ethical Theory and Moral Practice 9: 289–309. see also D. Bodansky. 1999. The Legitimacy of International Governance. The American Journal of International Law 93: 596–624.

[30] In positivistic point of view, law was nothing but coercive norms. Bentham states that '*Every law when complete is either a coercive or un-coercive nature. A coercive law is a command. An un-coercive, or rather a dis-coercive law, is the revocation in whole or in part of a coercive law*.' J. Bentham. 1948. An Introduction to the Principles of Morals and Legislation. 302. New York: Hafner Publishing Co.

[31] Bentham wrote that: '*the greater part of men are neither of sufficient strength of mind nor sufficient moral sensibility to place their honesty above the aid of the law. The legislator must supply the feebleness of this natural interest by adding to it an artificial interest more steady and more easily perceived*'. Bentham. 1864. The Theory of Legislation. 64. London: Trübner.

[32] *In ancient Chinese philosophy Taoism, however, law was not necessarily something desirable. The effect of law was negative also. In Dao De Jin, Lao Zi believed that 'the more the law, the more the thieves': 'In the kingdom the multiplication of prohibitive enactments increases the poverty of the people; the more implements to add to their profit that the people have, the greater disorder is there in the state and clan; the more acts of crafty dexterity that men possess, the more do strange contrivances appear; the more display there is of legislation, the more thieves and robbers there*

and punish something even worse. This idea was similar to Bentham's theory of law, in which law was to prevent the greater evil.[33] Such a consequentialist philosophy, however, led to the ignorance of the justice of a rule per se, or the inner morality of law. As in Tang Fujun's case that I discussed in Chap. 2, the *Regulation Governing Building Demolition and Resettlement* became the local administrative excuse to violate particular minority's right of property. The local administrative believed that they could deprive the minority's property on account of municipal construction, local development, or increase of local GDP. The minority's disobedience was defined by them as 'violent fight against law'. Even worse, a reporter who wrote a book to disclose the tragedy of such cases was arrested.[34] Chinese consequentialist justification of law and lawmaking caused the ignorance of particular minority's fundamental rights. For the happiness of the abstract concept of 'people', or the unclear majority, law became an instrument to force the particular minority to surrender.

Could codification contribute to the morality of law? In Bentham's theory of legislation, the answer was positive. I would like to examine this argument by referring to Chinese legal history. Codification was the major form of Chinese law. The codification movement happened early in 536 B.C.. It was the milestone in Chinese legal history of the codification tradition. Since then, every Chinese central government emphasized unified codes. From the Tang Dynasty to the Qing Dynasty, more than 1,000 years passed, there were not many substantive differences between the codes of each dynasty. The content of law developed in a more humanistic direction but the forms of law remained more or less unchanged.[35] In the end of Qing dynasty, the new codification movement was also the landmark of emperor's desire of transplanting Western laws in favor of making the country stronger.

From 1900 to 1911, during the last empire, the emperor was persuaded by scholars to reform the existing legal system by using Western ideas as a reference, to escape the fate of being colonized and subjugated. A new legal system was set up to replace the traditional classification of laws resulting in branches of law based on a modern Western style. New laws were codified in a short period of time to adjust the urgent

---

are.' Lao Zi, Dao De Jin. chapter 57. The English edition was cited from http://www.ebigear.com/news-479-62356.html. Accessed 02 Feb 2012.

[33] Bentham. 1864. The Theory of Legislation. 60. London: Trübner.

[34] Chaoping Xie, was arrested in August 2010 because of his book The Great Migration. He was released on 17th September 2010. Details of Xie's case see Xiuli Huang. 2010. Nanfang Weekend. September 23.

[35] Since the Tang Dynasty, every empire maintained four major forms of statutes: Lu, Lin, Ge, Shi. They can be seen as the criminal code, the administrative code, the detailed rules of the administrative law, and the common norms. Although the 12 sections were changed to seven sections since Ming Dynasty (1,368–1,644), the changed seven sections were also based on the previous twelve sections but in a more logical way, and more related to the ancient Chinese law of Zhou Dynasty (1046–256 B.C.). The seven sections were: (1) Ming Li, general rules (2) Li, rules of the officers (3) Hu, rules of the registered permanent residence (4) Li, rules of savoir-vivre/proprieties/etiquette (5) Bing, rules of the military, (6) Xing , rules of the penal punishment (7) Gong, rules of public works.

need to 'learn from the West and be strong'.[36] Unfortunately, the Qing Empire was overthrown rapidly by revolutionists because of the desperate diplomatic political situation of the time. Another new legal system was instituted by the Nanjing Government in 1927, named as a six-law-system, which contained six major branches of law: constitutional law, criminal law, civil law, commercial law, civil procedure law, and the criminal procedure law.[37] In less than 30 years, in 1949, another new government of the whole country announced the abolishment of the six codes made by the Nanjing Government. But the Nanjing Guomingdang government (1927–1949) and the present CPC government maintained the codification tradition of China.

China absorbed continental law model (especially German law) model in modern legal reform but did not choose Common Law as the reference.[38] A direct cause was that Chinese translated Japanese law as a reference for the legal reform in late Qing dynasty. And as we knew, modern Japanese legal system was based on the study of continental European law specifically represented by German law. Why did China chose German mode of codification? First of all, China had a long history of sophisticated codification, so that it would rather accept the German lawmaking model rather than the English model. German law was famous for its strict classification and definition of notions. It was much easier for Chinese to accept German style of lawmaking since it was similar to Chinese way of thinking, classification and definition. On the other hand, it was difficult for Chinese to accept a legal system constituted by 'messy' cases, because to Chinese, case law was in the 'undeveloped' lawmaking stage in its own legal history. To Chinese, absorbing case law would symbolize retrogression in law.

English Common Law's life embedded in its unique historical and social context which was totally different from China's context. It was difficult for Chinese to understand the principles behind those cases and even harder to use them properly in a Chinese context. Arguably, English Common Law had a 'loose' type of development and did not allow high-centralized governments (comparing with the continent Europe governments) in history. Abundant amount of precedents were acceptable in small territories in the early history. Common Law did not focus on law's social control function at the beginning because it did not face a large populace and it did not interrupted frequently from the outside legal systems, since it was an isolated island from the continent Europe.[39] In this sense, case law was sufficient

[36] Peng He. 2005. The Constitutional Thoughts, Efforts and Fate of Carsun Chang. 5. MA degree thesis of Zhongnan University of Economics and Law.

[37] After the Qing Dynasty, from 1919 to 1949 China was controlled by several warlords and there coexisted several governments as the Beijing Government, the Nanjing Government, and the Wuhan Government. The Nanjing Government ruled by the Guoming Party controlled the whole country later, but was defeated by the People's Communist Party of China. It receded to Taiwan in 1949 and was the leading party of Taiwan in the 1950s and 1960s.

[38] Weifang H. 2007. Common Law and Chinese Law. Comparative Law Studies. from http://www.hicourt.gov.cn/theory/artilce_list.asp?id=3815&l_class=7. Accessed 02 Feb 2012.

[39] See similar proposition in A. J. Toynbee and D. C. Somervell. 1957. A Study of History. Oxford: Oxford University Press. The part about remarkable achievements of civilization came from hardships and difficulties.

for England to solve problems. China, however, from the very early era had to value 'efficiency' in administration. It was important for Chinese ruler to solve problems quickly because he faced with a huge country which was covetously expected to be seized by other ambitious rulers from neighboring countries. Chinese rulers had to choose to use clear principles and explicated statutes and codes to solve problems, to rule the country. Relying on cases and precedents would add too much burden on common people's comprehensions of law. It would also require more legal professionals to spend abundant time on interpreting, debating and defending cases in court. Under the urgent requirement of efficiency in dealing with problems in the late Qing dynasty, China would not change its codification tradition to transplant or study the Common Law. Chinese traditional scholars were like German scholars who had higher reputations than judges and other legal professionals in history.[40] Scholars were the 'motor', the driving force behind Chinese modern legal reform.[41] They were more familiar with academic discussion on principles, definitions, and classifications in law rather than judicial practice. This academic tradition influenced Chinese modern legal reform also. China absorbed elements from continental legal systems rather than from the Common Law tradition.[42]

At the beginning of the codification tradition, Chinese scholars discussed the morality of publishing law. Shu Xiang denied the morality of publishing law and stated that law should not be publicized. Otherwise the common people would be able to use their knowledge of law to do wrong and avoid punishment. Zi Chan argued that the form of law should be clear and accessible to people, otherwise it was impossible for them to 'live under the law'.[43] Zi Chan also used the analogy 'law is better to be like fire rather than water' to discuss the justice of making law public and strict.[44] In this analogy, law should be like fire so that people could see it and feel afraid of it. They would be able to avoid being burnt by it. Law should not be like water, otherwise people would treat it lightly since it was tender like water. People knew not to play with fire, but they did not know if they played with water it could also swallow them. After the debate between Shu Xiang and Zi Chan, however, the justice of the form of law was not further debated. Chinese thought that law should be published and codified because it was the historical tradition. Previous emperors codified law, so later rulers should follow them also. There were not any further discussions on the morality of the form of law until modern legal reform in late Qing Dynasty. However, in Qing Dynasty, the question shifted from copying the ancestor's law to use the form of Western law. It was not about the justice of the form of law, but about the contributions of Western law to the purpose of developing

[40] Yinshi Yu. 2003. Scholars and Chinese Culture. 68. Shanghai: Shanghai Renmin Press.

[41] Peng He. 2009. The Father of the Republican Constitution and the Shattered Dream of Establishing Constitutionalism in the Republic of China. Chinese and Western Legal Traditions 7:530–542.

[42] Ibid.

[43] Hegao Yang. 2000. History of Chinese Legal Thoughts. 24. Beijing: Beijing University Press.

[44] Zuo Qiuming. 1993. Zuo Zhuan. Zhaogong Year twenty. Trans. Yang Bojun. 1486. Hunan: Yuelu Shuyuan Press.

a prosperous country with powerful army force. Consequentialism and utilitarianism dominated the discussion of the form of law. In Chinese context, the contribution of codification to the morality of law was limited.

Chinese consequentialism and utilitarianism in lawmaking although was similar to and influenced by Bentham's theory, the premises of two theories were different. Chinese lawmaking from the beginning focused on the necessity of forming a strong country. The principle of utility in Bentham's theory, however, was from the beginning concerned with human beings' desires. The purpose of lawmaking in Bentham's theory of legislation was to promote utility. Legislators should aim at this ultimate purpose. Therefore the strong country in Bentham's theory was rather the result of utility. The desire of individuals was the premise of utility. Chinese lawmaking, however, used to justify its legitimation on the premise of the strong country. The desire of individuals became the result, rather than the premise of utility. Individual's desires of happiness were not the starting point of lawmaking; and they were not considered as the cause and reason for lawmaking. The cause of lawmaking in Chinese legalism (and Chinese Marxism also) was stated as a plain fact of control: The ruler's law was law (as stated in Chap. 3, in Chinese Marxism, the ruler referred to CPC, the congress, and the working class; and the ruled referred to 'the enemy of the people' although they were also citizens of the country). It was not necessarily moral but was valid de facto. The purpose of lawmaking in Chinese legalism was to strengthening the ruler's control. Chinese Marxism was to promote the common prosperity, i.e., the collective good, rather than individual-oriented. Pleasure and pains in Bentham's argument were not vital in Chinese legitimation of lawmaking. In this sense, Chinese utilitarianism was based on a state-utility premise. Bentham's utilitarianism, as a contrast, still left space for individuals because the premise was based on individual's desires.

From the above two aspects, the purpose and form of lawmaking, I disclosed the deep difference between Chinese utilitarianism and Benthamnism. The purposive lawmaking in Chinese theories was too much stressed. It turned out to be an instrumental lawmaking. The legitimacy of the process and approaches were not emphasized and thoroughly debated. In Chinese legalism, injustice in the causes and approaches were tolerated for the sake of the justice of the result. As analyzed in previous chapters, in reality, the least advantaged group in China did not have the national treatment in aspects of medical treatment, education, working and pension funds. Chinese lawmaking policy admitted economic inequality caused by laws. Morality of law was less concerned because of the recognition of law (law as the justified evil). The ignorance of individuals' desire in Chinese legalism and Chinese Marxism although made a realistic and consistent argument, did not develop the purposive thesis of individuals' requirements. I could not help thinking of these problems: why should the individuals be abided by law if the purpose was not for them? Why the individuals' interests were consistent with the collective? Was it a slavishly acceptance of law? Chinese literatures did not go deeper into these debates of potential conflicts between individuals and the collective; not to speak the necessity and possibility of communications between them.

5.3 Hayekian Liberal Legislation

It was not until recent 20 years that discussion of liberalism and individualism became a centre of interests in Chinese academics. In the sphere of law, the translations and interpretations of Friedrich August von Hayek's *Constitution of Liberty, The Road to Serfom, The Fatal Conceit: The Errors of Socialism,* and *The Counter-revolution of Science* represented Chinese scholars' high interests in the new liberalism and the criticism of socialism. In the sphere of lawmaking, Hayek was also a representative Western theorist of liberalism which came from natural law tradition. From a positivistic perspective, the object of lawmaking was to create legislation and statutes, which were inside the man-made rule aggregation. Natural law theorists, however, separated secular, existing and state law with 'natural justice', 'higher law' and 'substantive law'.[45] To a natural law theorist, state law was part of the aggregation of law, as the Fig. 5.2 illustrates:

Different from the above two illustrations, the liberalistic theorist Hayek's thesis on law and legislation offered an 'organic law' perspective. In 1982, Hayek published *Law, Legislation and Liberty*, which was a significant development of a legal theoretical study on legislation. It was distinct from the utilitarian lawmaking conception, and was unique in its binomial conception of law. To Bentham, law was legislation; Hayek, however, renounced a natural law idea that some legislation was *not* law.

The 'contest territory' of the two different paths was provided to understanding law: the evolutionary teachings contrast to the rationalist constructivism. In Hayek's

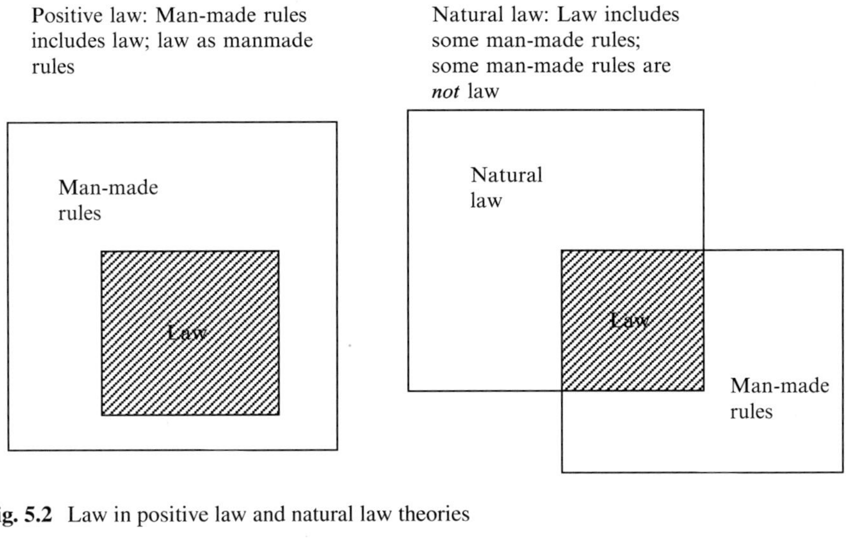

Fig. 5.2 Law in positive law and natural law theories

[45] About natural law theory see J. Finins. 1980. Natural Law and Natural Rights. Oxford: Clarendon Press.

last systematic monograph, *Law, Legislation and Liberty*, he stated a binomial concept of law: spontaneous rules versus legislation.[46] The concepts of law had in fact been speaking about different things because to some philosopher, law and liberty were inseparable, whilst to some others the two were irreconcilable. There was an obvious contrast between these two traditional ways of thoughts. One great tradition extended from the ancient Greeks and Cicero through the Middle Ages to the classical liberals like Locke, Hume, Kant and the Scottish moral philosophers, down to various American statesmen of the nineteenth and twentieth centuries, for whom law and liberty could not exist apart from each other. But to Hobbes, Bentham and many French thinkers and the modern legal positivists' law meant an encroachment on freedom. This apparent conflict between long lines of great thinkers did not mean that they arrived at opposite conclusions, but merely that they were using the word law in different senses.[47]

One of Hayek's basic arguments aimed to expose flaws in constructivist rationalism. Hayek's proposition on human beings' limitation of knowledge was his starting point to expand his legal theory. Hayek had a final conclusion after 40 years of thinking, which became the basis of his epistemology:

> *We ought to have learnt enough to avoid destroying our civilization by smothering the spontaneous process of the interaction of the individuals by placing its direction in the hands of any authority. But to avoid this we must shed the illusion that we can deliberately 'create the future of mankind', as the characteristic hubris of a socialist sociologist has recently expressed it. This is the final conclusion of the forty years which I have now devoted to the study of these problems since I became aware of the process of the Abuse and Decline of Reason which has continued throughout that period.*[48]

The constructivist rationalism was unable to help us up-build a system of 'substantive law' (the 'real' law in his theory) in Hayek's theory; it only made 'rules of organization' (i.e., legislation), as the opposite. From 1960s, Hayek started using pairs of Hellenic terms to differentiate what was real 'law' and what was only 'order'. He used the term 'cosmos' to define the spontaneous social order or the 'grown' orders. The word 'taxis' was used to describe the rules of organization or the 'made' orders. He also used 'endogenous order' and 'exoenous order', 'catallaxy' and 'demarchy', 'nomos' and 'thesis' to substitute 'spontaneous order' and 'rules of organization'.[49] All these pairs of terms were specifically used to finally strengthen the distinction between the 'law' (spontaneous order) and 'legislation' (rules of organization).

Such a binomial concept of law, i.e., law and legislation, was a well-illustrated theory on the different recognitions upon which the ontology of legislation was based. 'Organic law' or 'spontaneous law', as the Fig. 5.3 illustrates, was in contrast with 'man-made legislation' or 'artificial law'. A positivist would focus on the

[46] F. Hayek. 1982. Law, Legislation and Liberty. I: 35–37. 51–52. London: Routledge & Kegan Paul.

[47] F. Hayek. 1982. Law, Legislation and Liberty. I: 51–52. London: Routledge & Kegan Paul.

[48] Ibid. 152.

[49] F. Hayek. 1982. Law, Legislation and Liberty. vol.1 35–37. London: Routledge & Kegan Paul.

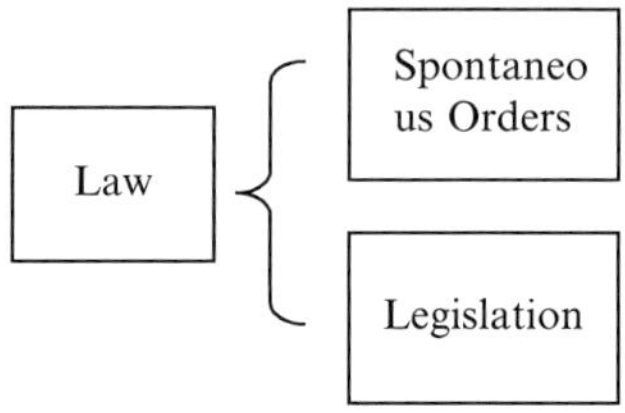

Fig. 5.3 Law in Hayek's theory

artificial man-made legislation; a natural theorist in contrast stressed the 'real law' idea to criticize the limitation of man-made order. They represented two different perspectives on the ontology of law. Hayek's concept of law, however, was different: Law included both of them: opposite to spontaneous rules, there is legislation, the man-made rules.[50]

The substantive law was therefore the 'spontaneous order', which differed from the 'rules of organization' or a 'made order'. Law was older than legislation and had never been 'invented' in the same sense as legislation, the deliberate making of law.[51] The invention of legislation came relatively late in the history of mankind, so

> *...law in the sense of enforced rules of conduct, on the other hand, is undoubtedly coeval with society. To modern man, however, the belief that all law governing human action is the product of legislation appears so obvious that the contention that law is older than lawmaking has almost the character of a paradox.*[52]

The idea that all law was, can be, and ought to be, the product of the free invention of a legislator, was recognized by Hayek as factually false because it was '*an erroneous product of constructivist rationalism*'.[53] This binomial conception of law was as a contemporary edition of interpreting the primary difference between natural law and positive law theories.[54] Hayek pointed out a limitation that both natural

[50] Ibid., 'Thesis: the Law of Legislation' (Chapter 6), focuses on artificial legislations and is in contrast with 'Nomos: the Law of Liberty' (Chapter 5). The rules of just conduct, the 'nomos' or 'law of liberty', or the substantive law in Hayek's definition, emerge from the judicial process.

[51] Ibid. 73.

[52] Ibid.

[53] Ibid.

[54] Hayek observed that in the second century a Latin grammarian, Aulus Gellius, rendered the Greek terms physei and thesei by naturalis and positivus, from which most European languages derived the words to describe two kinds of laws. The original Greek terms, physei and thesei, mean 'by natural' and 'by convention or deliberate decision'. In this way he differentiated natural law from artificial law. (ibid., 20.) Critics stated that Hayek's theory was neither in the sphere of natural law nor positive law because it was not a simple dichotomy of 'natural' and 'artificial'; it taked an 'evolutionary approach' which was different from the logic precondition of dimidiating 'natural' and 'artificial', to which natural law and positive law theories all obeyed. See J. Gray. 1986. Liberalism, Milton Keynes: Open University Press. The connection of Hayek's theory with natural law, especially his Kantian tradition, however, was obvious. See J. Birner, R. Zijp. 1994. Hayek, Co-ordination and Evolution: His Legacy in Philosophy, Politics, Economics and the History of

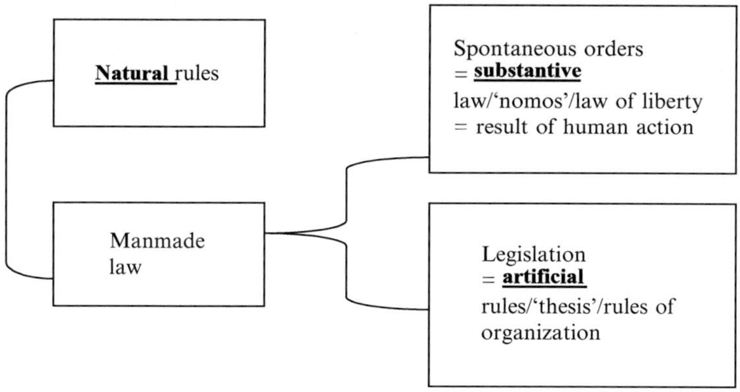

Fig. 5.4 Natural rules and Manmade law

law theorists and positivists shared, that was, the division of natural rules and artificial (man-made) rules. He put forward a middle ground between 'natural' and 'artificial' to break this natural-artificial dichotomy—customary rules which were not 'natural justice' or 'artificial design'—the objects which were the results 'of human action but not of human design'.[55] According to such objects, law was not something wholly and perfectly designed by human beings—it was the result of human action but not necessarily of human design. Hayek thus attempted to justify customary laws as 'real law', which was considered by him as better than natural or artificial rules, as illustrated by Fig. 5.4:

'Spontaneous orders' discovered by the judges were differentiated from legislation, which originated from the necessity of establishing rules of organization. The real law, which was observed by Hayek as the lawyer's law, emerged from spontaneous orders, and did not necessarily need a particular 'law-giver'.[56] Legislatures were primarily concerned with governmental matters rather than with giving law as 'substantive law', i.e., law of liberty.[57] He stated that, a '*thesis*', i.e., legislation, however, always presupposed the particular 'law-giver'; a '*thesis*', was the law that should be 'executed' or carried out.[58] The original meaning of legislature was also traced to state the relationship between legislation and the theory of separation of powers.[59] Hayek pointed out that the term legislature had become simply a name for representative assemblies occupied chiefly with directing or controlling government rather than as a lawmaking department.

Ideas. 297. London and New York: Routledge. See also J.C.W. Touchie. 2005. Hayek and Human Rights: Foundations for a Minimalist Approach to Law. 218. Edward Elgar Publishing.

[55] F. Hayek. 1982. Law, Legislation and Liberty. 20. London: Routledge & Kegan Paul.

[56] F. Hayek. 1982. Law, Legislation and Liberty. 122. London: Routledge & Kegan Paul.

[57] Ibid.

[58] Ibid.

[59] Ibid.128–130.

Based on this differentiation between 'rules of just conduct' and 'rules of organization', Hayek brought forward his division of public law and private law.[60] As an outstanding social observer, he pointed out the tendency of the private law sphere gradually transforming into public law by social legislation in modern societies.[61] This was recognized as common sense nowadays, but in the age of emphasizing governmental positive activities during the economic winter, Hayek's insistence of classical liberalism and his argument against the invasion by the 'public law' of the 'private law' showed his unique courage and wisdom.[62]

The final conclusions on law and legislation in *Law, Legislation and Liberty* were: there was an tendency of the public law to gradually interfere with or invade the private sphere; that legislation as the rules of organization was the result of purposeful invention and was aimed at solving governmental matters; and law generated from spontaneous orders and originating from long-standing historical practice ought not to be substituted by legislation—the 'nomos' should not be substituted or violated by the 'thesis'; otherwise, the individual's liberty protected mainly by the 'nomos' would be eroded.

Comparing the concepts of law in Fig. 5.2 with Fig. 5.4, we could see that Hayek's theory still remained within a positive law debate. Although he emphasized differences between 'results of human design', i.e., legislation, and 'results of human action', i.e., spontaneous rules, he put both into the man-made-rule aggregation. His conclusion that law was a subset of man-made rules was coincidental to the aggregation of positive law. He contributed, however, in his further separation of 'human design' from the unconscious results of 'human action' and thus stressed the importance of custom in the development of law.

In contrast with the criticisms on the positivistic monistic definition of law (i.e., that law was law), Hayekian binomial concept of law included two systems of laws, i.e., law and ideal law.[63] The ideal type of lawmaking was derived from the Common

[60] Hayek's classification is different from a traditional public law and private law classification. About Hayek's classification of public law and the private law, see ibid.131–144.

[61] About the tendency of private law transforming to public law, see also M. Tatsukichi. 2003. Public Law and Private Law. 234–251. Beijing: China University of Political Science and Law Press.

[62] In 1950s, Keynesian economics, interventionism and socialism were widely accepted. In this era of new liberalism and social democracy, most Western capitalist countries believed that a positive interference was better than free market. Hayek recognized the danger of having a blind faith in Keynesian economics and socialism and wrote series of books to defend the idea of economic liberty. The representative books were: F. Hayek. 1944. The Road to Serfom. Routledge. F. Hayek. 1960. Constitution of Liberty. University of Chicago Press. And F. Hayek. 1988. The Fatal Conceit: The Errors of Socialism. Routledge.

[63] See previous discussion on Bentham's theory: only legislation was counted as law, and that law should be recognized as the same as legislation. Bentham emphasized the prominent meaning of legislation and states in his Of Laws In General that the word 'law' was in some extent equal to 'legislation'. '*Judging…from analogy, it would naturally be expected that the signification given to the word law should be correspondent to that of its conjugates legislation and legislative power…* ', J. Bentham. 1970. Of Laws in General. 9.London: University of London, Athlone Press.

Law. The anti-rationalism attitude; suspicious perspective on governmental rules; rejection of constructivist rational legislation; preference of judge's law or lawyer's law and the statement that the substantive law (which emerges from spontaneous order) could only be discovered rather than designed (because they belonged to 'the results of human action' not 'human design'); the explanation that legislation was 'rules of organization' not 'rules of just conduct', 'thesis' rather than 'nomos', and was concerned with governmental matters rather than with making the law of liberty, all these propositions were emphasized to value Common Law.[64] It was logical for him make those conclusions because the starting point of his theory of liberty is *classical liberalism*.[65] An ideology which valued freedom and individualism also promoted the constitutionalism of Common Law.[66] Hayek's preference for classical liberalism was consistent with his choice of Common Law as the ideal lawmaking model while finding constructivist lawmaking dissatisfactory. The conclusion that law ought not to be substituted by legislation, however, strengthened his normative debate, or a preference for 'ideal law'. It therefore in the end became an *anti-positivistic debate on positive law*.[67]

However, the limitations of such a liberalistic theory should be noticed. One was the de-constructive attitude on existing legislations.[68] To Hayek, legislations were strictly deprived from the 'ideal law' category. The real law or substantive law should

[64] In Hayek's theory, spontaneous orders could only be discovered rather than designed. F. Hayek. 1982. Law, Legislation and Liberty. 20. London: Routledge & Kegan Paul.

[65] Hayek identified himself as a classical liberal, see F. Hayek. Why I am not a Conservative. 1960. The Constitution of Liberty. Chicago: The University of Chicago Press. S. Horwitz and F. Hayek. Austrian Economist. 2005. Journal of the History of Economic Thought:71–85.

[66] Common law was recognized as grounded in precedent and local tradition as well as reason; it stressed community. Liberal political theory was based on abstract, rational principles; it stressed individualism. Common law and liberalism both promoted constitutionalism. See J.R. Stoner. 1997. Common Law and Liberal Theory: Coke, Hobbes and the Origins of American Constitutionalism. Lawrence, Kans: University Press of Kansas; also see the synthesis of liberal theory with the common law, in B.P. Wilson and K. Masugi. 1997. The Supreme Court and American Constitutionalism. 52. Rowman & Littlefield. B.Z. Tamanaha. 2004. On the Rule of Law. Cambridge: Cambridge University Press.

[67] Anti-positivism as reactions against positivism had two basic forms: the hermeneutic science perspective and the mediating or interpretive structuralist perspective. M. Weber introduced the term anti-positivism. He believed that sociology should be a 'science', able to identify causal relationships—especially among ideal types, or hypothetical simplifications of complex social phenomena. As a non-positivist, Weber recognized that the selection and construction of ideal types was itself a subjective process, and realized that, unlike the causal relationships sought in positivistic science, those found between ideal types were not 'ahistorical, invariant, or generalizable'. See Ashley D. and Orenstein D.M. 2005. Sociological Theory: Classical Statements. 239–241. Boston, Mass.: Pearson Education.See also: I. Oliver. 1983. The 'Old' and the 'New' Hermeneutic in Sociological Theory. The British Journal of Sociology 34: 519–553. See also: J.A. Standen. 1986. Critical Legal Studies as an Anti-positivist Phenomenon. Virginia Law Review 72: 983–988. And also see: A. C. Wicks and R.E. Freeman. 1998. Organization Studies and the New Pragmatism: Positivism, Anti-positivism, and the Search for Ethics. Organization Science 9:123–140.

[68] 'Deconstruction' was central to post-structuralism, which was an umbrella term that came into use in the 1970's. Deconstruction was an attitude that doubts human artificial design, including

Fig. 5.5 A positive-sequence view and a reverse-order linear view

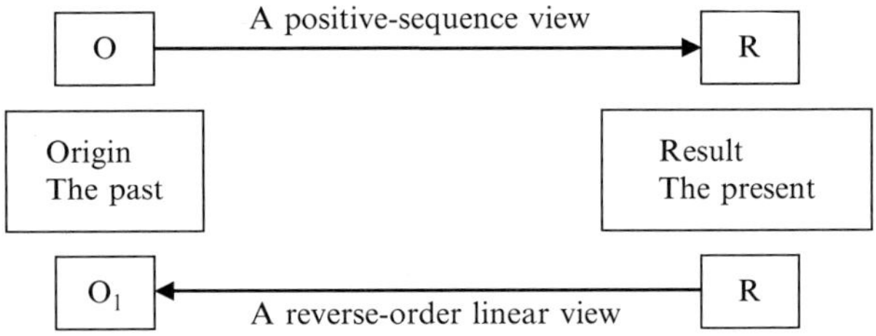

refer to the customs developed over a long period of human practice, such as the Common Law. If legislation was understood from this deconstructive attitude, or in other words, if the creative work and human design in law was totally excluded from the 'ideal law' concept, it would become difficult to justify the legality and legitimacy of modern legislatures and legislations. The deconstructive thesis, i.e., removing legislation from a normative study of law, ignored common people's understanding of law—'readers' response to law'.[69] Formal legislations could be easily recognized as law by people. The legislations, however, were sometimes different from the 'substantive law' or 'real law' interpreted by theorists or judicial elites. Even worse, to deny legislations' normativity was also to reject the fact that legislation was a reasonable, and most of the time a 'just' choice of the creators and the acceptors. If legislation and lawmaking processes were seen as reasonable problem-solving mechanisms, legislation (as the human design) could bring dignity to law.[70]

Apart from the de-constructive approach, Hayekian evolutionary perspective on law was at a disadvantage in interpreting modern legal systems because it denied one of their major characteristics: law as a positive institutional design. As observed by Professor Bankowski, '*For Hayek, societies and social institutions arise by evolution*'.[71] Hayek's cultural evolutionary approach should not be confused with the Darwinian species evolutionary theory, but both supposed a similar 'reverse-order linear view' on the research objects. The linear view (see Fig. 5.5), as defined in this thesis referred to a perspective which saw the present as a determined result from the past, and thus excluded diverse possibilities during the process. In Fig. 5.5,

---

language and legal doctrines. J.M. Balkin. 1987. Deconstructive Practice and Legal Theory. The Yale Law Journal 96:743–786.

[69] A reader-response criticism or a reception theory emphasizes the reader and the process of reading rather than on the author or the text. About reader-response criticism, see Buckley W.K. and Bracher M. 1986. Reader-Response Theory. Publications of the Modern Language Association of America 101: 250–251. See also P. Harkin. 2005. The Reception of Reader-Response Theory. College Composition and Communication 56: 410–425.

[70] It was also different from Waldron's thesis that I will introduce later. In Waldron's thesis, the dignity of legislation presented in the majority-rule principle, i.e., disagreements and diverse opinions. I believe that it was the problem-solving purpose rather than disagreement or diversity that brought dignity to law.

[71] Zenon Bankowski. 2001. Living Lawfully-Love in Law and Law in Love. 84. Dordrecht: Kluwer.

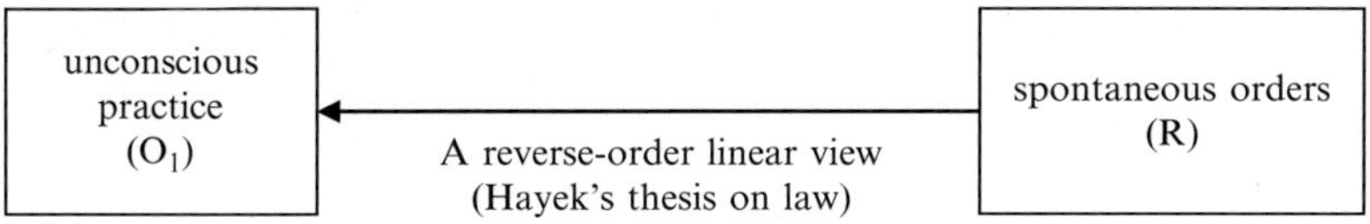

Fig. 5.6 A reverse-order linear view (Hayek's thesis on law)

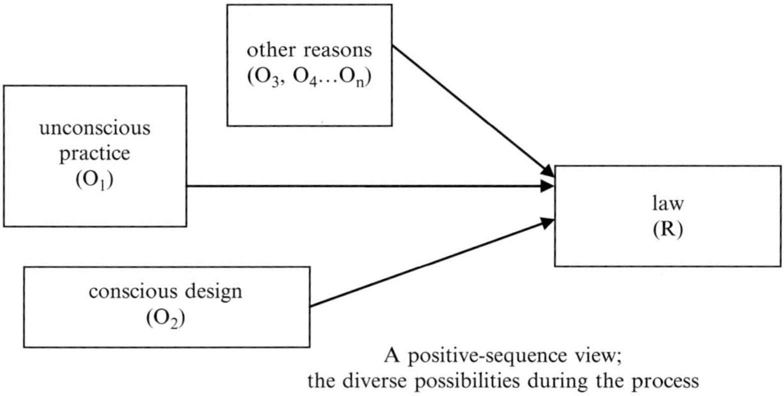

Fig. 5.7 A positive-sequence view: the diverse possibilities during the process

the aggregation of Origin in a positive-sequence view should involve more than one element: (O = O1+ O2+ O3 + … On), although the result (R) was one and only.

A reverse-order linear view deduced origin from result, past from present, and traced one potential source of the origins while ignoring other possibilities. For instance, if stated from this perspective, the proposition that: 'a human being (R) is a member of a species of bipedal primates in the family Hominidae (O)' would be stated like this: '*only* humans (O1) can be developed into wise humans (R)'.[72] Different from this perspective, a positive-sequence view admitted other various possibilities—other kinds of primates (O2, O3…On) could develop into wise humans (R). If stated from a linear view, Hayek's proposition that 'in early history human's unconscious practice (O1) developed law (R)' was stated like this: '*only* spontaneous orders (O1) are real laws (R) because they developed from human's unconscious practice but not human design' (see Fig. 5.6). A positive-sequence perspective, however, involved human artificial design (O2) and other causes (O3, O4…On) into sources of law (see Fig. 5.7).

[72] Taxonomically Homo sapiens—Latin: 'wise human' or 'knowing human', see Hominidae classification, http://animaldiversity.ummz.umich.edu/site/accounts/classification/Hominidae.html. Accessed 02 Feb 2012.

As Fig. 5.6 showed, the reverse-order linear view implied a deterministic deduction: only spontaneous rules developed law. The evolution was thus seen by him not only as the 'fact' but also as the 'tenet' that should be obeyed—Hayek emphasized the significance of unconscious human behaviours in the historical development of law, but exaggerated them as the exclusive 'tenet' of the growth of law and ignored the fact that human beings' initiative and creative motivation was also an important factor in the development of human civilization. 'Spontaneous rules' in his theory implied the proposition that law evolved without outside interference. Those self-developed laws were the real law according to his conception.

However, law could not grow spontaneously without interference in the past—during the codification movement in Western enlightenment era, law were transplanted to colonial territories; and as debated previously the development of law in China in the last two centuries could also support this argument. Even if the spontaneous growth of law were taken as a true proposition, it still could not explain the present and future development pattern of law. Would law develop in the same way as it did over history? A reverse-order linear view, which always began deduction from an existing result, could not 'predict' the future because the future result had not yet appeared! The reverse-order linear approach was therefore deficient for future-oriented deduction. The linear lawmaking perspective failed to consider the difference between developments of systematic rules with the self-development of a single rule. The idea of spontaneous law could interpret the development of rules *before* they were artificially classified and codified into a logical system, but it could not refer to an intended systematic lawmaking movement—rules might develop spontaneously; but a legal system could not exclude 'artificial' legislation.

Although the messy laws seemed to channel down to a straight and narrow path from variable path, in Bankowski's argument for the necessity of living the life under rules, 'de-simplification' of rules was not necessarily a bad thing.[73] However, he also pointed out that a linear perspective was influenced by rationalism, the ideology of seeing the society as a machine-like institution.

> *The past…is already fixed and can be described without loss of meaning in terms of behavioural co-ordinates. This makes us think that the future, where it is not past behaviours that are important but future actions which have to be described in terms of intention, can as well. However, just because you can retrospectively analyze behaviour as rule governed does not mean you can predict future action unless you see society as a machine like repetitive behaviour.*[74]

As we can see in the quote, the prediction of future (the linear perspective) is possible when the society was running like a machine. The problem of the machine-like rule system was not that behaviours were predictable and controllable, but that the system tried to get people to react in one particular way.[75] It was not about

[73] Zenon Bankowski. 2001. Living Lawfully-Love in Law and Law in Love. 119. Dordrecht: Kluwer.

[74] Ibid.123.

[75] Ibid.130.

'spontaneous rules' but 'spontaneous behavious'. In such a system, people acted without thinking about the law. The heteronomous rules made people stop thinking about whether their behaviours were wrong or not; they just followed rules. Although this displacement of thinking was not necessarily a bad thing—simplicity and predictability were positive effects of law, it can lead to bad results. In an organic perspective, life is not mechanized. The obedience to law should not be reduced to 'following law blindly'. To jump out of the linear and mechanized way of living, we should allow the creativity of people. It means people are following rules, but they can also make rules.

In ancient Chinese ideologies, the positive sequence view was stressed. Although the reason for wars among states was not justified in favor of the common people's interests, they emphasized the legitimate status of the ruler, who should come from the royal pedigree. Otherwise, in Chinese history, if a controller was not from the royal family, it could be a sufficient reason for other ambitious nobles to start wars to compete for a strongest conqueror for the country.[76] The new winner of the wars therefore would be justified as the legitimate new lawmaker without considering the justice of the approach he used. When the order of positive sequence was broken, 'law of the jungle' would start to rule. Force and art of control would be highly required in order to strengthen their de facto conquer. The history would become 'a history of conquerors', which was not about civilization and justice. The legitimacy of law would come from the winners' de facto victory over the losers. It was as much as to say that when a group of mobs robbed common people's wealth, if they succeeded, their immoral behaviors could be justified! In order to avoid this jungle rule, Chinese ancient theories emphasized that legitimate legislation should always come from the order of positive sequence of the royal perigee, rather than the 'law of the jungle'. In this sense, Chinese ancient theories embraced some elements of justice (for example, no to conquer by violence).

In contemporary Chinese theories, however, the reverse-order linear justification existed. The development of civilization referred to 'survival of the fittest' rather than other causes. In Chinese Marxism, for example, the working class was recognized as 'the advantaged class' and that the Communist Party (hereinafter the Party) was the representative of the working class. Therefore the working class should be the leading class and the Party should be the leading party. This justification was written in Chinese constitution as well: the task of the working class was to lead the whole population realize communism. This justification, however, was in conflict with two important facts that I discussed in Chap. 3: during the modern legislative reform, the working class was not the only leading class; and later, the working class did not have superiorities in reality. The working class in China was not strong enough to complete the reform in the past so they had to depend on the majority, the peasant. Later on, the working class was not the major party of the congress, and the industrial workers were among the weakest group. Therefore the working class was

[76]The famous history of the Three Kingdoms of China (220–265) was solid evidence. Luo Guanzhong. 2008. Romance of Three Kingdoms. 266. Beijing: Remin Publishing House.

not the 'survival of the fittest'. Although no one would deny that the Party (as the nominal represent of the 'working class') was the exclusive Chinese leading party, the justification of the 'survival of the fittest' was not ideal. Another problem was that this justification excludes the common and the disadvantaged persons' right of decision-making.

Hayekian liberal legislation although also held a reverse order liner perspective, differed from Chinese consequentialist justification. Hayekian theory did not ignore 'common peoples' understanding but relied on them. If we interpreted Hayekian spontaneous law as the law developed by the common people, rather by law itself (as Kelsen's normative theory described), we noticed that Hayek emphasized a contest of people's law against official laws. Professor Bankowski pushed this argument further in *Living Lawfully*. He argued that when someone (common people) had to rely on a cadre of experts working for the good of the people, this good gradually became their own good. Hayekian liberal legislation differentiated the people's law and the officials' law. If we considered them as two different systems, as an outside system and an inside system, what we need to do is to 'bring the outside in'. The lawmaking procedure should offer an arena for communications between them. They should not be seen as two isolated systems. Thus, we could develop Hayekian theory to a communicative theory.

5.4 Disagreements of Majority Decisions

Waldron's justification of majority decision-making was a theory relating to the legitimacy of Western lawmaking. The dignity of legislation was justified by the structure of legislature and its working progress in Waldron's argument. He concluded that democracy principle was worthy of dignity. Traditional political theories were criticized: Legislation and legislatures had a bad name in legal philosophy; and we had not developed a normative theory of legislation. More importantly,

> *[W]e are not in possession of a jurisprudential model that is capable of making normative sense of legislation as a genuine form of law, of the authority that it claims, and of the demands that it makes on the other actors in a legal system.'*[77] Normative or aspirational models of legislation are insufficient in that jurisprudence is pervaded by imagery that '*presents ordinary legislative activity as deal-making, horse-trading, log-rolling, interest-pandering, and pork-barreling—as anything, except principled decision-making.*[78]

Waldron compared two leading ideas of modern legal positivism—'*the sources thesis*' (Raz) and '*the rule of recognition*' (Hart), and criticized that they and their predecessors did not have interest in the structure and proceedings of legislatures.[79]

---

[77] J. Waldron. 1999. The Dignity of Legislation. 1. Cambridge: Cambridge University press.

[78] Ibid. 2.

[79] The 'source thesis' claimed that the existence and content of law can always be determined by reference to its sources without recourse to moral argument. According to this view, the sources of law included both the circumstances of its promulgation and relevant interpretative materials, such as court cases involving its application. J. Raz. 1979. The Authority of Law: Essays on Law and

The aspects that Waldron emphasized—size, diversity, disagreement, decision-making procedures—were not important to positivists. A strong positivism perspective influenced jurists, especially in the Common Law system, to disregard legislation as an object for legal research. Legislation was therefore considered an object for political science rather than the science of law so that '*the only structures that interest contemporary philosophers of law [were] the structures of judicial reasoning*'.[80]

In *Law and Disagreement* and *The Dignity of Legislation*, the jurisprudence of legislation argued for a wide range of propositions regarding legislation. In the former work, the concepts of legislation and legislature in political theory and legal philosophy were named as *Jurisprudence of Legislation*. In the latter, the reputation of legislation was restored by focusing on the writings of Aristotle, Locke and Kant. The conclusions on legislation were: legislation was a dignified mode of governance and a respectable source of law; 'large numbers' and the facts of diversity and disagreement should be central to the philosophy of legislation. The focus of the jurisprudence of legislation was primarily on legislation by assemblies: large gatherings of representatives who air their disagreements in adversarial debate before making laws by deliberation and voting; voting and majority-decisions were the pivotal points of legislation.

The *multiplicity* of different views rather than one mind or will was recognized by Waldron as the nature of legislation. Disagreement (rather than agreement) over the multiplicity of views was at the centre of his study of legislation. The principle of majority decision was justified as the basis of democracy. Waldron used Locke's reasoning to defend the argument that majority decision was unrelated to right or wrong, but conferred legitimacy or appropriation:

> *Just as the fact that a person consents to a proposal doesn't make the proposal right or wise, so the fact that there is majority support for a proposal doesn't make it right or wise or just either. Consent and majority-support are supposed to work in relation to the legitimacy of popular decision-making, not at this stage in relation to the wisdom of the multitude.*[81]

The majoritarianism behind modern legislation was considered as an effective and respected decision-making principle. Although legislation looked arbitrary when it was presented as the outcome of majority decision-making, Waldron's theory concluded that when an issue needed a common decision and there existed disparate individual views, majority decision-making could insure that the outcomes deserved respect rather than an arbitrary political procedure.

> *In the circumstances of politics, tossing a coin might be a way of settling on a common course of action. If the deadline for action was near enough and the need for concerted action sufficiently compelling, we might adopt any arbitrary method that made one course of action more salient. If the matter were particularly grave, we might even admire such methods...*[82]

Morality. 47. Oxford: Oxford University Press. The rule of recognition '*specifies some feature or features possession of which by a suggested rule is taken as a conclusive affirmative indication that it is a rule of the group to be supported by the social pressure it exerts*'. See H.L.A. Hart. 1994. The Concept of Law. 92. London: Clarendon Press.

[80] J. Waldron. 1999. Law and Disagreement. 9. Oxford: Oxford University Press.

[81] J. Waldron. 1999. The Dignity of Legislation. 146. Cambridge: Cambridge University press.

[82] Ibid. 157.

In *Law and Disagreement* Waldron put forward a *jurisprudence of legislation, a special jurisprudence*. A normative theory about legislation was discovered as: discussion of the difference between good and bad laws; attempts at determining the limits of legislation (the issues legislatures should address, and the issues that should be left to positive morality); and the sorts of things that ought to be taken into account when one embarks on the process of lawmaking.[83] In the two books, a central theme was that collective decision making was 'good'. The quality of the decision was likely to be higher the larger the number of individuals participating in the decision-making, 'the wisdom of the multitude'.[84]

Scholars noticed that Waldron was concerned with developing a vision of liberal democracy separated from the legal constitutionalism of the American model.[85] Specifically speaking, he disclosed the tensions between legislative authority and judicial authority and deliberated a profound question: the legitimacy of judicial review. He reminded us to characterize liberalism by legislative rather than judicial supremacy. By doing so, '*he upsets our standard assumptions about the inevitability and rightness of judicial review and asks us to rethink the foundations of our political order*'.[86] Waldron emphasized on the reality of political disagreement and the how political life should be conducted in the presence of fundamental disagreement. However, Whittington [224] criticized that Waldron did not consider the possibility that different political institutions may serve different functions within a coherent political system.[87] Or as Mendes [138] argued, why there were possibilities and necessities of dialogues among institutions, especially between the courts and the legislatures.[88]

In Michelon's book [140], Waldron's justification for democratic lawmaking was insufficient. He pointed out that Waldron put procedural justifications for the authority of law, i.e., particular accounts of the value of reasons produced through democratic procedures. However, '*Legal reasons produced by democratic procedures are, as a result, insulated from plain moral reasons*.'[89] The rational authority of the parliament was put prior to the rational authority of individuals and other sorts of groups that can be found in society. Therefore, '*Waldron's argument relies on an over simplified version of practical reasoning and, moreover, it implied an untenable position for practical agents living under the law.*'[90] Michelon emphasized an idea that even the procedural justice should enclose moral dimension. We could not

[83] Ibid. 23.

[84] Keith E. Whittington. 2000. In Defense of Legislatures. Political Theory 28.694.

[85] Ibid. 690–702.

[86] Ibid. 693.

[87] Ibid.

[88] Conrado Hübner Mendes. 2009. Is it all about the Last Word? Deliberative Separation of Powers 1 Legisprudence 3: 69–110.

[89] Cláudio Michelon. 2006. Being Apart from Reasons: The Role of Reasons in Public and Private Moral Decision-Making. 179. Springer-Verlag New York.

[90] Ibid.

justify the result by exclusively referring to the procedure of decision-making. Majority principle in democratic lawmaking should not be the only reason for the authority of law. He reasserted the value of Kantian categorical reasoning and stated that '*proceduralist accounts of the value of legal reasons, notably those put forward by discourse theory, are …not to be able to ground the exclusion of moral reasons from neither public nor private decision-making process*.'[91] Michelon disclosed the defect of discourse theory represented by Waldron (and Harbermas). They stressed 'dialog' but did not unearth the embedded justice of 'dialog'.

The key word in Waldron's jurisprudence of legislation was '*plurality*'. The structure of legislature and the disagreement and deliberation during legislation were noticed and justified. Waldorn concluded that modern legislature was a large multi-member assembly comprising hundreds of persons with diverse views, affiliations and allegiances. Therefore, majority decision-making was justified as a dignified way of lawmaking. However, in my view, it was not the pure procedural 'majority-decision', i.e., plurality, diversity and disagreement that justified democratic lawmaking, but the value of negotiation and compromise that also justified lawmaking. The authority of law, or the legal text, should be respected not because it came from 'messy opinions' but from people's effort to come to an agreement (I will re-address this point in the next chapter in my discussion of the social contract theory. Wintgens' version of social contract was the exact opposite of Waldron's perspective in this point). Waldron doubted the authority of legal texts and stated that the only thing which dignified legislation was its majority-decision method.[92] But if people did not rely upon the authoritativeness of the texts that had been passed through deliberate lawmaking procedures, why should legislations (the texts; the proof of compromise or agreement; the result of debate) rather than the various opinions during lawmaking be the final law? If the result, the texts of law were not reliable, was it possible to depend on the authority of legislature? In Waldron's argument, the text gained majority support despite continuing disagreement among legislators, and thus the text alone could have the authority of law—in contrast to the legislative intent expressed in floor debates or committee hearings. He believed that people recognized the authority of legislation not because they necessarily agree with its substance but because they respect the '*conditions of fairness in which a common solution was arrived at among those who disagreed about what it ought to be.*'[93]

In Austin or Hobbe's theories, the authority of lawmakers (commanders) was to justify the validity of law.[94] Waldron's special jurisprudence on legislation as a con-

---

[91] Cláudio Michelon. 2006. Being Apart from Reasons: The Role of Reasons in Public and Private Moral Decision-Making. 9. Springer-Verlag New York.

[92] Waldron wrote that '*…it strikes me that…'in a multicultural society, legislators are entitled to insist on the authoritativeness of the text and nothing but the text as the only thing that can be sure has been at the forefront of each member's legislative endeavours*.' J. Waldron. 1999. Law and Disagreement. 145. Oxford: Oxford University Press.

[93] J. Waldron. 1999. Law and Disagreement.85. Oxford: Oxford University Press.

[94] J. Austin. 1995. The Province of Jurisprudence Determined. 166. Cambridge: Cambridge University Press. As Cotterell observed, '*Austin's theory is not a theory of the rule of law—of*

trast questioned the authority of the institution. He stressed the authority of the democratic procedure, which was different from the recognition of the status of the authority. Legislature was recognized as a group of people holding multiple opinions—it although was worthy of dignity but did not necessarily gain authority unless majority's decision was made. Therefore in Waldron's theory, neither the authority of the institution nor the legal texts per se were considered to have dignity, unless they were supported by the majority.

In Waldron's special jurisprudence on legislation, the diverse opinions from individual legislators were to substitute the authority of the unified decision of a legislature. Legislators' intention was materialized as singular ones. However, from another perspective, individual lawmakers' opinions differed from the formal consensus decision of a group of persons, or what we call an institution. Waldron's special jurisprudence focused on the former part of a complex legislative process, but overvalued disagreement and diversity. He tried to save the dignity of legislation by arguing that disagreement and majority-decision in legislation were necessary and respectful. However, he overvalued the factors of 'plurality' and 'diversity', and extended these throughout the whole lawmaking procedure but ignored the fact that the later part of the lawmaking procedure, especially the final decision, i.e., an agreement rather than various opinions, should be of equal significance.

Waldron avoided the discussion of the part of lawmaking based on negotiation and compromise, which promoted a determinate law. As opposed to 'plurality' and 'disagreement', a determinate law and 'agreement' reinforced the authority of legislature also. In Waldron's theory individual legislators' disperse will was the ultimate source for understanding law. Ironically, the supposed problem-solving institution (legislature) became a headache to interpreters of law (courts and judges, the judicial), because the judicial and people needed to find out various intentions behind the law. It was in conflict with the requirement for legal certainty and predictability. In a harsh critique of *Law and Disagreement*, a Chinese critic said that:

> *[T]he book ignored several thousand years human intellectual accumulation and shake a stick to force us to go back to the war state, and the original state, where everybody was against everybody. Fortunately, there is at least one conception that the majority might accept or are reluctant to agree, that is, people have to live together…although the society is a net, it has gaps…otherwise we would keep wondering, why should we live together?! Why should we live together?*[95]

In my view, diversity could describe the nature of a democratic legislative process, but it should not influence the expectation of the certainty and predictability of the lawmaking institution and the laws it made. After the deliberate discussion of a bill, in which various and different opinions had been considered, law should

---

government subject to law. it is a theory of 'rule of men'—of government [and law] as an instrument of power'. R. Cotterell. 1992.The Politics of Jurisprudence: A Critical Introduction to Legal Philosophy. 74. Philadelphia: University of Pennsylvania Press.

[95] Ge Xiao. 2010. A Review of Law and Disagreement. at http://book.douban.com/review/3350529/. Accessed 02 Feb 2012.

be seen as containing a consensus behind it from the moment it was enacted. The dignity of legislation was reflected in its 'institutional way' of solving problems also. Lawmaking was 'institutional' and 'artificial', which was more than the 'natural' diversity and multiplicity among individuals. People accepted laws because they were derived from a prudent and consensus decision. Although there were many different opinions during legislation, law (the result of the procedure) should offer people a determinate, final agreement. The dignity of legislation therefore not only existed in its majority-decision method, but also in its institutional problem-solving agreement. Law was not only from diverse opinions but also from a final consensus and deliberate procedure.

Waldron's theory was therefore not sufficient for the justification of Chinese lawmaking. The justification of majority decision-making could not fit into the interpretation of Chinese 'democratic dictatorship' theory, for example. Waldron's theory would face difficulties in differentiating the means (majority rule) from the ends (a just result of lawmaking). It on the contrary would imply a substitution of the ends for the means. I disagree with Waldron's argument that democracy was reduced to disagreement. To me, democracy was not simply about majority decision-making and multiple different views, it was also a platform for the least advantaged group's opinions and requests being heard, as Rawls argued in *A theory of Justice* [167]. Democracy should be a platform for communications for the sake of agreements as well as disagreements. Lawmaking should aim at agreements although disagreements were important in the process of reaching to agreements. Disagreements were the means and agreements were the ends. Agreement through communication should be the principle of democratic lawmaking.

I agree with the critique that provided in *Living Lawfully* which argued against a simplified theory of majority: '*what conceptually is a majority*?'[96] The justice of law should not be tested by solely relying on '*the arithmetical sense of the term of majority*'; because '*looking at it from the point of view of the minority, this problem is insoluble*'.[97] As Professor Bankowski stated in the purpose and means of lawmaking:

> *If we are interested in bringing a society closer together, then we will be more interested in coming closer to the unanimity principle, whereas if we are just concerned with a decision making procedure which will, in a minimal sense, hold, then we will come closer to a simple majority system.*[98]

Therefore ruling by diversity and mathematic majority was not equal to rational lawmaking, unless certain substantial values were there to 'back up' the formalistic justice. 'Love' in *Living Lawfully*, 'mercy' in *Being Apart from Reasons*, and 'humanity' in this thesis were different from a pure procedural discourse theory. All those concepts emphasized the justice of dialog. Both the unanimity principle and

---

[96] Zenon Bankowski. 2001. Living Lawfully-Love in Law and Law in Love. 17. Dordrecht: Kluwer.

[97] Ibid.18.

[98] Ibid.18–19.

the principle of disagreements could reflect rational decision in different contexts. Therefore we should not refer the procedural majority principle exclusively to the justified dignified principle for lawmaking.[99]

[99] I stimulated a role-play discussion of lawmaking in my class of 48 students of Zhongnan University of Economics and Law in 2009. The specific situation of my case was stated like this: ‘suppose you were the passengers of a week-long ship. Before you got onto the ship, all of you passed the health examination so that you were healthy passengers. In the middle of the trip, however, two of you were sick and the only doctor of the ship diagnosed that the disease was new and infectious. One of the sick passengers died and five more passengers appeared symptoms. There were no medicines in the ship and the nearest shore was a two-day trip away. Now you have to decide, what should you do?’ I divided the students into two groups: Group A: those who support the decision of throwing the six sick passengers into the sea, and group B: those who would take a risk of keep the sick until they landed. I let the two groups stated their reasons and then made a decision together. Group A argued that the sick passengers already threatened most passengers' lives and should be killed. It was not a moral decision but it in the end could be justified for another moral value: the healthy people's (the majority's) lives. It was a right decision for the overall situation and also a legitimate defense of the majority (the healthy passengers) against the minority (the sick passengers). If this were the situation of a state, the state might make the same decision that they had made. In similar dilemmas, a nation always gave up few people for the sake of the interests of the nation. Group B argued that the healthy passengers did not have the authority to kill other people's lives, especially when the sick passengers were not guilty for any offences of laws. Killing them in the name of their disease was immoral and inhuman. If they killed the sick passengers, they murdered their lives and should be punished by law.

After half hour debate, I let my students to vote. Thirty-eight of 48 students made a decision for killing the sick passengers and 10 including the 6 ‘sick passengers’ stood by the minority's human rights for living. Then I asked them whether they all accepted this decision, the majority's decision? All of them agreed. Who would do the execution of the sick passengers? They believed that choosing by lot would be appropriate. What if the person who did the execution caught the infectious disease? Students still stood by the rationality of the majority decision and believed that if the person were chosen by the majority he did not have excuses of disobedience. I further asked them what if the person who did the execution faced with the death penalty of murder when the ship landed. Students then argued for a broader vote for the judgment: People should make their decisions based on the specific situation rather than exclusively according to legal texts. Those passengers were put in an extreme situation so that normal laws should not be used in this case. The majority's decision in that ship was the only justified reason for action. Therefore they should not be punished by normal laws that they would face afterwards.

Then I asked them to shift their roles to do another decision: ‘What if the situation of the case was quite the opposite? Let us suppose the minority, the ten students who voted for the sick passengers are healthy passengers now; and the majority, the 38 students who voted for the healthy passengers are the sick passengers. Now your roles have been changed. What decision will you make?’ They kept silent for a while because the reasons they argued for in the previous situation became a big obstruction of their new arguments. I gave them another half hour to think and then vote for their decision.

Ten students again voted for ‘not killing’ and the 38 students again voted for ‘killing’. The result was interesting and illuminative. According to the majority's decision, the minority healthy passengers should kill the majority, although the minority was in the beginning against this decision. When the minority did the execution, they were against their conscience of justice and would face the strict legal punishment when they landed. However, if the majority's decision was a sufficient reason for legitimate decision-making, like they accepted in the first instance, they had to accept this reason and be abided by this majority principle.

5.5 Conclusion

None of the theories about lawmaking that analyzed in this chapter started from a communicative mode. Principles of utility in Bentham's theory excluded negotiations from the least advantage groups. Law was regarded as the unconscious discovery rather than active creations of society by Hayek. Therefore in Hayek's theory, lawmaking as administrative behaviors lacked communication. Disagreement was the core concept of Waldron's justification of lawmaking. However, it emphasized conflicts rather than co-operations during lawmaking. The principle of majority decision in Waldron's theory excluded negotiations from the minority. Such justifications were insufficient for a communicative lawmaking mode.

If we have doubts on the legitimacy of majority-decision, we may realize that in the first situation the majority probably made a wrong decision. There must be something value in lawmaking except for the majority votes, if we all agree that the minority sick passengers deserve to live in the first case, and that the minority healthy passengers have a right to disobey the majority's decision in the second. When we consider the Great Cultural Revolution movement that happened in China from 1966 to 1976, we see how wrong lawmaking could be if it was exclusively about the majority's decision. Multiple opinions of the majority during that era were ideological. Even there were different and opposite voices during decision-making procedures, as long as the majority's vote was the final decisive standard, multiple opinions would be an inferior factor. The principle that the minority should submit to the majority was not in conflict with the requirement of diversity during the debate stage of lawmaking. If the dignity of justice was only connected with numbers, even if the minority's opinions being heard, they were not treated seriously. If on the contrary we accepted that justice was irrelevant to the numbers, the principle of majority decision and diverse opinions were not enough for lawmaking.

Chapter 6
Lawmaking in Jurisprudence (II)

—A binding duty can appear as a limitation only in relation to indeterminate subjectivity or abstract freedom, and to the drives of the natural will or of the moral will which arbitrarily determines its own indeterminate good. The individual, however, finds his liberation in duty. On the one hand, he is liberated from his dependence on mere natural drives, and from the burden he labours under as a particular subject in his moral reflections on obligation and desire; and on the other hand, he is liberated from that indeterminate subjectivity which does not attain existence or the objective determinacy of action, but remains within itself and has no actuality. In duty, the individual liberates himself so as to attain substantial freedom…[D]uty is not a limitation of freedom, but only of freedom in the abstract, that is, of unfreedom: it is the attainment of essential being, the acquisition of affirmative freedom.

(G.w.F.Hegel)

6.1 Introduction

In this chapter, I will introduce another legitimation route developed by Professor Luc J. Wintgens. Legisprudence was distinct from the previous theories I discussed in Chap. 5 in its deliberations on freedom and the legitimacy of the social contract. Bentham and Waldron debated on a collective sense of legislation: the principles of utility and the majority decisions were more or less relate to 'collective morality'. Hayek debated on a social sense: the customary rules in his theory were the genuine rules. Legisprudence, as a contrast, started from 'individual morality': a conception of freedom. In legisprudence, freedom, social contract and the legitimacy of law-making were deliberated inseparably interconnected: Freedom was the fundamental basis for 'an alternative version of social contract'. The chain of legitimation of the social contract started from freedom.

P. He, *Chinese Lawmaking: From Non-communicative to Communicative*, Understanding China, DOI 10.1007/978-3-642-39507-9_6, © Springer-Verlag Berlin Heidelberg 2014

6.2 Legisprudence

Legisprudence was defined as: '... *the name for the branch of legal theory that deals with legislation from a theoretical and a practical perspective*'[1] and '...*a rational theory of legislation*'.[2] The object of legisprudence was legislation and regulation, and it made use of the theoretical tools and the insights gained from legal theory which predominantly dealt with the question of the application of law by judges.[3]

The hermeneutic interpretation was employed to solve the difficulties caused by legalism on legislation. By relying on the distinction between the internal and external points of view, a legal hermeneutic approach, legisprudence was a theory began with a clarification on the distinction between scholars', judges' and legislators' points of view.[4] These three kinds of groups that influenced legislation were introduced to explain the idea of the hermeneutic approach.[5] An external point of view was suggested to break through the limitation of the internal point of view presupposed by strong legalism. The theoretical way of showing how law was linked with social reality opened an avenue for a legisprudential approach to law, that was, the study of rational legislation.[6] The hermeneutic approach, which included the external point of view of the observer and the internal point of view of the actor, was therefore considered a better precondition to a theory of legislation. The position of the legislator as a legal actor is thus articulated.[7]

Legisprudence started from freedom to justify social contract. Based on the classification of conceptions of freedom (*hereinafter cof*) and conceptions about freedom (*hereinafter caf*), traditional social contract theory provided by Hobbes and

[1] L.J. Wintgens. 2002. Legisprudence: A New Theoretical Approach to Legislation. 10. Oxford: Hart Publishing. See also Wintgens. 2005. The Theory and Practice of Legislation—essays in Legisprudence. London: Ashgate Publishing Limited.

[2] L.J. Wintgens. 2004. Legisprudence as a New Theory of Legislation (presentation for the discussion group of jurisprudence at Oxford). http://www.trinitinture.com/documents/wintgens.pdf. Accessed 02 Feb 2012.

[3] L.J. Wintgens. 2002. Legisprudence: A New Theoretical Approach to Legislation. 2. Oxford: Hart Publishing.

[4] About legal hermeneutics see N. MacCormick. 1994. Legal Reasoning and Legal Theory. Oxford: Clarendon Press. See also F. Atria and N. MacCormick. 2003. Law and Legal Interpretation. London: Ashgate Publishing Company. And see also R. Dworkin. 1982. Law as Interpretation. Texas Law Review 60: 527–560.

[5] Wintgens. 2002. Legisprudence: A New Theoretical Approach to Legislation.15–39. Oxford: Hart Publishing.

[6] '*Legsiprudence has both a theoretical and a practical aspect. The theoretical aspect involves questions on the concept of sovereignty, the relation between the legal system and social reality, both from a judicial and a legislative perspective (and the similarities between both). This relation, as was argued, is based on a conception of coherence of a legal system. The practical aspect of a legisprudential approach of law concerns the elaboration of concrete criteria of rational legislation. They are gained from within the legal system relying on its own dynamics according to the hermeneutic point of view of authoritative actors.*' ibid., 39.

[7] Wintgens. 2005. The Theory and Practice of Legislation—Essays in Legisprudence. 7. London: Ashgate Publishing Limited.

Rousseau were analyzed: in their theories, concretizations of freedom by the sovereign (i.e., *caf*) predominate over conceptions of freedom (i.e., *cof*) by the subject[8]:

> *From the moment of the contract on, subjects primarily act on conceptions about freedom. Their consent to the contract includes a proxy to the sovereign. On this proxy, they consent to abide by any of the sovereign's external limitations of freedom whatever their content may be.*[9]

Discovering this crisis of the internal recognition of the outside, an alternative version of the social contract theory was then provided to re-discover the priority of the *cof* and the necessary justification when the conceptions *caf* predominated over the *cof*. The discussion on the meaning of freedom implied that, if freedom in the moral sense was considered as the general purpose or the *leitmotiv* of the legal system, the social contract could also be regarded in this 'thinner version'. A challenge to the absolute priority of *caf* referred to an alternative model of the social contract, which Wintgens called the *tradeoff model*. In this model, subjects did not give a general proxy to the sovereign:

> *On the contrary, the model says that freedom is traded off with each and every external limitation. Put differently, the proxy model contains a general and a priori trade-off of freedom. The trade-off model on the contrary qualifies the proxy character of the social contract, in that the subjects do not trade off their capacity to act on conceptions of freedom; they only trade off a conception of freedom.*[10]

Therefore, in the moral dimension of freedom, moral autonomy meant that acting on conceptions of freedom should have relative priority over acting on conceptions about freedom (i.e., *cof* prior to *caf*), because in a thinner version of the social contract individuals did not signed away all but some of their freedom. The morality of freedom should have a priority over law.[11] The *cof* and *caf* and the social contract theory were preconditions to interpret 'the chain of legitimation'.[12] Legisprudence was therefore a theory to interpret the existing *phenomena* (lawmaking and lawmakers) as well as the *meaning* of them.

Four principles were proposed in legisprudence to further deliberate the reason of introducing the chain of legitimation: the principle of alter nativity (PA), the

---

[8]After clarifying the premise of freedom, Wintgens articulated the contours of an alternative version of the social contract theory. The social contract model as Hobbes and Rousseau conceived was aimed to solve the problem of political integration from individualism. Wintgens concluded that '*in Razian language, the reason for entering the contract is an exclusionary reason. While Hobbes can be read to hold some utilitarian version of rationality, Rousseau's most obviously is of a more purified brand. It is reason itself that unfolds and induces to the adherence to the true principle of public law as he calls the social contract.*' '*Both variants of the contract result however in the same: the sovereign's rules are morally true.*' ibid. 5.

[9]Wintgens. 2005. The Theory and Practice of Legislation—Essays in Legisprudence. 8. London: Ashgate Publishing Limited.

[10]Ibid. 10.

[11]Wintgens. 2005. The Theory and Practice of Legislation—Essays in Legisprudence. 9. London: Ashgate Publishing Limited.

[12]Wintgens. 2007. Legitimacy and Legitimation from the Legisprudential Perspective. Legislation in Context: Essays in Legisprudence. 19. London: Ashgate Publishing Limited.

principle of normative density (PN), the principle of temporality (PT), and the principle of coherence (PC).[13] PA as a principle of justification was based on the subject's capacity to act on *cof*. The sovereign could only intervene on the condition that due to a failure of social interaction an external limitation was preferable to an internal limitation of freedom as a reason for action. PN submitted an external limitation to justification as far as the density of the normative impact was concerned. It required that the means of realization of the rule's end, purpose, or goal result from a process of weighing and balancing of the alternatives. If the essential connection between a rule and a sanction was broken, PN should establish a connection between the end, goal, or purpose and the means to realize them. PT brought a temporal dimension into the legal system. Therefore, on PA, the justification focused on the *external justification* as an alternative for failing social interaction. On PN, this *normative density* of the external justification should be explained. PT on its turn stressed the general *historical* character of any justification.[14] PT constrained normative proposition submitted to justification on PA and PN from the perspective of time. PC was a principle of justification of external limitations from the perspective of the legal system as a whole.

Therefore, a legal system was not a static chain of external limitations; it was on the contrary a complex and dynamic set of intertwined propositions concerning what ought to be done and how it ought to be done. Wintgens compared differences between consistency and coherence, and illustrated four levels of coherence. More recently, Wintgens further classified the last principle (PC) into four levels. The first level was the basic level to differ coherence from non-coherence, the level below which nothing made sense. The second level added a time dimension into the first level. The third level chose the point of view of the judge especially. In this level the meaning of coherence to a judge was that he had to make a systematic interpretation of a legal system rather than gave an interpretation of singular unconnected things. The fourth level, coherence meant 'making sense as a whole'. In this level of coherence, an external perspective was required while the second and third level of coherence referred to the internal rationality.[15]

> So, '*legal rules or external limitations of freedom are submitted to justification on the principle of alternativity, the principle of celerity (the principle of temporality), and the principle of normative density. This justification comes to a positive implementation of the moral autonomy of the subject. The supplementary justification on the principle of coherence underpins the connection between the concept of freedom as part of the analytical theory of the legal system and the system's rules*'.[16]

[13] Wintgens. 2004. Legisprudence as a New Theory of Legislation (presentation for the discussion group of jurisprudence at Oxford). http://www.trinitinture.com/documents/wintgens.pdf. Accessed 02 Feb 2012.

[14] Ibid.

[15] Wintgens. 2005. The Theory and Practice of Legislation—Essays in Legisprudence. 15–20. London: Ashgate Publishing Limited.

[16] Ibid. 24.

The above four principles (PA, PT, PC and PN) could also be read as providing four arguments of jurisprudence: (1) why should people follow law, (the morality of freedom should have priority over law); (2) If law should be obeyed (the morality of the obedience to law), why should people obey *legislators'* law (rather than other people's mandates), (conflicts were better to be solved by the *agents* themselves in the first instance)[17]; (3) Why should legislations be changed (the historical background of lawmaking is depended); and (4) Why should legislations be systematically coherent (in order to make the rational understanding of law possible)?

The chain of legitimation was deliberated to further examine the first two questions. In the chain of legitimation, the moment of entering a social contact was the starting point of legitimating. From this moment on, the *meaning* of legislator and their legislative behaviors need justifications and the subjects should also be abided by their consent to the content of the contract. From an empirical interpretation of the authority of the social contract, Wintgens pointed out that in a 'realistic' world, whatever the legislators rules would be, they were valid.

> *From the moment of the contract on, subjects primarily act on conceptions about freedom. Their consent to the contract includes a proxy to the sovereign. On this proxy, they consent to abide by any of the sovereign's external limitations of freedom whatever their content may be.*[18]

The proxy model of social contract was to weigh and balance the *cof* (the conceptions of freedom of the subjects) and *caf* (the law of the sovereignty). The four principles were therefore disclosed to justify the other parts of the chain since the moment of entering a social contract. The legitimation chain continued to be effective, as long as the contract was valid.

6.3 *Promissory Estoppel* in the Social Contract

From the above brief introduction of legisprudence, we could see that the conflicts of freedom and submission were disclosed. In Legisprudence, the main line of argument was formed by the attempt to interpret and harmonize the conflicts of freedom and submission. The legitimacy of lawmaking relies on the reason of submission to the social contract. However, the social contract should aim at realizing freedom. This argument embraced the Aristotelian Rule of Law tradition, in which the Rule of Law means obedience to the laws laid down and well enacted laws laid down by which people abide. This legitimation chain also differed from the one which put the emphasis on the authority's justification or the sovereignty's legitimacy. It interpreted the core of social contract theory as a theory of freedom.

---

[17] This question was initiated in Wintgens. 2009. Freedom and Legisprudence—a More Substantial View: a Reply to Professor Perju. Boston University Law Review 89:1804.

[18] Wintgens. 2005. The Theory and Practice of Legislation—Essays in Legisprudence. 8. London: Ashgate Publishing Limited.

Suppose a simplified social contract existed between a nation of laws and a subject. The contract was signed before he was born, when long time ago his ancestors decided to constitute a community and rule the nation by laws. The nation of laws was legitimated from the moment the contract was signed. This simplified edition of the modern social contract was different from a classical social contract theory which based on differentiation between the State of Nature and civil governments; and also different with the alternative version that legisprudence supposed (contract on freedom).

In this simplified social contract, the starting point of legitimation chain was the state founding fathers' agreement (rather than free will of subjects of later generations) on signing the contract; the subject had to be abided by the contract whatever the content it might be, as long as he was maintaining in this nation of laws. If it were the essence of the social contract, a subject as a subordinate member of a society, was in nature a dependent rather than the decision-maker of the contract. He was thus born non-free, but endowed with limited freedom and equality defined by law. In this simplified social contract, the first responsibility of the subject should be the duty of observance of the law.

Therefore in a simplified social contract, submission rather than freedom was the core value of the contract. From the egoistic perspective, individuals' freedom was not the ultimate goal (*principium*) of the contract because the founding fathers made laws for themselves rather than for others. From altruistic perspective, however, if the ancestors constituted the contract for the good of later generations, it was not for the freedom of contract-makers: their freedom was *again* not the starting point (*principium*) of the contract. If the contract-maker made the contract for the good of both themselves and the successors, the successors' conceptions of freedom should be consistent with their ancestors, otherwise the contract was a violation of their own freedom—but when their conceptions were consistent and unanimous with others, the individual conception of freedom was identical with a collective sense of morality, i.e., liberty of the whole community. In this sense individuals' freedom (of both the contract-maker and contract-accepter) could be the *principium* of the contract but it was in the end identical with the collective morality and the good of the society, which became a utilitarian justification and was meaningless to differentiate it with the collective morality.

In contrast to the previous simplified model, a social contract could be justified by individuals' tacit consent to the legal system built by their ancestors; their tacit consent lied in the fact of *remaining in the society*. They had the freedom of *entering* or *leaving* the society. In this alternative mode, individual rights of freedom and equality could gain vital significance.[19] In fact, this model attempted to rectify the unbalanced right and duty in the social contract by asserting the priority of individual's freedom, which was indeed an alternative version of social contract theory. Put differently, it made an attempt to use contract theory, especially the doctrine *promissory estoppel*, which was distinct from a classical social contract theory or

[19] See Wintgens' version of the alternative social contract, in Wintgens. 2005. The Theory and Practice of Legislation—Essays in Legisprudence. 8. London: Ashgate Publishing Limited.

the reductive version of the modern social contract that discussed previously, to re-interpret the legitimacy of lawmaking. Contract theory, as a chief cornerstone of the private law, took the principle of the autonomy of will and the freedom of contract as the foundation. Relying on this tacit consent model and the doctrine *promissory estoppel*, legisprudence re-built the social contract theory by emphasizing the importance of freedom and equality of the subject in interpreting lawmaking.[20]

The doctrine *promissory estoppel* was a legal principle that permits enforcement of a promise made without consideration in order to prevent injustice. In legisprudence the legitimacy of a social contract was interpreted alike the doctrine *promissory estoppel*. Individuals should not fight against the authority's law because they had agreed to follow the law when they decided to enter into the society. They should be abided by any law that the legislature would make although at first they would not know the concrete laws that the latter would make. They were bound by the social contract they signed. Or in other words, they should be bound by their own commitment or promise to the contract. They entered into the society and 'abandoned' their free status and went into a state of 'slavery'. The decision was a 'free' choice and the contract was made under a 'genuine' will. Therefore they should not arbitrarily draw back from the agreement (to the Rule-of-Law) once the contract was signed. The value of promise, agreement, or commitment could support the justice of obeying rules. The doctrine *promissory estoppel* was employed here to interpret the reason (or cause) of submission. Submission was made by a free decision of a free will before an individual entering into a social contract. From freedom to submission, the subject was bound by his own agreement of entering into the society.

6.4 Conceptual Freedom and Concrete Freedom

In *Legitimacy and Legitimation*, concrete freedom was interpreted as rights. Wintgens referred rights to political rights, (equal) participation rights (the right to participate in the ruling of the state), the right to resist violence, right to survival, and finally freedom as a right.[21] In contrast with those concrete freedom (or rights),

[20] In his reply to Perju's comment on legisprudence, Wintgens deliberated different layers of freedom and supposed that 'law should act only as a subroutine' and that 'law should not a priori determine social relations at the price of destroying social interaction', law should act as a subroutine 'only interferes when interaction breaks down'; 'law must be kept distant from social interaction'; 'rules should be constructed so as to leave the priority of solving conflicts to the agents themselves'; '...(it requires) a legislator to abstain from intervening'; '...it includes prudence in the intervention of state power in social interaction'. Wintgens. 2009. Freedom and Legisprudence—a More Substantial View: a Reply to Professor Perju. Boston University Law Review 89:1804. All those expressions were private law ideas which emphasized the individual's autonomy and freedom, and denied the (positive) intervention of the nation.

[21] Wintgens. 2007. Legitimacy and Legitimation from the Legisprudential Perspective. Legislation in Context: Essays in Legisprudence. 25–30. London: Ashgate Publishing.

freedom was debated in its philosophic and abstract sense also. An interesting argument, i.e. freedom as both *a terminus ad quem* and *a terminus a quo,* was further debated in Wintgens' reply to Perju's question about 'freedom as a starting point'.[22] Here freedom was debated in an abstract and conceptual way. In his defense, Wintgens described freedom as a starting point, i.e. freedom unlimited in legisprudence from a pure conceptual analysis: freedom was a formal and reflexive concept and it was indefinite.[23] '*The meaning of freedom*', however, '*is subject-related, in that it follows from interaction, not from deduction*'.[24] 'The meaning of freedom' therefore referred to concrete freedom. This classification of different freedom was to interpret that concrete freedom or rights were different from a theoretical construction of a social contract theory. 'Freedom as the starting point' referred to the starting point of a theoretical deduction rather than an empirical interaction.

The emphasis on right (prior to duty) and the deduction from freedom to the Rule of Law in legisprudence was impressive. Freedom as *a terminus a quo* of legisprudence was obvious. Even legal positivists would admit that there were some purposes that law should pursue. The enterprise of the Rule of Law should aim at a purpose: the rule of '*good*' (good content or good in the form) law in the end. An impressive argument that Wintgens made in his conceptual analysis of freedom was that freedom '*does not refer to any ultimate value. On the contrary, it refers to the absence of ultimate values.*'[25] This perspective differed from an instrumental rationalistic perspective which took freedom as a 'tool' or 'media' to realize other values. Utilitarianists and free market economists including F.A. Hayek were inclined to agree with the latter debate of freedom. Wintgens apparently disagreed with instrumental rationalistic freedom. He also differed from an argument that took freedom as an inner independent value, or ***value-independent freedom*** that debated by Joseph Raz in *The Morality of Freedom*. Raz argued that if the value of freedom depended on other values, then freedom per se lost its value—therefore the value of freedom should be independent. In Raz's argument, freedom has some value, although the value was independent.[26] Wintgens' argument was different: in his argument freedom was value-free. In legisprudence freedom was debated in a sense of a philosophical study of '*being*', rather than in a system of values.

Freedom in legisprudence was therefore started from a conceptual unlimited 'free natural status of human being', a point of view that classical social contract theories held. It also discussed the ultimate freedom. There were two kinds of freedom indeed: one at the starting point and the other at the end. Logically, it seemed strange to make efforts to pursue something already there (freedom as the starting point but also as the end). Freedom as the purpose should not be something already

[22] Wintgens. 2009. Freedom and Legisprudence—a More Substantial View: a Reply to Professor Perju. Boston University Law Review 89:1796–1805.

[23] Ibid. 1798.

[24] Ibid. 1801.

[25] Ibid. 1799.

[26] Joseph Raz. 2006. The Morality of Freedom. Oxford: Oxford University Press. 13. Chinese edition: 2006. Ji Ling People Publishing House.

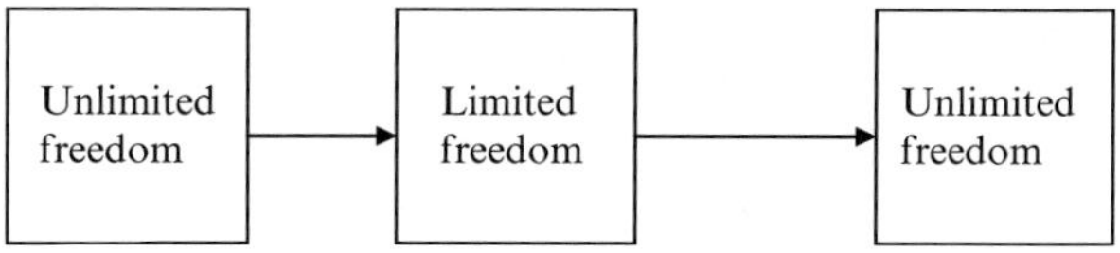

Fig. 6.1 Three stages of freedom

existed from the beginning. In other words, 'freedom as the starting point' should have essential differences when comparing with 'freedom as the end'. However, if we came along this route, we misunderstood Wintgens' differentiation between the starting point and the end of legitimation.

To understand these two kinds of freedom, we need to notice that there was an important stage between the starting point and the end in legisprudence, which was the unfree stage (see Fig. 6.1). The stage of unfree referred to the reality while the starting point and the end were debated in the conceptual analysis. Classical natural status or the original status of man in the original stage was recognized beyond question in a social contract theory. But since the man decided to enter into the social contract, they were unfree. Freedom as the starting point could be understood as a pre-condition of entering the society, that the man's choice of entering was (or should be) based on his free will. Freedom as the end did not mean to deny the justice of the social contract, but aimed at a transcendental value: the man did not enter to the contract for slavery; he chose to be unfree because of the purpose of realizing a 'higher' freedom, i.e., the freedom beyond a natural being's original free status. Therefore, freedom as the end (purpose, goal) was not the same freedom at the starting point. Three different stages were deliberated to justify the reason of entering the social contract, while at the same time pointed out the limits of freedom (concrete freedom in a political society). The three stages disclosed three levels of freedom: freedom in the natural or original status; freedom in a political society; and freedom as the ultimate ideal.

External restrictions including law were limitations to freedom, and were not the ultimate purpose (freedom as the end). Freedom as the opposite of law was argued in the second sense of freedom. In legisprudence, the argument for the conceptual freedom was much similar with Hayek's epistemological argument for the free market. The latter argued that things could only be known through abstract categories and therefore there was an infinite amount of facts in the world. This was also described as 'the void of particularity' in Professor Bankowski's book.[27] The conceptual freedom in legisprudence was defined by negative freedom (which meant the absence of limits; or freedom *from* restrictions); while concrete freedoms (which referred to rights) were positive freedom (freedom of what we can do). Unlimited freedom as the starting point of legisprudence was therefore not aiming at an empirical debate but a philosophic debate. The differences between the two kinds of freedom, therefore, explained Perju's thought that freedom was not sufficient to be the starting point of a realistic debate; and Wintgens' argument that a theory of freedom

[27] Zenon Bankowski. 2001. Living Lawfully-Love in Law and Law in Love. 169. Dordrecht: Kluwer.

could defend his philosophic pre-condition. They were both right in their argument but they discussed freedom in different perspectives.

In an abstract philosophic debate, individuals were presupposed to be conceptual equal. Therefore concrete freedom of specific persons was not in the realm of discussion. Wintgens made contributions to develop a theory of freedom especially in its conceptual sense. We here turn to Bankowski's argument of concrete freedom to complete the discussion of freedom. The latter pointed out that a particular person's understanding of freedom should also be very particular. Bankowski pointed out that 'conceptual individual' also appeared in Marx and Pashukanis criticisms of capitalistic theories.[28] Conceptual freedom was sufficient when we talked about the abstract bearer of right or 'the legal person' in a formal equality.[29] In a substantive principle of equality and a positive conception of liberty, however, people should not be treated as conceptual equal individuals because of their respective needs:

> ***Freedom is not just freedom from, but the freedom positively to fulfill oneself.*** *This means we cannot just apply a measure to people and treat them equally in respect of it. The rule that everyone is free to go to the Ritz is no use. We have to treat each person individually and see whether they need to go to the Ritz and what they will gain from it. The implication of this is that society is a co-operative venture, where people confront each other in all their facets and not as buyers and sellers or bearers of rights and owners.* ***The freedom of each becomes the condition of the freedom for all and distribution occurs naturally: from each according to his abilities, to each according to his needs***.[30]

From the above quote we can see that the problem of conceptual freedom and equality was that they see a real person as an abstraction. In this reductive perspective, the law ignored the complexity of the particular concrete individual. In the end, '***treating unequals equally merely compounds inequality***'.[31] Self also disappeared into this conceptual freedom. Relationships among persons were transferred to duties and rights rather than love or hate. Freedom thus became irrelevant to one's love of free status, but the right to be distant from others.

6.5 Values of/Behind Freedom

An obvious difference between legisprudence and other theories appeared: Utilitarianism aimed at common prosperity; individualism aimed at individuals' rights; or legalism aimed at the maintenance of a social order. The purpose of interaction in legisprudence, however, led to 'freedom as distance'.[32] In an extreme way

[28] Zenon Bankowski. 2001. Living Lawfully-Love in Law and Law in Love. 87–88. Dordrecht: Kluwer.

[29] Ibid. 88.

[30] Ibid. 89.

[31] Ibid. 95.

[32] Wintgens. 2009. Freedom and Legisprudence—a More Substantial View: a Reply to Professor Perju. Boston University Law Review 89:1801.

of interpretation, 'freedom as distance' means others should be kept at a distance because they would interfere with a person's own conception of freedom. Therefore the purpose of interaction aimed at non-interaction in the end. Related individuals were thus 'conceptually' separated for the sake of freedom.

This edition of freedom, i.e., 'freedom means distance' defended the individual's independence and subjectivity. This version of freedom was also defended by 'right-wing' liberalists. Henry David Thoreau practiced this philosophy at the Lake Waldon in late nineteenth century. He chose to leave the society and live a simple life. In the sense of the second freedom that analyzed before (freedom in a political society), Thoreau broke the chain of slavery of flourishing life and social activities, and in this sense he practiced freedom. This freedom was still practiced by those who chose reclusion, i.e., a life 'far from the madding crowd'.[33]

This 'distant freedom' was different from Bankowski's argument of 'bringing the outside in'. In Bankowski's theory, the interruption and intervention from the society (the outside) could and should be transferred into 'the inside'. Freedom did not mean distance. On the contrary, freedom should not exclude communication and interaction. In a 'left-wing' liberal camp, freedom (liberty) was for the collective (although it could benefit individuals in the end). Communication and cooperation were necessary for practicing freedom.

Therefore we could understand freedom in twofolds, a purely conceptual freedom which is value-free as defended by Wintgens; or concrete and value-dependent freedom defended by Bankowski. When we discuss a question about values behind the law of lawmaking, we apparently did not see legitimacy as a pure conceptual and value-free topic. Legisprudence was not a pure conceptual theory either. It had its normative debates on legislation: freedom should be the basis of lawmaking. Even though it did not claim to be a reproduction of reality, its normative debate was more than conceptual: freedom *should be* the beginning and the end of the legitimation chain. However, we should notice that the concept of freedom per se was defended value-free in legisprudence. It further deduced another value-free argument: freedom referred to distance or non-interaction.[34]

---

[33] Recent news disclosed a married Chinese couple who both graduated from Peking University secluded themselves in remote mountains for more than ten years. They resisted any pollutions of the outside world and depended on themselves. http://news.163.com/11/0417/03/71QFHVM500014AED.html. Accessed 02 Feb 2012.

[34] Here I saw loneliness and isolated 'free' individuals. In fact, loneliness and the isolated feeling were exactly what I felt when I was living in a Western environment. People were distant because of privacy, freedom and independence; those ideas were more valued than interactions. Relations were loose and casual in this environment. In a society where relations among family members and friends were closer and the interactions were more frequent, a person would not feel happy when he was kept distant from others. On the contrary he would feel ignored, disrespectful, and marginalized. The Western environment for freedom might not bring joy to a person who preferred a 'close-relation' society. To me, a conceptual freedom was not freedom at all; it was just a concept without any meaning and contents. It had a beautiful name but when we attempted to endow this name any positive meaning, it should have contents that can be realized: such as 'when I speak, I have a right to be heard and my speech would not be interrupted' (a freedom to speak); 'when I stand at the bus station, other people will not slap me or kick me if I refuse to donate twenty pounds

In legisprudence, heteronomous and autonomous norms were represented by law and freedom, an opposition which also reflected in classic Marxist theories and liberal theories. In Bankowski's argument, as a contrast, the social life and its institutions were based upon a mixture of principles which were in tension, one with the other. '*Particular social institutions will resolve this tension in different ways. They will balance the principles in particular ways in different concrete circumstances. But this will not be a compromise in the sense that more of one will mean less of the other*'.[35] In this line of argument, which I also agree, freedom and law were not absolutely isolated but could transform each other commutatively. Particular circumstances would decide the nature of law and freedom. I employ Bankowski's 'particular freedom' in *Living Lawfully* here to further support my argument against conceptual freedom:

> *When we come to looking at political institutions we will not necessarily justify them by the grand and abstract principle of 'freedom' or 'welfare'. Thus the market definition of [the] absence of coercion will not be the one always applied. Freedom from poverty, freedom to organise, etc. will also be in play. These particular freedoms will be pursued at particular times and places and will be weighed against each other. Likewise with welfare, this will mean different things in differing circumanstences and differing concepts will be balanced against each other.*[36]

We thus see the articulation of legalism and love, i.e., the concept of legality. Law should not be seen heteronomous and moral autonomous solely but rather law and morals should both be seen as a mixture of them.[37] In this sense,

> *We need to be dependent upon people, who are beings that need other people and cannot live without them. But this dependency means that we must not think of ourselves as wholly autonomous, dependent upon our will alone. Nor does it mean that we have to surrender our autonomy and live a wholly heteronomous life. We are neither slave nor lord of all.*[38]

As defended in legisprudence, which I also agree, the *meaning* of freedom was subjective. Therefore different subjects in diverse cultures would have particular understandings of freedom. In other words, a particular person's conception of freedom was particular. If freedom as distance were Western people's ideal life, the conception of happiness in Western culture was very different from that of China. If freedom meant the unavoidable distance from others, it meant unhappiness and bitterness in Chinese culture. Thoreau liked to live alone beside Lake Walden; Heidegger liked to live alone in the woods; Tao Yuanming's ideal living place was

---

to a child-saving organization' (a freedom to refuse); 'when I ask sufficient guidance I can get the information' (a freedom to get information); 'when I am unfairly treated I can ask a fair hearing and judgment' (a freedom to have justice); 'when I am hurt and am suffering, I can ask others to stop injury and if they refuse I can fight back' (a freedom to self-defend). If those contents were not in the idea of freedom, the conceptual freedom meant nothing to me.

[35] Zenon Bankowski. 2001. Living Lawfully-Love in Law and Law in Love. 107. Dordrecht: Kluwer.

[36] Ibid.

[37] Ibid. 108.

[38] Ibid.

Tao Huayuan; but if freedom meant cutting off connections with a Chinese person's family and friends, he would rather abandon some of his freedom.

Freedom was interpreted in legisprudence as a formal and reflexive concept which had no content and was indefinite.[39] Therefore in legisprudence freedom should not be 'exchangeable'. Otherwise, if it could exchange with other things it was not reflexive. Suppose we were free as the conceptual freedom meant, would we sacrifice our freedom for other values? On the one hand, if we could not choose to give up our freedom, we were not free at all, because the conceptual freedom meant absence of any limitations. On the other hand, however, if we had a choice and we did choose to give up freedom for other things, we were exchanging sacrifice our freedom for something else, and thus freedom had some content and was not 'indefinite'.

Socrates chose death and sacrificed freedom for his ideal Rule of Law: when he made his decision he had a choice to run for freedom, therefore his choice was a free choice to give up freedom. Free men chose to become soldiers to fight for their country. Un-married persons chose to get married and gave up their freedom of living alone. Women chose to have children and gave up their freedom of being alone. Parents chose to die for their children and gave up their freedom of life. If we admitted that those facts were truly existed, we would agree that a free man would sacrifice his freedom for other things—and most of them were about love: love for their country, partner, and child. People also exchanged their freedom for desires of power, beauty, fame and fortune. Freedom was exchanged not only for positive values like love but negative desires too. Therefore freedom was not only conceptual without any contents; it had some values and contents and could be exchangeable according to different subject's desires.

We could argue that when those men exchanged their freedom for other values, they were not free because they were in chains of love and desires. But conceptual freedom meant no ties and restrictions, so they were actually unfree if they were in chains of love and desires. Indeed, a man as a social being was from birth in chains of particular culture and was later restricted by his knowledge of the world. I did not see any men without desire and love. To me, not only the meaning of freedom was subject-related, the concept freedom per se was man-related from the beginning. We would not say a mountain was free or a river was free because freedom was meaningless to those objective beings. A man-related fact from the beginning was delimited.

In my point of view, the conceptual freedom as principium, which had no content, reflexive and absence of any values that defended in legisprudence was possible when it referred to God-related things. Only God was free. For man-made rules, freedom was not the starting point of legitimation, and should not be the exclusive purpose. The ultimate principium should be the value that we could not abandon. To me, it was not freedom but love. I would give up my freedom for the lives of my loved persons. A society that was formed by persons like me would not take

[39] Wintgens. 2009. Freedom and Legisprudence—a More Substantial View: a Reply to Professor Perju. Boston University Law Review 89:1798.

freedom as the ultimate principium of lawmaking. Subjectivity, therefore, brought the difficulty to the legitimation chain: how could we compare and balance different individuals' different desires?

I would like to use Bankowski's analysis of 'indifference' and 'exchange' to further support my argument. In his analysis, liberal theorists tended to describe the market individuals relationship as 'mutually indifferent ships sliding by in the night'.[40] In such an indifferent relationship, the connection between persons was nothing more than the satisfaction of each other's wants. Otherwise, interaction was un-necessary. A person did not engage with others except in so far as those others could satisfy some need of one's own. Therefore 'keeping others at a distance' was reasonable because there was no obligation and necessity for interaction. We did not need other persons' interruptions unless we need their assistance. It was a world of the principle 'no use, no discourse'. In such a relationship, people were not interested in others requires: 'in the exchange of A and B I want you A and you want me B but I am not interested in whether my B is of real value to you and you are not interested whether your A is of real value to me'.[41] As a contrast, the idea of exchange built mutuality of regard into it. Fuller stressed the 'good' of the exchange in the idea that law was something about reciprocity and connection. Law was no longer something outside us, or as restrictions and limitations, but an enterprise that we could contribute to. Our freedom was thus shaped by law but at the same time shaping the law: the exchange of the inside and the outside.

> *The Rule of law becomes something more than a one way street of norms standing above us and is a shared interaction that not only protects and facilitates, but also enriches us through our participation in its life, through living lawfully'*[42]

Therefore we were less under the external control but more open to the outside and to the transformation. The separate atomic self was thus transformed to interactive and communicative beings. The self should be located and constituted in a social context and interactive within it.

> *For the self is constituted by and is in a continuous process of construction by exchange. Like everyone else, I develop by the process of giving and receiving in my interaction and encounter with others. In the process of giving myself to others I also receive input from them and it is in that process that I constitute myself and develop and grow. This process of exchange can be characterized also as the process of encounter. Since it is with the other, an outside, that encounter will be unexpected and transformative. This process of mutual penetration whereby we develop and grow continues from the personal to the social and societal level.*[43]

I agreed with the argument that freedom makes it possible for an individual to communicate with 'the outside'. If a law tried to control the 'exchange' or

---

[40] Zenon Bankowski. 2007. Bringing the Outside in: The Ethical Life of legal Institutions. Law and legal Cultures in the 21st Century: Unity and Diversity. Wolters Kluwer Polska. 193–217.

[41] Ibid.

[42] Ibid.

[43] Zenon Bankowski. 2007. Bringing the Outside in: The Ethical Life of legal Institutions. Law and legal Cultures in the 21st Century: Unity and Diversity. Wolters Kluwer Polska. 193–217.

communication between us and the outside, or 'keeping others in distance', the law as well as our freedom became a closed system—but freedom should never be a closed system in its formal sense (see previous discussion about freedom means absence of limits). In Bankowski's discussion of the limits of freedom, he pointed out that the fear of exchange and communication further limited our freedom. We might not be selfish when we refused to communicate; but we might fear of the return of the uncertain consequences that might involve in communication. It was the fear of exchange that makes people act selfishly. People were scared of effects and the ways that would change and make them different. The reason we chose not to communicate might be that 'we are happy in the worlds we inhabit and do not want to leave them.'[44] When we started to communicate and interact with others, and with the law, the outside restrictions start to change; and through interaction we transformed the outside into the inside, and vice versa. Thus the supposed two closed and clear-cut categories of freedom and law started to have intersection. In an interactive theory, law was an essential element of our freedom. According to law we connected with people. Through communication and interaction we were truly in touch with each other and practice our freedom under the law.

6.6 Limits of Freedom and Limited Freedom

Man was born *unfree* and everywhere he was in chains. Oedipus made efforts to get off the chain of his fate but failed. He was born unfree. If there were a destiny of everyone, everyone was unfree. If there were no destiny but plain fact of survival, a person was 'free', but this freedom was not different from other creatures 'free' status. It was not a conceptual freedom either because survival conditions objectively limited the content of 'freedom'. Creatures were abided by the 'natural rules' of birth, growth, age, sickness and death. When we considered those 'natural rules' as destiny, a person could never be free in the sense of conceptual freedom. Destiny imprisons freedom because freedom supposed to be absence of any restrictions. If 'destiny' and 'natural rules' were 'true', the 'unlimited freedom' should be 'false'.

If freedom was not referred to an objective fact which was in contrast with destiny and natural rules, but was a subjective feeling, could freedom be 'true'? A person could claim that he felt free. His statement was the direct proof of his will. Freedom in this case could be 'true' if his statement reflected his feeling. Other external observers' judgments of this person's feeling would be more or less distant from his true feeling and thus became a bias. Therefore, the most credible proof was the person's own judgment of his free or unfree status. However, if the person was imprisoned by any of his desires, his statement of freedom was not true because his will was not free. A teleological argument defended that a social being's action was driven by desires. Utilitarianism further interpreted such desire or purpose as

[44] Ibid.

seeking happiness. The desire of seeking happiness was also justified as the principium of lawmaking. In this teleological perspective, a person was restricted by his desires.

We could interpret the tragedy of Oedipus in two senses: objectively, Oedipus was not free because he was restricted by his destiny; furthermore, he was 'subjectively' unfree because of his desires to break up his destiny. The unfree Oedipus was tragic in both objective and subjective situation. He faced an ironic dilemma: when he was seeking for freedom, his desire for freedom limited his freedom in turn. Or in other words, subjective freedom became a restriction of objective freedom.

Wintgens noticed the difficulty of discussing freedom in epistemology so he admitted that the 'meaning of freedom' was different. He focused his argument on the objective free status. Here I attempt to extend the discussion of freedom by introducing the subjective freedom into the argument. Why would an objectively free person choose to enter into a political society, or in other words, an unfree status? If the 'objective' freedom was 'good', why did the subjects chose to enter into an unfree contract? Or if freedom was absence of any value like legisprudence supposed, i.e., it was not good or bad but a plain fact of no limitations, why should lawmaking (as a purposeful human activity) aim at this ultimate goal? The social contract theory attempted to answer those questions. It attempted to justify the moment when a freeman chose to be unfree. In legisprudence, Wintgens further attempted to connect the obligation (result of social contract) with freedom (the starting point and the goal of the contract), and to justify the obligation and social contract through freedom. His theory, in my opinion, highlighted two issues: first of all, obligation was temporary; and secondly, freedom as right was eternal. He thus proved that lawmaking should aim at the ultimate purpose of freedom. Law as the external limitations although supported temporary obligation was tolerable.

Was the argument 'freedom as the principium of legislation' in legisprudence an objective description of a 'future' fact? If it referred to a future fact, did it mean that in the future the law and the state would eliminate, as one of the conclusions that classical Marxism held? We would notice that in classical Marxism, the law and the state were not value-free. They were necessary tools for class struggle and control. This recognition of law (law as a tool of control) was different from the precondition of lawmaking (law as a contract of freedom) in legisprudence. The latter did not attempt to picture or justify anarchism. 'Freedom as the principium of legislation' implied a normative argument, or a moral judgment: *freedom was better than constraints.*

Constraints were everywhere in social activities. We were raised in family rules. We grew up in a society and should obey the society rules. We were abided by the state laws to keep our citizenships. Our status in the family, the society and the state restricted our 'natural' freedom. In this sense, social contract and law were limitations to freedom. When a natural being 'entered into' a society, he started an unfree life. From that moment on, freedom referred to the political and legal right to have free will and make free choice. It was no longer a 'natural' freedom, the one which was irrelevant to the goal of social communication and cooperation. Freedom in the society became an 'artificial freedom'.

Therefore, freedom of a natural being changed into the *rights* of freedom in the social contract. The contract was to settle down the rights and duties between a social being and the state, i.e., between an individual and the collective of other particular persons. In this perspective, an individual's freedom was his compromise with the law which was supposed to represent the free will in the collective sense, i.e., the conception about freedom. Here we can see the apprehension that Wintgens reminded us, that the conception of freedom would be replaced by the conception about freedom. This argument disclosed the fact that in such a contract, an individual's political or legal freedom was grounded on his free will *as long as* it was consistent with the collective's consensus. This kind of free will was *not* free in nature.

6.7 The Opposite of Freedom

The political or legal freedom was limited freedom. We should not disregard our limited freedom though, because we spoke for ourselves through it. Although it was limited, the restrictions of freedom should be acceptable for us when we signed the social contract. Otherwise we were in slavery and the limited freedom became a fake freedom. As long as the limited freedom was approved by us when we signed the contract, it could be a genuine freedom. In other words, it was our own decision to abandon some contents of 'natural' freedom and to accept the limited freedom. As analyzed earlier, the *promissory estopple* doctrine contributed to this legitimation. Here I would like to further develop the theory of legisprudence by arguing that the opposite of freedom was neither unfree in a conceptual sense, nor law as the external limitation, but *status* in realistic legal contexts.

In political and legal freedom, the opposite of freedom was status. Or in other words, law and contract were *reflections* of freedom rather than *restrictions* of freedom. In Maine's *Ancient Law*, status referred to the relation with the collective while contract related with individual free will. The essential nature of status was the subordinate relationship between an individual and his (family, ethical, religious, political, etc.) group. As long as the individual belonged to a group, he was not free. When the group was disassembled, individuals became independent. They subordinated to their own (separate and independent) wills only. '*The movement of the progressive societies has hitherto been a movement from status to contract*' was a classical argument for the relationship between modernism and individualism.[45] Since the traditional societies based on status transformed to the modern societies based on contracts, collectivism gave place to individualism accordingly. The movement from status to contract could also be interpreted as a shift from 'collective morality' to 'individual freedom'. In this sense, the argument of 'the movement

[45] Henry Maine. 1861. Ancient Law. 165. John Murray publishing. the last paragraph of Ancient Law, chapter 5. see texts from http://en.wikisource.org/wiki/Ancient_Law#Chapter_5_Primitive_Society_and_Ancient_Law. Accessed 02 Feb 2012.

from status to contract' was the opposite of the argument that 'the conception about freedom substituted the conception of freedom'. The latter argument implied that the collective will would be imposed to the individual. The former description, however, disclosed the rise of individualism in modern history.

The movement from status to contract, however, should not be understood as an irreversible movement. In modern society, the (social) contract also authorized new status of individuals. We would defend equality as a pre-condition of the contract. Realistic contracts, however, approved inequality tacitly.[46]

In ancient societies, individuals got their property through their status; while in modern societies, contracts authorized individual's approaches to get the property. Contracts in modern society also established new status. Two parties of a contract were unequal: they had different economic status and information channels. When a social contract was concerned, an individual's status was not the equal of the other party of the contract. When he was supposed to sign the contract with the society, he was either supposed to sign a contract with the particular majority or to sign a contract with the state (the state as a *persona* subject as the other side of the contract). Therefore, equality was absent when he signed the contract. The other party of the contract was much stronger than him. A defense could say that an individual was supposed to sign the contract with other equal individuals, a multiple-subject contract. However, we need a further debate about the equality of every human being of the multiple-subject contract in such a pure fictional situation

Status was considered as the opposite of the contract in *Ancient Law*. However, status in modern societies could be changed. New status could be created by individual's efforts, and was thus *not* the opposite of the contract. In this sense contract could authorize new status. Therefore status reflected the free will (represented by the contract) and was thus no longer a restriction of freedom. The contract could also protect the status of the least advantaged group. The recognition of status could help the weak to negotiate with the advantaged. If the realistic inequality of status was ignored, individuals would be put into a worse situation. They would have to compete with those realistic powerful persons in a same arena, while the latter's privileges were not restricted. Such equality ignoring different status or situation would lead to unfairness.

When Maine wrote 'the movement from status to contract' in *Ancient Law* in the nineteenth century, it was ironically the era for the trade union movement. It was the age of the first modern trade union law, the Trade Union Act of 1871. It also had a successful cooperative society paradigm: the Rochdele Society of Equitable Pioneer

[46] As analyzed in chapters about Chinese lawmaking reality and its legitimation by Chinese Marxism and Chinese legalism, law established and differentiated status. An obvious example was that city folks' status were pre-supposed to have more privileges than the status of peasants. In China, every city person could get allowance from government but peasants could depend on themselves exclusively. Law thus established different status to treat people differently. See also similar arguments by domestic famous scholars Shang Jiang and Guodong Xu, in Guodong Xu. 2009. Humanistic Spirit of Civil Law. 109. Beijing: Law Press.

in 1844.[47] Status in modern society was different from that of ancient societies. As stated in the *Humanistic Spirit of Civil Law*, '*In the nineteenth century, people enjoyed a very short period of individualism right after the dissolution of guilds. They associated several unions and gained new contractual status to protect their interests and rights. Modern societies became a new status society. However, the status in modern society is essentially different from ancient societies.*'[48] The new status of modern societies differed from the old in its source: modern contracts. Different from ancient status which was *priori* decided by others exclusively, modern status could be gained through individuals' own efforts. The ancient status was a statistic and unchangeable fact while modern status was a dynamic and changeable fact. Status in ancient societies meant that an individual had no choice. The old status was thus a restriction to freedom. Modern status, however, could reflect the subject's free will and could be a protection of his freedom. Therefore, the new status as the result of a 'free will' was reflected in the contract.

6.8 A Chinese Case

In the Chinese context, however, status was *not* a reflection of the free will. When I was writing this chapter, a piece of news caught my attention. A Chinese peasant Mr. Youde Yang built a fortress in his cultivated land to stop the 'demolition workers'. He lit fireworks to frighten them off and in this way to safeguard his land and properties.[49] Mr. Yang said that he was a peasant and his life was on his land. He would allow the demolition work if he got his compensation according to the law. But he was given no compensation and would lose his land soon, and he had to steal and rob for survival. The law would punish him then. The demolition department did not offer him a negotiation arena but forced him to agree to the harsh terms. 'I do not have any power of discourse.' He said. He worried that if he did not safeguard his land, when his properties on the land were pulled down, and when his cultivated land was leveled by the bulldozer, he would lose evidence of his rights. He could not apply for any compensation then. 'Did you try to sue them to the court?' The reporter asked him. 'I could not pay the costs of litigation as the plaintiff. I asked the demolition department to sue me instead. Then they should pay the cost first. I could not leave my land just in case they would pull down my house and confiscated my land. So I hope they sue me first and let the law give me the discourse arena. But they did not sue me, so I had to stay here to safeguard my land by myself.' The reporter asked him whether he still believe in law, he replied yes: 'I believe the law is good. After reading law I have my confidence to fight against them.' The law,

---

[47] About The Rochdale Pioneers see http://www.bbc.co.uk/dna/h2g2/brunel/A2764424. Accessed 02 Feb 2012. about trade union movement see Encyclopaedia Britannica International Chinese Edition. 2007. Encyclopaedia Britannica, Inc. 17:188.

[48] Guodong Xu. 2009. Humanistic Spirit of Civil Law 126. Beijing: Law Press.

[49] News from http://news.sina.com.cn/s/2010-06-09/044420438816.shtml. Accessed 02 Feb 2012.

however, did not engage in the fights between Mr. Yang and the demolition department. Mr. Yang was still staying at his fortress to fight against the demolition workers' 'invasion' that happened once a month.

This case showed that *The Regulation Governing Building Demolition and Resettlement 2001* (hereinafter the Regulation 2001城市房屋拆迁管理条例) was in conflict with the Property Law and the Constitution. The legitimacy of this law was questionable. This law, however, was valid because it was made by the authority. According to the argument of a traditional legal positivism, people had to admit the validity of the Regulation 2001, although it was not a just law. According to the natural law theories, the Regulation 2001 was not a law at all because it violated basic rights including the right of living without interruption and the right of private ownership. Both positivism and the natural law theory simplified the problem in a degree. The Regulation 2001 was a valid legal basis or justification of official demolition. However, it injured particular individuals' rights indeed. It should be changed or annulled according to just lawmaking procedures. Either way was not enough, to ignore the justice of the law or to ignore the validity of it. How to judge Mr. Yang's self-protection behavior? His intention was to use fireworks to frighten the officials rather than to really hurt them. But his behavior endangered their lives and that was not right. If he gave up his self-protection, however, he would lose everything. Therefore it was not a kind suggestion that he should give up his last practical resistance. He was thus pushed into an impasse.

Lawmaking may solve this dilemma and contribute to both the legitimacy of the law and the justification of Mr. Yang's behaviors. The Regulation 2001 was not an appropriate law. But it was law and should be changed through formal procedures. The lawmaking procedure should offer a fair discourse arena for interested parties including Mr. Yang. In defense of non-interventionism, lawmaking was not necessary to Mr. Yang because he could execute his freedom through self-protection and in this way he could negotiate with the agent of demolition. The Regulation 2001 was an external limitation of Mr. Yang's freedom of living (it was therefore a conception about freedom), Mr. Yang in this case did not give up his conception of freedom. Therefore his case was not a situation that 'conceptions about freedom substitute conceptions of freedom', so that we could not use directly the principles defended by legisprudence to justify the Regulation 2001 or other new lawmaking activities.

When Mr. Yang was fighting against the official demolition, he was not only fighting against a 100 demolition workers directly but also the law. He was the absolute minority in his defense. He was thus in the least disadvantage group. In the next chapter I will discuss the reason why his request should be involved into lawmaking, and how. What should be noticed here was that Mr. Yang's case was a miniature of Chinese peasants' experience. If Mr. Yang represented them, he represented the majority. The legitimacy of Regulation 2001 and the demolition official's behavior could not be justified then. Mr. Yang therefore should have a right to question the justice of the law. When justice was absent, his resistance and self-protection should be forgivable. Most importantly, people should have the right to participate into the progress of changing old unreasonable regulations and creating new regulations.

6.9 Conclusion

Legisprudence started from the concept of freedom to justify lawmaking. It attempted to make freedom the ultimate purpose of lawmaking, and was thus related with morality and kept a distance from a pure positivistic tradition. It was an attempt to defend the objectivity of legitimation. Although I doubted the practicability of such a route in the Chinese context, I agree with the objectivity of lawmaking enterprise. I believe that modern lawmaking should aim at providing the public good rather than for private desires. If there were some values that lawmaking was aiming to, it must be applicable to the commons. However, as I criticized in the previous chapter, majority rule was not sufficient either because justice was not exclusively about numbers.

If we connected Waldron's majority rule with Wintgens' freedom, we could have a new concept: freedom for the majority, i.e., liberty. Or it became what Bankowski had discussed in the relationship between the individual and the collective, '*collective individual*': '*there is no space between the individual and the collective, they collapse the one into the other and produce a sort of collective individual*'.[50] Professor Bankowski interpreted that 'collective individual' was discussed in a negative sense. It, however, was a realistic situation in China and was also justified by Chinese legalism and Chinese Marxism, as I analyzed previously in Chap. 4. Chinese theories attempted to justify the collective morality, or liberty rather than individual freedom or conceptual freedom. The collective sense of freedom, i.e., liberty in lawmaking should be justified through a just procedure. Otherwise individuals could not recognize what the collective morality was. Chinese legalism and Chinese Marxism therefore needed further amendments. Lawmaking should safeguard and substantiate participation. Justifications through political propaganda were not enough. People should be able to participate in the declared democratic lawmaking procedures.

Since Mr. Youde Yang's case became typical, and because more people executed their natural rights of self-defense, resistance and noncooperation, the discussion of civil disobedience became necessary.[51] Different theories provided different answers to the topic of civil disobedience. In Waldron's jurisprudence of legislation, the majority rule substituted the reason of action, and the representative democracy procedure was recognized just. Minority's disobedience was hard to be justified in a procedural theory. Traditional positivism, although was persuasive in its discovery of the validity of law, did not soften the tension between free will and the external restrictions. In legisprudence, the tension between the free will and law was noticed, but their opposite status was over-stressed, and possibilities of connections or exchanges between them were less discussed. Freedom was deliberated as an

[50] Zenon Bankowski. 2001. Living Lawfully-Love in Law and Law in Love. 22. Dordrecht: Kluwer.

[51] Theories of civil disobedience focus on the minority's disobedience to the majority's rule. About theories of civil disobedience, see J. Rawls. 1977. A Theory of Civil Disobedience. The Philosophy of Law. 89–112. Oxford: Oxford University Press.

exclusive individual-related concept so that it was not used in an interpretation of collective wills.

Some laws were created from civil disobedience. Laws made through civil disobedience were *not* the external limitation of freedom. A law created from civil disobedience could be a content of 'the conception of freedom'. It was also a good example of a community's practice of liberty. In Mr. Youde Yang's case, suppose Mr. Yang and other peasants' noncooperation finally led to a new lawmaking event. Suppose a new law was made to substitute the old law. The new law respected Mr. Yang's requests and protected his private ownership. This new law was therefore consistent with his will. It was no longer an external restriction. The law became a *reflection* of freedom rather than the opposite of freedom.

In these two chapters I discussed Western theories of lawmaking represented by four different legitimation routes. From my analysis we could see that communication per se was not necessary in Bentham's consequentialist moral reasoning for lawmaking. If a non-communicative mode can provide utility, it could still be justified as an appropriate mode. Therefore the *result* rather than the *process* of communication in Benthamian legitimation was crucial. Hayek's theory implied the justification of a communicative lawmaking mode, when the 'spontaneously grew' customary laws were included in the topic of lawmaking. However, in the Hayekian mode, the discourse between the official law and social rules was not necessary. The exchanges between the two systems of law were not discussed. Both Hayek and Waldron deliberated through categorical moral reasoning. Waldron pointed out the importance of disagreement during lawmaking and in this sense he stressed the dignity of dialogue per se. However, in his procedural theory of lawmaking, disagreements were over-valued, and the communication to achieve an agreement was not recognized. In my point of view, communication and agreement were also the significant content and supporting value of lawmaking. Wintgens employed freedom as the ultimate principle to justify democratic lawmaking. He contributed to a lawmaking theory in its discovery of the doctrine of *promissory estopple* in social contract, which was different from the arguments of Hayek and Waldron. However, as disclosed in this chapter, Wintgens tended to argue for 'distant' and 'non-interactive' freedom. In this sense he implied that communication was impossible or unnecessary. In the next chapter I would further discuss the importance of rediscovering a theory of communicative lawmaking.

Chapter 7
Communicative Lawmaking in China

—By and in himself a man can accomplish very little; he is like Robinson Crusoe on a desert island. It is only in society that a man's powers can be called into full activity. (Arthur Schopenhauer)

—法治概念的最高层次是一种信念,相信一切法律的基础,应该是对于人的价值的尊重*(陈弘毅)*

Hongyi Chen: On the top of the rule-of-law there should be a faith; according to which the respect of the value of human bengs should be the base of all laws.

7.1 Introduction

In this chapter I aim to discuss the possibility and necessity of a communicative lawmaking of China. The possibility of Chinese communicative lawmaking relies on the recognition and acceptance of Chinese communitarism or republicanism. Different from individualism and liberalism, Chinese law and philosophy were based on the idea that no one was isolated from others. Chinese people laid much stress on the individual's status in a family, a community and a society.[1] The status reflected a person's cognition of himself. This cognition depended on his recognition of others and his relationship with others. Therefore, in Chinese ideology, independent and atomic individuals did not exist.

As a result, the communication in Chinese lawmaking was not mainly about the relationship between an individual and another individual, but between an individual and a community (society). In legisprudence Professor Wintgens rightly concluded that equality was an important principle for achieving freedom. We could also

[1] In Chinese philosophy, there were Three Cardinal Guides (ruler guides subject, father guides son and husband guides wife) and Five Constant Virtues (benevolence, righteousness, propriety, knowledge and sincerity). They were all about a person's status and relationship with others in the society. See also my discussion of Chinese humanism in Chap. 3.

P. He, *Chinese Lawmaking: From Non-communicative to Communicative*, Understanding China, DOI 10.1007/978-3-642-39507-9_7,

speculate that equality was the important pre-condition for communications in a liberalistic lawmaking. In an individual-prior lawmaking system, a social contract signed between individuals. The principle of equality made communication possible and fair in that system. In a community-prior system, however, a social contract meant an agreement signed between an individual and a community, the principle of equity was significant. The possibility and necessity of communicative lawmaking in China therefore depends on the clarification of the relationship between an individual and a community.

7.2 Necessity of Communicative Lawmaking

Communicative lawmaking is necessary for Chinese legal reform. Let me explain how my arguments in the previous chapters reach to this conclusion: I start from a dichotomous classification between non-communicative lawmaking and communicative lawmaking. This dichotomous relationship is designed to highlight the exclusiveness nature of non-interactive lawmaking. We should notice that neither the top-down nor bottom-up lawmaking mode is non-interactive *unless* it makes communication impossible. A top-down or bottom-up mode could be communicative in nature if they tolerate and absorb sources from their 'external'. The top-down lawmaking mode, if welcomed sources of 'the down', could be a communicative mode. A bottom-up mode, if considered sources from the 'up', should also be recognized as communicative. Therefore I aim to argue against the non-interactive mode represented by Chinese lawmaking rather than the formal top-down mode.

However, there exists an inseparable relationship between the Chinese top-down mode and its non-communicative characteristic. The Chinese one-dimensional mode is different from another mode: a bottom-up but communicative lawmaking mode. In Western representative democratic theories the possibility of communication is embodied in the bottom-up lawmaking. Formal laws and laws from the society are not opposed to each other diametrically. One could influence and transform to the other. However, in China, hidden rules and laws from the society (laws from the bottom) could not compete with the official laws. The Chinese top-down mode in this sense is a non-interactive mode, and thus becomes the opposite of the communicative mode diametrically.

Here I reach to the first conclusion: *In China, the unidirectional lawmaking mode is the opposite of communicative lawmaking mode. (L1)* We should notice that this proposition *depends* on Chinese contexts. I used empirical research basis to disclose the close connection between the Chinese top-down mode and its non-communicative nature. This proposition is proved in Chinese contexts, but not necessarily true in other contexts.

Then a hypothetical syllogism could disclose the relationship between Chinese traditional non-communicative lawmaking and contemporary legal reform. Suppose the syllogism (I will explain that it is a valid but unsound argument) contains the following premises and the conclusion: (1) The non-communicative lawmaking is necessary for contemporary legal reform; (2) Contemporary legal reform is necessary for the increase of well-being and the protection of human rights; So, (3) non-communicative lawmaking is necessary for the increase of well-being and the protection of human rights. (L2) In this syllogism, if the first premise were true, the conclusion should be true because L2 is a valid syllogism. However, as I analyzed in the first four chapters, although the second premise is true, the conclusion is not true, therefore the first premise should be false. Therefore L2 is a valid but unsound argument. So, the non-communicative lawmaking is *not* necessary for contemporary legal reform (L3).

I thus come to the second conclusion: *the non-communicative lawmaking is not necessary for contemporary legal reform in China. (L3)* Combining L1 and L3, we have a disjunctive syllogism (L4): (1) Either non-communicative or communicative lawmaking mode is necessary for contemporary legal reform in China; (2) Non-communicative lawmaking is not necessary for contemporary legal reform in China; so, (3) communicative lawmaking mode is necessary for contemporary legal reform in China. I thus reach to my last conclusion: *The communicative lawmaking is necessary for Chinese legal reform.*

7.3 Communication Under Communitarianism

We may recall Aristotle's classical question that Bankowski reiterated in his argument for the exchange between law and love: how to living righteously. Living freely, or living under rules, which equaled living righteously? In the previous chapter, I discussed the liberalistic view of living lawfully proposed by Wintgens, which was based on the value of individual freedom. In this chapter, I would like to discuss another perspective represented by communitarianism, which was concerned as the pre-condition of Chinese philosophies and policies. As discussed in previous chapters, philosophers debated different pre-conditions. Waldron argued for the majority's decision and was close to utilitarian liberalism; while Hayek and Wintgens tended to defend Kantian liberalism and individualism. Communitarianists objected to the assumptions of the above two liberalisms. The relationship between an individual and a community was well discussed in communitarianism.

To bring communitarianism into focus, I want first to briefly review the Western line of argument. Since 1970s, the common assumptions of liberalism have been put into question by philosophers including Charles Taylor, Alasdair MacIntyre and Michael Sandel. Hegel philosophy noticeably influenced many of them, which was reflected in their insistence on the social character of humans and on the connections between morality and the customs of each society. Aristotle's ideal of moral life was absorbed into their arguments also, since many of these communitarian philosophers defend a conception of the good related to a teleological vision of human nature and reflected on a set of virtues.

Communitarianists pointed out that liberals insufficiently appreciate the social nature of persons.[2] Challenging the liberal stance on individualism and human rights, communitarians insisted that '*we cannot justify political arrangements without reference to common purposes and ends, and that we cannot conceive our personhood without reference to our role as citizens, and as participants in a common life*'.[3] Based on this recognition of self-in-the-community, communitarians rejected rights-based liberalism in part because of their interpretation of the liberal approach to the self. In *Liberalism and the Limits of Justice*, and in his criticism of Rawls's *A Theory of Justice*, Sandel argued that deontological liberalism misunderstood the nature of self because it deracinated persons from the community.[4] Sandel said that the liberal view of freedom was 'thin' and 'devoid of inherent meaning'.[5] MacIntyre also argued that the liberal self was disembodied from 'narrative history' lacking 'character' and 'social identity'.[6] Communitarians thus stressed a 'thick self' conception that the self was not only constituted by society, but also was '*open, indeed vulnerable to growth and transformation in the light of revised self-understandings*'.[7]

Communitarianism as a school of Western philosophy was new to China. As an ethical thought, however, it rooted in Chinese predominant ideologies. In contrast to liberal and right-based morality, Chinese philosophies especially represented by Confucianism emphasized a person's responsibilities to the community rather than his rights, and the virtues of caring and benevolence rather than freedom. A person in Chinese philosophy never stood up as a person-qua-autonomous-being, but in relationship with other persons and creatures and the nature (*Tian Ren He Yi*).[8] Chinese philosophies gave priority to becoming a 'good' person (a responsible person) over being a right-claimer. Chinese communitarianism built a 'thick self' conception of an individual since it emphasized the social contexts of a particular being. In contrast to the liberal concept of freedom (freedom as the absence of external limits), Chinese communitarianism focused on the 'internal freedom'. It disagreed about the idea that more options and less interference brought up a genuine sense of

---

[2] Alasdair MacIntyre. 1981. After Virtue. Notre Dame: Notre Dame University Press. See also Michael Sandel. 1984. The Procedural Republic and the Unencumbered Self. Political Theory 12: 81–95. And Charles Taylor. 1990. Sources of the Self. Cambridge: Cambridge University Press.

[3] Michael Sandel. 1984. Liberalism and Its Critics. 5. Oxford: Basil Blackwell.

[4] Michael Sandel. 1982. Liberalism and the Limits of Justice. 62. New York: Cambridge University Press.

[5] Ibid. 175.

[6] Alasdair MacIntyre. 1981. After Virtue. Notre Dame: Notre Dame University Press. esp. chap.6, Some Consequences of the Failure of the Enlightment Project.

[7] Ibid. 172.

[8] Chinese Tian Ren He Yi, may be literaterly translated as 'oneness of heaven and man'. The origin of the thought of 'Tian Ren He Yi' came from Daohism. Literaturely the concept of Tian Ren He Yi expressed in Zhang Zai. Wang Fu Zhi (commentary). 2000. Zhang Zi Zheng Meng. 239. Shanghai: Shanghai Ancient Books Publishing House.

freedom. One might fail to be free even if open options were provided unless one could overcome his inner constraints, i.e., to lower desires.[9] To achieve genuine freedom, one had to overcome conflicts of desires, through self-mastery, self-government, self-cultivation and self-realization. Like Mencius said:

> *There is nothing better for the nurturing of the heart than to reduce one's desires. When a man has but few desires, even if there is anything he fails to retain in himself, it cannot be much; but when he has a great many desires, then even if there is anything he manages to retain in himself, it cannot be much.*[10]

Mencius pointed out that the most important factor that prevented a person from being free was not external obstacles but internal ones. The self-overcoming of conflicting desires and the cultivation of character would naturally lead one to be free. In Chinese communitarianism, a person who possessed virtue was freer than a person who lacked it, in the sense that one would act out of one's significant desires without frustration and internal conflicts. Otherwise, a person would become a slave of desires.

In Chinese communitarianism, the self was related to others, the outside, with the other creatures and nature. A person was not an atomic being, but connected to the community. The purpose of life contained the self-realization, in his contact with others. One should become a person of excellence (*Jun Zi*), and a person of love (*Ren Ren*), but first of all he should live in a community. A man was a social being. The value of life and self-realization connected with a person's responsibility to his community. Self-realization for the community-being was not about achieving non-disturbance or non-interference from others, but maintaining harmonious relationships with other members in the community.

In this perspective, a community was not the means but the end. The community was more than a factual existence. It was an ideal life style. A community in Chinese communitarianism should be a 'good' community, the one that helped its members to achieve their personal goals. In a liberal perspective, as a contrast, an individual's right was the premise of the good life and therefore the community was the means rather than the end. The group right or the justice of the community was less important than the right of an individual in this line of argument. Another extreme argument was to reduce the individual right to the community good. As discussed previously in Chinese lawmaking reality and problems, I pointed out that a fault of Chinese lawmaking was that it ignored individual's rights and took the individual as the means rather than as the end. I believe that both the individual and the community should be the end of an ideal life. None of them should be reduced to as the means.

---

[9] Confucians maintained that genuine freedom could be achieved not by securing more options but by overcoming one's lower desires while spontaneously and intentionally internalizing community norms. Analects II.

[10] Mencius. 2002. Jin Xin Zhang Ju II: 35. Meng Zi. 215. Zhuhai: Zhu Hai Publishing House.

Is communication under communitarianism possible? To answer this question we need to discover the relationship between an individual and the community that he belongs to. The relationship between the individual and the community in communitarianism highlighted the individual's submission, responsibility and sacrifice to the community. It was not much about the right but virtue. In communitarianism, the communication thus happened generally between an absolute minority (the one) and the absolute majority (the others; or the community). Without virtue, or without the majority's benevolence, the communication was impossible since the two parties of communication were too unequal.

The possibility of communication was different in liberalism. For liberals, the purpose of law was to prevent individuals from harming each other. The purpose of morality was to secure options in action and choice by securing a maximum degree of non-interference. Therefore as long as one did not inflict harm on others, and one did not violate the rights of others, one might do whatever one wanted. We thus saw an interesting phenomenon that communication was not necessary in this perspective. However, what was lacking in liberalism here was a vision of a good or virtuous life. Communitarianism, as a contrast, required that one should benefit others by overcoming one's own selfish desires. Both the liberalism and communitarianism might cause bad results. Extreme liberalism would lead to anarchism since it cut the necessary connections between a social being and the society; while extreme communitarianism would lead to authoritarianism because it tended to change the individual's purpose of a good life into blind submission. In an ideal liberalism or communitarianism, we need a coordination of rights and virtues. In the ideal communitarianism, communication was possible because there was 'right' to protect individuals and to restrict tyranny of the majority, and there was 'virtue' to promote a constructive dialogues between them.

7.4 Social Contract in Communitarianism

Chinese lawmaking is based on communitarianism. In communitarianism, a social contract presupposed the legitimacy of the social contract between a subject and a community, and was less concerned with the content of the contract. The 'improved social contract' that proposed by legisprudence started from the free will of an individual. Chinese social contract theory started from the 'will' of the community. These two kinds of social contract theory led to different routes of legitimation. In Chinese ideology, the community's good was a priority consideration. It put the collective morality over individual freedom. The collective good and its relation with law were what justifications or legitimations about. It was also a utilitarian perspective, in which security and order of the community should be the criterion of the validity of law. Freedom and the violation of it were *not* vital in this kind of social contract, as long as the community's good could be ensured. In this sense, the doctrine *promissory estoppel* could justify either a free or unfree contract as long as the promisor keeps his words.

Therefore we need another doctrine besides promissory estoppel, which is *Culpa in Contrahendo.*[11] It was about the liabilities for wrongs in conclusion of contract and fault in the negotiation process. Relying on the doctrine *Culpa in Contrahendo*, people would be able to escape from the rigid principle *promissory estoppel,* especially when the content of the social contract was no longer just. In a social contract that the individual's good was a priority consideration, freedom and right were justified apriori. Therefore if the nation made laws against the original purpose of protecting individuals' freedom and right, for instance, arbitrarily increasing taxes, those laws needed *ex post* justifications. Legisprudence provided four principles to support the doctrine *promissory estoppel*. The doctrine *Culpa in Contrahendo* offered another route to solve the problem. As we know in a contract theory, wrongs in conclusion of contract and the breach of the contract could cause the contract void, and when a contract became void it could be cancelled. It meant that if a contract was made against a person's good/will/interests, this person (rather than the other side of the contract) could claim that he would not be abided by the contract because it was void.

Under the doctrine *Culpa in Contrahendo*, the individual could take the official justification of law in consideration; or simply ignore it. He could make a complementary announcement further, that whether the social contract was still binding. He could choose whether to sign a new contract or re-sign the old one. Therefore, it was not about the justification of laws, but the justification of the validity of a social contract. If *Culpa in Contrahendo* was employed, the person (rather than the collective, the nation, or the society) could have freedom to admit or refuse the justification when the contract was already void. The question of the legitimacy of law was therefore transformed into the legitimacy of lawmaking. It would be a question of re-confirming the validity of the old (social) contract.

Therefore, the doctrine *Culpa in Contrahendo* stressed the appropriate content of the contract and the default responsibilities that an ideal contract should include, apart from an agreement (or a promise). The agreement or the promise was the formal condition, while the content and the default responsibilities were the substantial conditions. The binding force of a contract should exist when both of the two parties kept *their own commitments* to the contract. If one party broke the contract, the other should have the right to ask for compensation from the wrong-doers.

---

[11] *Culpa in Contrahendo*, can be briefly summarized as follows: a party who, through culpable conduct, prevents a contract from being formed or causes the contract to be invalid, should be liable for damages suffered by the innocent party who relied on the validity of the forthcoming contract. *Culpa in contrahendo* doctrine has strong influence in civil law countries especially Germany and Italy. The doctrine was firstly stated by Rudolf von Jhering in his 4 Jahrbrucher Fur Die Dogmatik Des Heutigen Romischen Un Deutschen Privatrechts I (1861) reprinted in I von Jhering, Gesammelte Aufsatze 327 (1881). See also Bao Anh Thai. Culpa in Contrahendo In English Law, http://www.baolawfirm.com.vn/dmdocuments/Culpa%20in%20contrahendo%20in%20English%20Law.pdf. Accessed 02 Feb 2012. See also J. Dietrich.2001. Classifying Precontractual Liability: a Comparative Analysis, *21 Leg. Stud.* 153–191. http://www.heinonline.org/HOL/Page?handle=hein.journals/legstd21&size=2&collection=journals&id=155. Accessed 02 Feb 2012.

The innocent party should reserve a right of cancellation of the contract. To apply the doctrine *promissory estoppel* strictly exclusively would be unfair in this situation because it provided no compensation for default, but required a blind obedience to law.

We may argue that the subject did not consent to the content of the contract if it were against his free will.[12] However, this argument would lead to a situation that we were not *picking up* or recover the infringed freedom, but maintaining the situation (the four justifications provided by Wintgens in legisprudence were to justify the reasons for letting the external limitations dominate the internal one, i.e., why should law substitute freedom). The doctrine *promissory estoppel* was re-discovered in legisprudence. The offer and acceptance of the contract was the starting point of the legitimation chain of legisprudence. It was important for the contractor to keep their promises. However, the content and the purpose of the contract should also be taken in the consideration of legitimacy. The doctrine *Culpa in Contrahendo* was also important. A person would not accept an unfair contract if he had a choice to cancel it. If he, however, were born in a society where an unfair legal system were already there, under the doctrine *promissory estoppel*, he could not rectify the content of it but to accept the official legitimacy. The only choice for him to preserve his natural freedom was then to leave the community.

'*Take it, or leave it*' was the only freedom a person had in such a situation. He had no right or freedom of resisting or changing any contents of the supposed social contract. The contents of the social contract were not really negotiable. It therefore did not constitute a real agreement that required by a common contract. It was not really a free contract at all. Is it possible for a social contract theory to cover these topics: liabilities for wrongs in conclusion of contract and fault in the negotiation process, i.e., *culpa in contrahendo,* and other remedies of contract in relation to pre-contractual liability, or tort of fraud, or deceit such as misrepresentation, mistake and unjust enrichment? I believe those topics should be included into a social contract theory. The principle of good faith and the duty of best efforts, the concepts of course of dealing and performance, the usage of trade and reasonableness, all these conceptions of contract law could be introduced into the social contract theory.[13] Lawmakers' legislative activities were therefore *not priori* legitimate by the offer and acceptance of the contract. The content of the social contract was also important and it should be negotiable. The remedies of contract in relation to *Culpa in Contrahendo* or pre-contractual liability could make up for the deficiency of the doctrine *promissory estoppel.*

As discussed earlier, in an ideal communitarian social contract, both right and virtue are important. The virtue of the community and that of the individual has equal importance. The virtue of the community relies on the realization of individual's wellbeing and the community's good. The virtue of the individual requires him

[12] For example, four principles were discovered to offer justifications in this situation in legisprudence.

[13] About contract theory and social contract theory, see also Ri Tiangui(Japanese). 2005. Qi Yue De Zai Sheng (the Revival of the Contract). 137. Beijing: China Legal Publishing House.

to live righteously for himself and for the community. The goal of the community and that of the individual should aim at a same direction rather than in conflicts. 'They are in a same direction' does not mean that 'they are one thing'. The community's goal and the individual's purpose can be different but they should not be conflicts. *Culpa in Contrahendo* in an ideal communitarian social contract therefore requires that the community should value individual's rights rather than sacrifice the individual for the community. Therefore we need to differentiate an individual's freedom and the collective's liberty. This differentiation is helpful for us to further understand this theme.

7.5 Freedom, Liberty and Law

Firstly let us recall the concepts of freedom and law that discussed in legisprudence. Formal logic was employed in legisprudence to define freedom and law: '*freedom unlimited logically includes the absence of any limitation*'.[14] '*[T]he concept of freedom allows any action*'.[15] '[*A*]*ny rule of the sovereign is an external limitation of freedom*'.[16] A syllogistic deduction was imbedded in these definitions (Fig. 7.1):

Wintgens noticed that it was unprofitable to discuss 'freedom unlimited' in a legal society. He stated that 'freedom unlimited is only a concept' and must be supplemented by a concretization, i.e., a 'conception'.[17] Therefore the conceptions of freedom (*cof*) and conceptions about freedom (*caf*) in his definition were both limited freedom. None of them excluded the interference of law. In other words, the two conceptions (*cof* and *caf*) were homogenous in nature (both of them were limited freedom).

cof and *caf* were different in the definition: the conceptions of freedom were the internal limitations of a person; while the conceptions about freedom were the external limitations that were imposed by the sovereign. Therefore they were supposed to have no intersections in the definition. However, I discover that the relationship between the two *conceptions* could be more complex (see Fig. 7.2):

Freedom unlimited (S) is the absence of any limitation (M)
Law (P) is a limitation (M)
Freedom unlimited(S) is the absence of law (P).

Fig. 7.1 A syllogistic deduction

[14] Luc J. Wintgens. 2007. Legitimacy and Legitimation from the Legisprudential Perspective, in Legislation in Context: Essays in Legisprudence. 23. London: Ashgate Publishing Limited.

[15] Wintgens. 2005. The Theory and Practice of Legislation—Essays in Legisprudence. 7. London: Ashgate Publishing Limited.

[16] Ibid. 10.

[17] Ibid. 7.

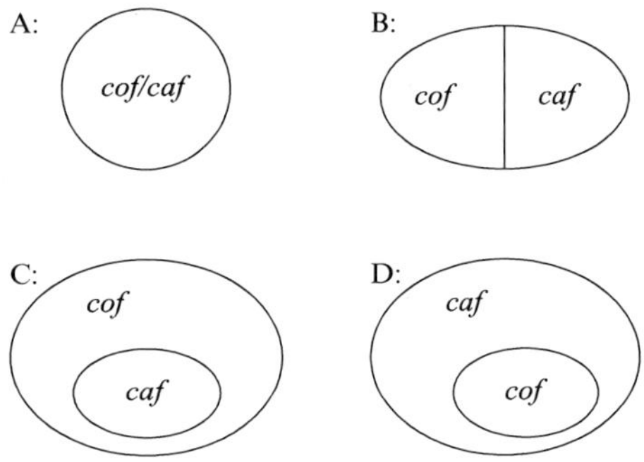

Fig. 7.2 Relationships between cof and caf

Logically, when they are equal in extension:

A. *cof*=*caf*; or,
B. *cof*≠*caf*;

Or when they have different extension:

C. *cof*⊃*caf* (when cof had the broader intension than caf);
D. *cof*⊂*caf* (when cof had the narrower intension than caf).

In legisprudence only situation B was considered, i.e., when the extension of two conceptions were equal plus their intension were just opposite to each other (cof≠caf). In a reply to legisprudence, an interesting question was proposed but not elaborated. It was about the situation that in homogeneous cultural groups members shared a conception of freedom [15]. [18] This question was about the situation A, when the intension and extension of the two conceptions were equal, i.e., cof=caf. Legisprudence excluded discussion about situation A, when the two conceptions were exactly equal in extension and intension. In my point of view, the definition of *caf* and *cof* in legisprudence also neglected the other two possible situations, when the extensions of *cof* and *caf* were *not* the same (situations C and D in Fig. 7.2).

Let us suppose that the unlimited freedom of speech meant absence of any limitation on speech. A person in a community, however, had to be restrained by conventional, cultural, moral, legal rules and other limitations when exercising his freedom of speech. Suppose: legal rules were what conceptions about freedom (*caf*) about, while the other factors referred to conceptions of freedom (*cof*). Let us suppose in this community the vocal insult to the sovereign was a crime. If a person respected the sovereign sincerely and felt guilty of insulting it, then to him *cof equals caf* (that is situation A). In this situation, *caf* although was an external limitation, was not really against his own conception of freedom. If, however, there were another person who hated the sovereign and felt happy of insulting it, then to him it was the situation B: *cof*≠*caf*. In this situation, *caf* became a real limitation of freedom. *Caf* became a reason of restricting his temptation of exercising his *cof*, i.e., insulting the sovereign.

[18] Vlad Perju.2009. A Comment on Legisprudence. Boston University Law Review 89:428.

Morality should have a priority over law
If not, a justification (PA) is needed
In some situations (B and C) law is prior to morality
So, a justification (PA) is needed in situations where law is prior to morality (B and C)

Fig. 7.3 An implicit syllogisitc deduction in legisprudence

Or if the person did not mean to abuse the sovereign but he spoke of its name directly—he thought he was acting according to his *cof*, but the community's law regulated further in details that directly speaking of the sovereign's name was also an insult. Then in this occasion, the intension of the person's conception of freedom was broader than that of the sovereign, i.e., $cof \supset caf$ (C). On the contrary, if a person believed that speaking of the sovereign was an insult to the sovereign, but the law punished negative criticisms only, then the subject's conception of freedom was narrower than the law, i.e., $cof \subset caf$ (D).

In situations A and D, the subject's own conceptions (the internal limitations) *coincide with* law or *stricter than* the law, therefore the supposed external limitations were not really extra limitations. Only in situations B and C the problem of justification of legitimacy existed. In situations B and C, the *caf* added extra responsibilities to the person. In these situations he should abandon his own *cof* and act according to *caf*. The first principle of legisprudence, the principle of alternativity (PA) was a justification of external limitations of freedom.[19] PA was exactly necessary for situations B and C. In the above four different situations (see Fig. 7.2), situations A and D were not covered by principle of alternativity (PA). In other words, PA was not necessary for them, although a person's morality was prior to law in situations A and D. The justification of external limitations (PA) was needed in situations B and C when law surpassed morality (see Fig. 7.3).

The above premise, i.e., morality should have a priority over law, needed a further justification. The justification could be that freedom should be the starting point of action and should be taken as the *principium* of a political organization, as defended by Wintgens. But the justification could be considered in two different ways: the specified way or the nonfigurative way. In the specified perspective, *every* lawmaking activity should be legitimate. Therefore the justification or the legitimation should apply to *each* and *every* law. On the contrary, in the nonfigurative perspective, legitimation was applied to the whole lawmaking system. It did not require a justification of a law's specific content or the justice of an activity.

This premise (morality should have a priority over law) could be an 'indisputable' starting point of a theory, which could avoid further examination. Or it could be examined as a true or false statement. I believe that Professor Wintgens employed the former way of deduction. Therefore it was sufficient to support his argument for freedom. From another perspective, when we consider the facticity of the argument, the

[19] Wintgens. 2009. Freedom and Legisprudence—a More Substantial View: a Reply to Professor Perju. Boston University Law Review 89:1795.

conclusion could be different. Morality *was not* always prior to law. A differentiation between *freedom* and *liberty* was thus useful for a consideration of the facticity of this proposition.[20]

Let us suppose we were talking about an individual's conception of freedom (*hereinafter icof*), not his conceptions about freedom (*hereinafter icaf*). They both were different from the collective morality (the collective conceptions of freedom, *hereinafter ccof*) or law (the collective conceptions about freedom, *hereinafter caf*). Based on my previous discussion about the relationship between *cof* and *caf* that showed in Fig. 7.2, we could see that four basic different logical relationships were possible between *icof* and *ccof*:

When they were equal in the extension, $icof = ccof$, or $icof \neq ccof$; or when they were not equal in the extension and the intension of *icof* was broader than *ccof*, $icof \supset ccof$. Or on the contrary, when the intension of *icof* was narrower than *ccof*, $icof \subset ccof$. When law (*caf*) was added, the results of the three (*icof*, *ccof* and *caf*) were more complex (see Fig. 7.4):

Therefore here were at least 28 possible relationships among an individual's conception (*icof*), collective morality (*ccof*) and law (*caf*).[21] When the proposition 'morality should be prior to law' referred to individual morality, only in the section (a1) did a person's conception of freedom coincident with the collective morality, or in (b2) had it been covered by the collective morality. Therefore in (a1ii), (a1iii), (b2ii) and (b2iii), law needed justifications (like PA in legisprudence) because law was against morality or had narrower intension than morality. In other situations, especially when the individual freedom was against or broader than the collective morality, plus the collective morality was coincident with or stricter than law, an individual's morality should not necessarily be prior to law, as (a2ii) or (a2iii) showed.

We should differentiate collective morality (*ccof*) from law (*caf*). A person's own conception was an internal limitation. Collective morality, when coincident with his conception, could be regarded as an internal limitation. When it was not, it was an external limitation. If 'morality should prior to law' meant a person's own conceptions of freedom (*icof*) should prior to law (*caf*), it would be difficult to justify itself (*icof*) when the collective morality (*ccof*) was coincident with law (*caf*), or even stricter than law, as (a2ii) or (a2iii) showed. The proposition therefore needed another supporting argument: An individual's morality (*icof*) should be prior to collective morality (*ccof*); or freedom should be prior to liberty.

[20] About the differentiation between freedom and liberty, see also Hanna F. Pitkin. 1988. Are Freedom and Liberty Twins. Political Theory 16:4. cited from Ying Qi. A Third Concept of Liberty. 2006. 312–345. Beijing: The Eastern Publishing Co. Ltd. Freedom in Hanna's definition is 'personal liberties', 'private liberties' and 'negative liberties'. In this thesis I also use this differentiation between liberty and freedom, to discuss the relationship between an individual's cognition of freedom and a collective consciousness or unconsciousness.

[21] In the above 16 possibilities, 12 of them were certain, 4 of them were not certain (b1ii, b1iii, b2ii and b2iv) and led to another 16 possibilities, therefore 12 + 16 = 28 possibilities in total.

A. When icof and ccof had equal extension:

(a1)When icof=ccof, there were four results:

(a1i) icof(=ccof)=caf;

(a1ii) icof(=ccof)≠caf;

(a1iii) icof(=ccof)⊃caf;

or, (a1iv) icof(=ccof)⊂caf.

(a2)When icof≠ccof, there were four results:

(a2i) icof=caf but ccof≠caf;

(a2ii) icof≠caf but ccof=caf;

(a2iii) icof⊃caf but ccof⊂caf;

or, (a2iv) icof⊂caf but ccof⊃caf.

B. When icof and ccof did not equal in extension:

(b1) When icof⊃ccof:

(b1i) icof=caf, ccof⊂caf;

(b1ii) icof≠caf, *ccof?caf* (? Means:in this situation, the relationship between ccof and caf are not certain; it means all these following four results are possible: ccof=caf; ccof≠caf; ccof⊃caf; or ccof⊂caf);

(b1iii) icof⊃caf, *ccof?caf;*

or, (b1iv) icof⊂caf, ccof⊂caf

(b2) when icof⊂ccof:

(b2i) icof=caf, ccof⊃caf;

(b2ii) icof≠caf, *ccof?caf;*

(b2iii) icof⊃caf, ccof⊃caf;

or, (b2iv) icof⊂caf, *ccof?caf.*

Fig. 7.4 Relationships among icof, ccof and caf

The argument ‘freedom should be prior to liberty’ therefore would face difficulties in defending the rationality of the existence of a community. An extremely self-centered person would not agree with the commitment to respecting *other* persons’ opinions and wills. If this person intended to take the convenience of the community but rejected inconvenient aspects (for example, other persons’ conceptions of freedom), other self-centered persons or the community would not welcome him. From a radical liberalistic view, this person would not want to join the community because entering the society required him to abandon his freedom from the beginning. From a utilitarian communitarianism perspective the collective morality should be prior to an individual’s freedom because the society should aim at the greatest happiness for the greatest number (rather than the individual).

The differentiation between freedom and liberty was used here to reflect the relationship between the individual and the collective. In a society that individuals were supposed to be atomistic units gathering together, each atomistic individual had to give up some of its autonomy in order to enter into the society. But as Professor Bankowski pointed out, which I agree, and which was also a reflection of the Chinese legal system and modern social contracts, an individual was born in a society, where his autonomy was defined and influenced greatly by the society in the first place.[22] The atomistic individual was 'shaped' by the society, so that he was not came exclusively from the outside of a society—

> *Thus one cannot think, as in the first case, of his giving up something that was previously his and his alone…the individual is viewed not as sovereign but as part of the community and it is that person-in-the-community that must take into account when working out a solution. The fact that I want (or don't want) something is never perceived as the final determining factor.*[23]

The content of *icof* and *ccof* were not identical, therefore the reductive proposition that *ccof* dominated *icof* was insufficient. More problems appeared: When law (*caf*) was in line with the individual's conception of freedom (*icof*), but was in conflict with the collective conceptions (i.e., when $icof \subset caf$, plus $icof \neq ccof$), like situations a2i, a2iv, b2i and farfetched b1iv and b2iv showed in Fig. 7.4, was the law still just? Was the law legitimate? Did such law need justifications? Principles debated in legisprudence were unable to answer these questions since they focused on the situation when $icof \supset caf$ but ignored the relationships between *icof* and *ccof.* They did not differentiate various situations a1iii, a2iii, b1iii and b2iii that were supposed here in Fig. 7.4.

To interpret the possibility of the coincidence of an individual's conception (*icof*) and the majorities' (*ccof*) and their conflicts with the law (*caf*) further, i.e., a possibility that legisprudence did not refer to ($icof = ccof \neq caf$), I would like to use an example of the reform that happened in 1990s in China to defend my argument. It was about conceptions of 'private property'.[24] Before 1990s, most Chinese including me believed that private property was the origin of inequality. This belief was formulated since our primary school education about the legitimacy of the socialist public ownership. Personally, I did not think it was questionable although at that time I did not read the famous theme wrote by Rousseau in his *Discourse on the Origin and Basis of Inequality among Men.*

My own conception on freedom of possession (*icof*) was identical with the (old) constitution (*caf*) and the collective conception (*ccof*). The law said any property belonged to the country; the country belonged to the people; thus any property belonged to the people. I was very proud of this conception of rights of property and

---

[22] Zenon Bankowski. 2001. Living Lawfully-Love in Law and Law in Love. 19. Dordrecht: Kluwer.

[23] Ibid.

[24] In China, there is a differentiation between 'private property' and 'public property'. As professor Bankowski noticed, it is 'a vocabulary of the old communist law'. At the same time we should notice that in ancient China, all the property belonged to the Emperor but the property was at the same time 'public property' because the Emperor belonged to the public. Not until the Spring and Autume period, did the private ownership of land appear and be admitted. Law was then seemed as the tools for the public rather for the private. Different from the Western property concept, in the beginning property was not 'private' to the public in China. about 600 B.C. Shijing. Xiaoya (Gufeng Zhi Shi. Beishan).

satisfied with my right of proportionate possession of the country. Later, however, I felt confused, because in the late 1990s the law suddenly changed and it supported the transformation of state-owned enterprises to private companies. More than 21 millions of workers were laid-off from state-owned enterprises and faced difficulties in livelihood because of the transformation.[25] Law was changed to persuade us to accept the conception of limited private property (without clarifying which groups of the people in society should gain this brand new privilege first).

The new law (*caf*) was thus in conflict with my own conception (*icof*) and conceptions of most people (*ccof*; please notice that our conceptions were greatly influenced and formed by the *old* law). But the new law became valid without consent of the people since it already gained the consent of the lawmakers (please also understand that the referendum never existed or happened in Chinese history). In legisprudence, the new law as the external limitation needed justifications from four principles, PA, PN, PT or PC.[26] None of them, however, could justify the legitimacy of the new law, since firstly it was not happened because of ineffective social interaction but because of few lawmakers' decisions (therefore PA failed to justify it); secondly it was not consistent with the constitution (the constitution was changed later; therefore PN failed to justify it); thirdly it had no historical roots in China (therefore PT failed to justify it); and fourthly it was not harmonious with the legal system; the legal system changed accordingly *afterwards* (finally PC failed to justify it). The four principles all failed in interpreting this Chinese lawmaking. But if we simply denied the legality or legitimacy of this law, we ignored the reality: It was lawful because the law was passed by the authority and people tolerated this fact. Positivism might interpret the validity of law in this case. The conception of freedom or individual freedom, however, could not interpret the legitimacy of the new law.

To interpret the legitimacy of this new law, we need to hold a dynamic perspective of lawmaking. The strict opposition between law and freedom needs to be softened. Different from a pure logical definition of freedom, Bankowski's argument of law and love discloses an exchangeable relationship between law and freedom: law could fulfill freedom, and vice versa. '*Law and going beyond it are inseparable and, …in breaking the law you are fulfilling the law. Truly to follow the law implies being able to break it and recreate it anew-in breaking the law you are following it*'.[27] In this line of argument, both freedom and restrictions were the base of law and lawmaking. Law and freedom were not the opposite of each other. They were connected by a reciprocal transformation.

Bankowski's theory of the relationship between law and love disclosed the relationship between heteronomy and autonomy. It could be used to interpret the

[25] According to the report of the Ministry of Labor and Social Security 2000, from 1998 to 2000, there were 21,370,000 workers became laid-off. See Chang Kai. 2004. The Right to Work and its Realization in the Market Economy. China Labor 6:4–9.

[26] Wintgens. 2004. Legisprudence as a New Theory of Legislation (presentation for the discussion group of jurisprudence at Oxford). http://www.trinitinture.com/documents/wintgens.pdf. Accessed 02 Feb 2012.

[27] Zenon Bankowski. 2001. Living Lawfully-Love in Law and Law in Love. 10. Dordrecht: Kluwer.

relationship between right and virtue, and the relationship between freedom and liberty in communitarianism. Law was not exclusively about heteronomy; the love of law, or the purpose 'living lawfully' embedded the requirement of autonomy. Unlike freedom in legisprudence which emphasized philosophic autonomy from a formal logical perspective, Bankowski described the meaning of freedom (as a combine of heteronomy and autonomy) in practical reasoning: '*[T]he tension between heteronomy and autonomy is part of the grammar of practical reasoning and an underlying premise of social organization and institutional design-accepting that is the way forward. That, …is what gives our lives and our institutions integrity and unity*'.[28] Both law and love should reflect heteronomy and autonomy. Liberty should be a combination of heteronomy and autonomy.

Lawmaking should reflect both the heteronomy and autonomy. It would be partially true if autonomy was exclusively stressed. It would be bias also when a compulsory theory neglected the autonomy. Communications and discourses could be one of the approaches (if not the only one) to contribute to the articulation of autonomy and heteronomy in lawmaking. Unlike contemporary legitimation theses in Chinese politics, traditional Chinese legalism, or non-negotiable social contract, a discourse thesis would re-emphasize an idea that it was us (people in a real democratic legal system rather than hypothetical rational beings in a state of nature or behind a veil of ignorance) who could make and change the rules. At the same time we (in this realistic context) promised to be abided by them. On the one hand, the subjectivity of creating rules should not be substituted by rules—the demand for autonomy. On the other hand, we should make a promise to live under the rules—the demand for heteronomy.

7.6 Conclusion

Communicative lawmaking in China should absorb Western lawmaking ideas and experiences, but most importantly it should emphasize the communication between the individual and the community within the system. China has a long history of communitarianism that the collective interests or the group rights were prior to individual's rights. Chinese lawmaking theories highlighted 'order' and 'public good' as the supporting values. It appeared to be the opposite of a liberal theory of lawmaking based on freedom. However, Chinese lawmaking might slide into a totalitarian justification; therefore I believe that an ideal communication in communitarianism should admit the value of right and virtue. When the community ignores or sacrifices some members' rights, the minority can rectify the social contract based on the doctrine *culpa in contrahendo*. An individual's right and virtue should not be detached from that of the community. A free individual and a liberal community can coexist.

[28] Ibid. 12.

Chapter 8
Retrospect and Prospect

In this book I discussed and criticized different legitimation for lawmaking, including ancient and contemporary Chinese theories, as well as Western representative perspectives on lawmaking. From my previous discussion we saw that the reality and popular theories of lawmaking in China were not for communicative lawmaking and did not provide mechanisms to build dialogues between the top (the legislature, the Party and the rich persons) and the down (common people). I also disclosed the links between contemporary justifications of collective lawmaking and the essential topics of Chinese legalism. I focused on the origin of Chinese top-down lawmaking model: Chinese legalism. Chinese legalism was a historic school arguing against Confucianism in its hypothesis of human nature. It denied the necessity of 'loving' people but focused on punishments. In Chinese legalism people were in nature 'bad' so that it was better to use harsh punishments to control them. In such an instrumentalist philosophy and its political design, rights and freedom for individuals were not important.

I attempted to introduce a communicative structure of lawmaking to balance individual rights and state interests, by arguing for a system that individuals' voice could be heard and paid attention to. This structure would go against the grain of the traditional top-down legislation that was defended in Chinese theories. I turned to Western theories for help. Western theories of lawmaking including Benthamian utilitarian lawmaking, Hayekian liberalistic lawmaking, Waldronian democratic lawmaking and Wintgensian freedom-priority lawmaking could contribute to Chinese future legal reform.

However, they would also face difficulties in solving realistic problems in China. Utilitarian lawmaking was close to Chinese legalism and Chinese official justifications. Its ignorance of the least advantage group, or the persons in the worse situation should be criticized. Hayekian liberal lawmaking although stressed the necessity of recognition of customary laws, or laws came from the society and from common people rather than from official laws, did not say much about the possibility of communications between these two kinds of laws, the official law and the laws of the society. Waldron re-discovered the dignity of representative democracy, but as

P. He, *Chinese Lawmaking: From Non-communicative to Communicative*, Understanding China, DOI 10.1007/978-3-642-39507-9_8,

criticized by Bankowski, which I also agree, he overlooked that democracy was more than representation. In cases relating to basic human rights and freedom, the majority voting might be against humanity and should not be a sole principle of justice. Freedom as the ultimate goal of lawmaking in Wintgens' theory could contribute to Chinese legal reform. But it should be applied cautiously also since it was against Chinese dominant ideology for the collective good.

After my introduction and analysis of these theories, I attempted to escape from pure theoretic discussion about law and legality, and try to provide a practical application of communicative lawmaking in China. I believe that the top-down lawmaking mode in China was insufficient in its justifications for legitimacy; neither was it beneficial for increasing the degree of individual freedom and rights. Therefore it is better to absorb positive Western lawmaking elements, especial taking a shift to a more interactive and cooperative mode. Theories of disagreement and individual freedom in this sense have positive contributions to this proposed shift.

Based on Bankowski's two arguments in *Living Lawfully*, that is, the relationship between love and law and the procedural design for 'Bringing the Outside in', I believe that humanity and procedural justice were important values for communicative lawmaking. The humanity value emphasized the subjectivity purpose of lawmaking while procedural justice contributed to the interactive, reversible and cooperative lawmaking. The legislative procedural justice focused on the process values, 'the means' rather than 'the results'. It emphasized that apart from the result, there were independent values for the legal process per se, including participatory governance, process fairness, procedural legality, and procedural rationality. Whether or not a procedure could guarantee a good outcome was a result-oriented proposition. It was concerned with the 'good result efficacy' of the process. The procedural justice, however, emphasized a process-oriented theme. The procedural justice required that the lawmaking process itself should be publicized. If focusing exclusively on substantive justice, it was not necessary to design fair procedures because the approach to get the result was not important. A process-oriented theme, however, required a just design of the procedure.

Therefore 'the law of lawmaking' should not refer to a code of lawmaking (like Legislative Law of China 2000) exclusively, but should contain legitimation justifications. For the sake of the procedural nature of lawmaking, the initial rules that guiding lawmaker behaviours should design a just and acceptable procedure also. Law in general attempted to perpetuate the value of order, justice, equality, freedom, convenience or efficacy. Specific laws emphasized different values in light of their particular primary reasons for existence. The law of lawmaking in a democratic society should aim at promoting harmony in a society and smoothing the information exchange between lawmakers and other people. It should secure legal equality by offering people a fair chance to present and debate their opinions. It should restrict arbitrary lawmaking and safeguard freedom by establishing punishments and remedies to legislative misbehaviours.

Relying on the contributions of Western lawmaking theories, but at the same time realizing their difficulties in their application in Chinese contexts, I believe that Confucianism and a love philosophy of law could contribute to a discourse theory of lawmaking. The core of Confucianism, Ren (loving the people) provided a possible theoretical background for a discourse theory because it required that we should take the responsibility of our treatments to other people. In Confucianism we were not isolated atomic individuals with absolute free will. We were in a relationship with others and should consider others. Bankowski's argument for the interplay of law and love, the inside and the outside systems, also initiated a debate for communicative decision-making, and could be employed to solve the difficulty of applying Western theories into Chinese contexts.

In the recent 30 years economic reform from 1970s, the Western capitalistic political and legal theories were discussed further and deeper in China. However, conflicts between Western values and Chinese traditional justifications of the law became more obvious. The gap between the ultimate hidden rule in China (i.e., the rule of recognition as the CPC's affirmance) and Western recognitions of democracy and the Rule of Law became wider. This gap reflected conflicting values imbedded in the Western Rule of Law and Chinese rule-by-law. We could not simply copy the West to China. For example, the discourses that I supposed in this book were not simply about voting for different parties. The Chinese lawmaking system was unlike the one that Professor Bankowski described about the decision-making reality.[1] Chinese contemporary party system did not offer such different programs among different parties since the Communist Party of China was the exclusive leading party. Therefore, we could hardly copy Western bilateral and multiple-party system of lawmaking directly to China.

However, elements of Western lawmaking could be introduced into the Chinese mode. Indeed, we at least shared those procedural elements in a legislative process including: (1) a pre-legislative stage: the process of choosing lawmakers usually occurred before making a specific law; (2) a legislative stage, including the process of initiating or sponsoring a bill; (3) a process of deliberate consideration and debate of a bill; (4) a vote and passing of the bill; and (5) a post-legislative stage: the promulgation of law. Besides, China also valued legislative fairness and other substantive justice of lawmaking. It is therefore possible for Chinese lawmaking absorbing elements of Western lawmaking.

In the previous chapter I argued for the necessity and possibility of communicative lawmaking. I concluded that relying on 'right' and 'virtue', communications between an individual and the community was possible. Communicative lawmaking was necessary for Chinese legal reform. Here I would like to introduce the recent trend of Chinese reform to support my previous arguments. The present leader of CPC and the president of China, Mr. Jingtao Hu re-emphasized the importance of Confucian humanity and stated *Yi Ren Wei Ben* (humanism;

[1] 'We are implicated in the decision-making process because it is the general line of decisions that we approve in voting for a particular candidate. If we vote for a socialist party we cannot complain if we are taxed more to organize better social welfare provision, even if we do not want to give up our hard earned money. If we vote for a conservative party, we cannot be surprised when the return to individuals is given priority over provisions for society in general; when privatization is more important than providing public service'. Zenon Bankowski. 2001. Living Lawfully-Love in Law and Law in Love. 16. Dordrecht: Kluwer.

people-oriented) principle as the core of 'scientific development'.[2] People's subjectivity should be respected and the law should promote all around human development. President Hu pointed out that the economic and legal reform stressed the socialistic development of the country, but the modernization development should work for the people, depended on the people, so that all the people could share the fruit of the development. President Hu's statement thus deepened and developed Xiaoping Deng's theory about the common prosperous. It shifted from pure instrumentalism (which focuses only on the development) to humanism. It also shifted from opposition to unity (between the people and the 'enemy'). Colors of class struggle and the democratic dictatorship were not that intense in President Hu's interpretation of contemporary Chinese Marxism. Under the principle of humanism, President Hu's report implied that the majority, the minority and the weakest group should all be concerned. Chinese lawmaking therefore would be based on a solid moral ground.

The Chinese lawmaking practice also showed the shift from the economic priority to humanism. Basing on the principle of *Yi Ren Wei Ben* (humanism), amendments of the Constitution added contents about human rights, protections to legal private properties, and compensations to land expropriation. In the policy of investment, sustainable development of environment and resources was emphasized; on finance and taxation, the peasants interests were more valued; more assistance was given to agriculture; people's livelihood, health and safety were considered prior to economic construction.

Chinese local legislatures also started to execute communicative lawmaking and gained favorable comments. The standing committee of the people's congress of Shanghai invited 21 junior students to discuss the Regulation of the Protection of Juveniles of Shanghai. During the meeting, Gao Jianling, a high school student suggested that the law should forbid the schools to randomly publicize students' transcripts and ranking. Law-drafters did not realize the students' psychological pressure under the prevailing ranking and transcript system. The law finally absorbed Gao Jianling's suggestion. It was the first time a regulation absorbed a teenager's legislative advice into Shanghai's local lawmaking practices.[3] Before making the Administration of the Leasing of Urban Premises of Beijing, the local legislators took advices through website, and discovered that most people held opposite opinions, so they decided to postpone the schedule. It was also a new attempt in Beijing legislative practice.[4] Since September 2005, citizens of An'Hui province could write, email or fax to the local legislature of An Hui, to submit their individual opinions of bills. All these practices showed a development of communicative lawmaking.

---

[2] President Jingtao Hu, the Report to the 17th CPC National Congress, http://news.xinhuanet.com/newscenter/2007-10/24/content_6938568_2.htm. Accessed 02 Feb 2012.

[3] News from Xinhua News, http://news.xinhuanet.com/legal/2005-09/08/content_3460751.htm. Accessed 02 Feb 2012.

[4] News from Sina China, http://news.sina.com.cn/o/2005-04-10/11555609189s.shtml. Accessed 02 Feb 2012.

However, although official laws were created and changed to be more humanity by paying attention to people's voices, those who lacked power, authority, status, fortune, and knowledge had few channels and approaches to express their rational requirements. The attempts and examples mentioned above were still initiated from the 'top', rather than initiated from the 'bottom', which implied that the channel and arena for communication were not 'communicative' but still relied on the decision of the 'top'. When the 'top' stopped or closed the communicative channel, communicative lawmaking would return to unidirectional lawmaking. We therefore need to establish and institutionalize a more equal and fair arena for a discourse between the 'top' and the 'bottom'. It should be a long-term goal of Chinese construction of the Rule of Law.

In Chinese lawmaking reality and theories, the means of lawmaking (i.e., the top-down and irreversible lawmaking) had conflicts with the ends (i.e., the purpose of 'common prosperity'). An interactive, reversible and cooperative lawmaking mode could contribute to the further development of the Chinese legal system and improvement of Chinese people's livelihoods. In this last chapter, I attempted to offer possible solutions based on arguments deliberated in previous chapters for the contemporary Chinese lawmaking system. I believe two principles could contribute to an interactive and cooperative lawmaking: the principle of a fair exchange of information between the internal and external systems in lawmaking; and the principle of full debate between adversary parties.

Before I discuss the principle of debate and its meaning to Chinese lawmaking, I believe it is helpful for us to read the analogy that Bankowski illustrated in *Living Lawfully*, the debate of the reform of the (fictional) Law school at the University of Auchenshuggle.[5] The Law Faculty itself was not as an overseeing entity, but rather as a department or individual administrative unit. A new movement for unification arose to abolish all the departments and to have one single Law School, one administrative unit, and one department. However, the problem arose in a democratic debate of the reform: '*The individual voices would be lost in the representative and, the more one tried to prevent that, the larger that committee would become until it became the Faculty as a whole.*'[6] In order to satisfy the necessity of efficient management and control of the Law school without losing concerns with the particular requirements and contributions of the average staff, Bankowski offered a solution, which claimed that a porous architecture enabled different units of the school to be open and exchange with the outside—thereby restructuring themselves. Thus the separate different small units of the school 'drag the outside in' while at the same time ensure their voices being heard.

Chinese current legal reform was like the reform of the Law School of Auchenshuggle. The aim of the current legal reform should establish a principle that people's voices being heard rather than being represented simply. Thus, just as the Law School of Auchenshuggle, Chinese lawmaking process might be seen as a

[5]Zenon Bankowski. 2001. Living Lawfully-Love in Law and Law in Love. 216. Dordrecht: Kluwer.

[6]Ibid.

complex interaction of groups at differing levels, functionally and territorially. People interacted with each other through and in different groups in a series and family of connections which in the end led to the general identity

Democratic lawmaking procedures should consist of negotiations and compromises. The Chinese lawmaking system lacked the tense adversarial atmosphere. When discussing a bill, Chinese lawmakers represented the whole community. They had similar status and task although participants were more or less influenced by different interest groups. Legislators considered the overall situation and long-term interests. They valued compromise among diverse parties and attempt to reduce conflicts. The first and foremost concern of lawmakers was whether or not a bill should be passed as a law. They handled the bill together although they might represent different interest groups. Their overlapping work lightened the degree of antagonism. Lawmaking was unlike trial: In a trial the appealers were not the decision-maker. Lawmakers, however, were 'representative appealers' of a bill but at the same time 'the judge' of it. The dual role of lawmakers, i.e., as both 'appealers' and 'the judge' of a bill, was not distinguished clearly.

As 'the judge' of a bill, whether the representatives of NPC could say 'no' to a bill reflected the degree of democracy in lawmaking also. In Yan'an times in China (1935–1948), Chinese peasants put soybeans, green beans, broad beans into a bowl to represent their different opinions (because at that time most of them were illiterate).[7] From 1949 to 1966, voting by applause or a show of hands were popular approaches. Especially in the Cultural Revolution period, voting by warm applaud was the exclusive vote mechanism. From 1979 to 1990, secret ballot and electronic voting appeared in Chinese lawmaking, but not until 1980s appeared the negative votes in Chinese lawmaking. For the first 30 years of 'new' China the applause for the solid unanimous vote was the dominant form of voting. Especially in local congresses applaud-votes were still a major form of voting. Yujie Wang, a NPC representative stated that the absence of negative votes in the 50 years of local congresses showed that Chinese lawmaking was abnormal.[8]

Negative votes started to appear in Chinese lawmaking since 1990s. In 1989's voting for independent legislative power of Shenzhen special zone, negative and abstain votes were more than a thousand and was seen as a great development in Chinese lawmaking history. In 1997, negative and abstain votes for the report of the Supreme People's Procuratorate was also above a thousand, and were about 40.4 % of the whole votes.[9] Since the development of electronic voting, negative votes increased. Siwei Cheng, the previous vice chairman of SCNPC, stated in his speech in the New Year 2002 that in the age of applaud-vote, all decisions were almost passed without any negative opinions. A representative who applauded for years admitted that in the old voting atmosphere, representatives were machines of putting up hands. They did not express real thoughts. They were afraid of saying no to

[7] Biyao Tian. 2008. The Development of Voting Witness Democracy. Gong Ming Dao Kan (Guidence for Citizens) 02:52–53.

[8] Ibid.

[9] Ibid.

issues of 11th NPC	session	Affirmative	Negative	Abstain	affirmative degree
the report of government work	1	2,885	32	12	98.5%
	2	2,824	42	22	97.78
the execution of national economy and social development	1	2,747	125	25	94.17
	2	2,669	145	71	92.51
the budget of local and central governments	1	2,462	362	102	84.14
	2	2,440	315	124	84.75
the work of NPC and SCNPC	1	2,846	57	23	97.17
	2	2,721	99	68	94.22
the work report of the Supreme People's Court	1	2,287	521	142	78.11
	2	2,172	519	192	75.34
the work report of the Supreme People's Procuratorate	1	2,270	514	142	77.58
	2	2,210	505	162	76.82

Fig. 8.1 The rate of affirmative votes in NPC

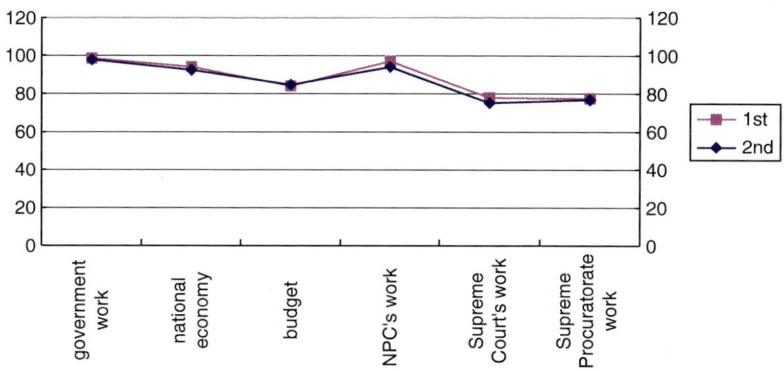

Fig. 8.2 Satisfactory rate of different reports by the NPC representatives

a bill. They were also ashamed of being a candidate of 'no' in front of the whole rostrum. The development of electronic voting improved the situation and made the negative public votes possible.[10]

The negative votes in NPC, however, were still not common in China. From the following Figs. 8.1 and 8.2 we could see that: In the first session of the 11th NPC, the votes for the report of government work were 2,885 affirmative, 32 negative and 12 abstain; the proportion of affirmative votes to the whole vote was 98.5 %. The votes for the execution of national economy and social development were 2,747 affirmative, 125 negative and 25 abstain; 94.17 % affirmative. The votes for the budget of local and central governments were 2,462 affirmative, 362 negative, and 102 abstain; 84.14 % affirmative. The votes for the work of NPC and SCNPC were

[10] Bifei Zang. 2009. Expecting Electronic Voting in 'Two Congresses'. People's Congress Studying 04:37–38.

2,846 affirmative, 57 negative, and 23 abstain; 97.17 % affirmative. The votes for the work report of the Supreme People's Court were 2,287 affirmative, 521 negative, 142 abstain; 78.11 % affirmative. The votes for the work report of the Supreme People's Procuratorate were 2,270 affirmative, 514 negative, and 142 abstain; 77.58 affirmative.[11] In the second session, the affirmative degree was 97.78 %, 92.51 %, 84.75 %, 94.22 %, 75.34 % and 76.82 %.[12] From these recent statistics we could see that NPC representatives' votes were harmonious. Disagreements rarely appeared. NPC's lawmaking work was highly approved by NPC representatives especially when compared with their judgments on the work of the other two legal institutions, the Supreme People's Court and the Supreme People's Procuratorate.

From the Chinese reality we could see that the disagreement and diverse opinions that suggested in Waldron's legitimation of lawmaking were rare in Chinese lawmaking. The problem, however, was not about the diversity of autonomic individuals, but rather 'individuality gets lost in the collective', a problem that discussed by Bankowski: 'The collective life took over in such a way that the individual was lost'.[13] In my previous critics of Waldron's theory I disagreed with his argument that disagreement represented nobility of legislation. As far as Chinese situation was concerned, however, absolute harmonious and consistent opinions also had problems in justifying a fair lawmaking. Either way was wrong when we considered lawmaking as an absolute disagreement or an exclusive agreement. In my opinion, Chinese lawmaking put too much emphasis on harmonious opinions. It should better absorb some of the Western democratic elements such as a hypothetical polarity opposition system. Such a 'formal' polarity oppositions could contribute to a relatively fair design of the procedure of Chinese lawmaking.

Another principle, the principle of exchange, emphasized a fair arena to present opinions and get information through the legislative process. By increasing publicity and transparency of legislative processes, people could have more time and channel to express opinions from the 'outside'. The deliberate consideration and debate stage in lawmaking was a process of exchange of information among all relevant parties. Lawmakers in a democratic system should absorb outside information and opinion to estimate the consequences of passing a bill. Externally, relevant groups also needed a platform to fully express their will. The discourse between the outside and inside system of lawmaking was thus built.

It would cost more to change a valid but unjust law, and it would denigrate the dignity of law and its maker through publishing an unjust law. Therefore it was rational to let people express their will and exchanged opinions *before* a law was made. Mr. Youde Yang's case that analyzed in Chap. 6 was an example of disobedience to an unjust law. A law related to demolition should consider Yang's opinions and requests and provide discourse channels for him. People should have channels to participate into lawmaking that concerns with their rights and interests. Otherwise, unjust

[11] Statistics from the official report of NPC http://www.npc.gov.cn/npc/zhibo/zzzb8/node_4306.htm. Accessed 02 Feb 2012.

[12] Statistics from http://www.npc.gov.cn/npc/zhibo/zzzb9/node_5826.htm. Accessed 02 Feb 2012.

[13] Zenon Bankowski. 2001. Living Lawfully-Love in Law and Law in Love. 20. Dordrecht: Kluwer.

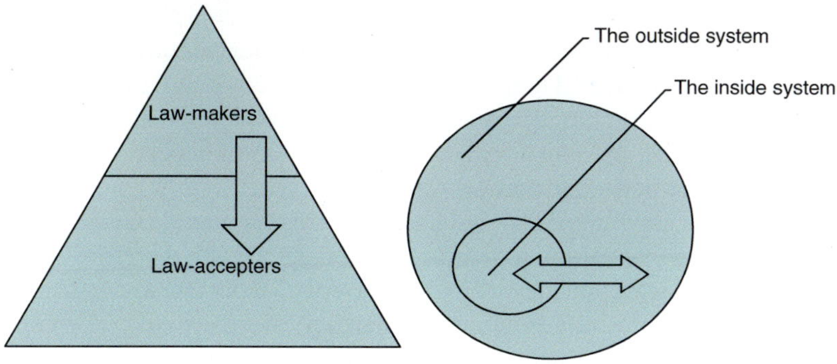

Fig. 8.3 Top-down mode and communicative mode

laws would lead to negative effects like Ms. Fuzhen Tang's case that discussed in Chap. 2. If an unjust law were obeyed, people submitted to the authority of an unjust law. They could not trust that law. People should have the right to disobey unjust laws, but the authority, legitimacy or justice that should be represented by the law became uncertain. The law would lose its dignity or efficacy in either way, so it was better to avoid these negative effects by communications *before* a law being made.

I believe that if people were given the opportunity to express and exchange their opinions, and if they participated in the procedure, they would feel respected and fairly treated. Thus they were more likely to accept the results of the procedure. For the sake of argument, it was better to divide lawmaking into two reciprocal systems: an internal system and an external one. The internal system referred to lawmakers who directly participate in lawmaking. The external system referred to those whose interests are affected by this law. In Youde Yang's case, representatives in the National People's Congress (NPC) was the internal system; while Mr. Yang and other peasants whose lands and properties were demolished was the external system. Interaction between the two systems meant that before the law of demolish being made, opinions of Yang and other related persons should be heard in the lawmaking progress.

Lawmakers as the 'internal system' should be at the same time rule-followers rather than using their position to gain a detached privileged status. Unlike the 'one-way' transmission model in Chinese legalism and Chinese Marxism, the exchange model depicted the bilateral communications between lawmakers and law-accepters. It thus was different from a commanders' law model or other one-way transmission models (Fig. 8.3).

A people-oriented lawmaking should be the purpose of a communicative thesis. The most direct way to understand people's real request, I suppose, was to listen to their discourse. But it was more than an argument for direct democracy. It was for deliberative democracy. My argument referred to the legitimacy of representativeness of lawmaking. To reframe the question, the argument for people-oriented lawmaking was about the moral ground of representativeness and democracy of lawmaking. Why representative lawmaking was legitimate? Why the majority's decisions were prior to a subject's own judgment? The four justifications in Chinese Marxism that I discussed in this book were not sufficient to offer satisfying solutions to the above questions. I believed that it was better to return to the people's real requests rather than searching for outside justifications.

How to understand people's real request in the communication? Deliberative democracy was justified when people were provided with a sufficient, equal and fair arena to discourse about their law and morality. This fair arena should be provided as the first necessary condition to realize real democracy. We therefore come to the debate of deliberative democracy against representative democracy. In Chinese ideology, the conception of representative democracy was discussed. The concept of deliberative democracy, however, did not attract public attention. It was therefore especially important for Chinese scholars to pay attention to deliberative democracy because democracy was not necessarily with representation. If we misunderstood democracy as the majority rules or the representative decision, we might ignore the deficiency of democracy.

The most prominent nineteenth-century advocate of 'government by discussion' (John Stuart Mill) was rightly considered one of the sources of deliberative democracy. But Mill preferred that this discussion be led by the better educated. It was not until the early part of the twentieth century that deliberation came to be decisively joined to democracy. In the writings of John Dewey, Alf Ross, and A. D. Lindsay, deliberation and discussion were regarded as a necessary part of democracy, or 'the essential of democracy' [66] . Jürgen Habermas provided deliberative democracy a solid foundation. His theory was based on the argument that the fundamental source of legitimacy was the collective judgment of the people. Some critics, however, complained that his conception did not adequately protect liberal values, such as freedom of religion or human rights; they criticized proceduralism in deliberative democracy. But the bond that held deliberation and democracy together was not pure proceduralism. What made deliberative democracy democratic was an expansive definition of who was included in the process of deliberation—an inclusive answer to the questions of who had the right (and effective opportunity) to deliberate or choose the deliberators, and to whom did the deliberators owe their justifications.

In *Living Lawfully*, Professor Bankowski discussed associative democracy and deliberative democracy. Associationist democracy was supposed to promote governance through democratically legitimated voluntary associations, and reducing the greatest democratic deficit—we had organizations running our lives without consent and corporate control and without representation. Representative democracy was no longer a mode of constraint or co-ordination, but rather a mode of legitimation. Representative democracy concentrated on the Rule of Law above everything else and in that sense excluded the voice of the individual.[14] So that associationalism aimed to extend liberalism.

> *Democracy should be seen as to do with communication and not necessarily with representation—all representative democracies construct, in some way, 'the represented. Thus…the*

[14] Zenon Bankowski. 2007. Bringing the Outside in: The Ethical Life of legal Institutions. Law and legal Cultures in the 21st Century: Unity and Diversity. Wolters Kluwer Polska. 193–217.

answer is a system of communicating networks, split across the public/private divide, interacting with each other and it is this which will be the foundation of co-ordination. It will enable society to be organized and goods to be delivered by voluntary associations which would be democratic and self-governing…[P]eople need others to realize themselves but it would encourage voice since entry and exit would be relatively easy. It would cope with the fact of the decentralization of political authority and the rejection of the sovereign state. It would mean more mutualism.[15]

Deliberative democracy was used to describe a mode of decision-making which privileged participation in debate or dialogue (as opposed to mere polling or casting ballots) as the desirable means for arriving at public judgment. In deliberative democracy, the collective decisions were taken in arenas where local people took part but in so doing must take into account other people in similar situations. Gutmann and Thompson, in their focus on deliberative democracy, offered a detailed diagnosis and persuasive prognosis of public debate and civic virtue. Presenting an alternative theory to the prevailing utilitarian perspective, the authors proposed a model for public policymaking that must be taken seriously by citizens and public officials alike. In *Why Deliberative Democracy*, Gutmann and Thompson discussed the characteristics of deliberative democracy [66]. Deliberative democracy affirmed the need to justify decisions made by citizens and their representatives. Both were expected to justify the laws they would impose on one another.

The first and most important characteristic of deliberative democracy, then, was its *reason-giving* requirement. In deliberative democracy, individuals were offered a fair term of cooperation. The reasons required were neither merely procedural (for example, the majority decision rule) nor purely substantive (the result promoted the greatest good for the greatest number). They were reasons that should be accepted by free and equal persons seeking fair terms of cooperation. Deliberative democracy stressed the idea that persons should be treated not merely as objects of legislation, as passive subjects, or the subjects to be ruled, but as autonomous subjects who could take part in the governance of their own society, directly or through their representatives. In deliberative democracy an important way these persons took part in to lawmaking was by presenting and responding to reasons, or by demanding that their representatives do so, with the aim of justifying the laws under which they must live together. The reasons were meant both to produce a justifiable decision and to express the value of mutual respect.

Secondly, the reasons given in the lawmaking process should be accessible to all the people to whom the rules were addressed. Rules should not be simply imposed to us. The reasons to make those rules should be comprehensible to us. It was a form of reciprocity which meant the reasons given during lawmaking should be public. In contrast to Rousseau's conception of democracy, in which individuals reflected on their own on what was right for the society as a whole, and then came to the assembly and voted in accordance with the general will, deliberative democracy happened in public through open discussion and dialogues among individuals.

[15] Ibid.

Thirdly, deliberative democracy made a dynamic and continuing dialogue possible. It meant individuals did care as much about what happened after a decision was made as to what happened before. The decision-making process was therefore open. It was different with the classical social contract theory which denied 'afterwards changes'. It admitted that some results of lawmaking were imperfect and could be changed in the future, if we would realize their defects in the future. We therefore understood that the decisions we made today might be wrong tomorrow, and the decisions appeared most sound at the time might appear less justifiable in light of later evidence. We should remind ourselves that decisions justified by the majority rules were not all consensual. Those who disagreed with the decision accepted the majority's decision. But we should tolerate this possibility: if they want, they should have a chance to reverse or modify it in the future, by persuading the majority to join their camp.

Therefore in deliberative democracy, lawmaking should not be an exclusive top-down and irreversible official procedure, but a fair arena for exchanging opinions. In China's context, it meant the weakest group, the 150 million poor population should have a channel to request their rights; the majority of the Chinese population, 900 million peasants should discuss their opinions in the lawmaking procedures; the 95 million industrial workers at the production line and 145 million peasant-labors in the cities should be able to choose their peer representatives to discuss their requests at the congress.[16] The strict unchangeable social contract in the Chinese context could only be justified to the real will of the 'contemporary' people, if the deliberative democracy could be accepted in Chinese lawmaking. People's autonomy could make the second justification, i.e., the people's congress, a reasonable legitimation of Chinese lawmaking.

An opposite argument, however, was that the common people were not as good as the elite in self-government because common people had a lower degree of education, lacked financial support, and had deficient ability to make decisions. A famous argument 'political tutelage' was made by Dr. Yat-sen Sun, (or Zhongshan Sun, the Father of the Republic of China 1912–1949) in the *Constructive Scheme for the Country* in 1924. In Article 5, the constructive scheme was divided to three stages: military administration; governmental tutelage; and constitutionalism. In the military administration period, the task of the government was to unite China. The political tutelage in Sun's theory was a temporary stage. During this period, the government needed to train the people of the Qing Dynasty to be the owner of Mingguo, a new China. When people understood democracy and could practice autonomy, the society came to the last period, the era of constitutionalism. According to this theory, people needed to be trained to be democratic. This argument was alien to Western democratic theorists. However, in a state that paternalism and monarchy had the absolute authority for several 1,000 years, democracy was also a

[16] Statistics of the poor, peasants and peasant-labors see data resources in chapter 2. Statistics of the industrial workers were from Peilin Li etc. 2002. An Investigation of Contemporary Social Class Classification and Structure Advanced Research of Xiaoping Deng Theory Report No.2. Beijing: Social Science Academic Press.

totally new life style. It was an enlightenment era in China. The Chinese needed to learn to make their own decisions without asking permissions of their patriarch, the emperor or officials. In Sun's theory, the implied authorized lawmaking power was returnable since the tutelage period was temporary.

The people's genuine thoughts might not be rational—I suppose this was the major reason of Dr. Sun's theory of political tutelage. My point was, if people were provided with the fair arena of discourse, their genuine thoughts could be rational. If I were born in a closed environment and had no chance to learn the benefits of education, I probably might not vote for education. But if I lived in a more open environment and could compare the two systems basing on my own experience, I could make a more rational decision.

However, a common person did not have such an open and fair arena to compare different choices because he was already assimilated by the system where he stayed in. And it would be difficult for him to jump out of the system and make a rational and objective decision concerning other choices. But if he were provided with the fair arena, the results might be different. However, in the beginning of new China it was difficult to persuade subjects of Empire Qing to vote for democracy. Dr. Sun's Tutelage theory was rational because at that time China lacked the fair arena and it was necessary to teach the subjects what democracy was about at that time. It did not mean political tutelage was right; it was just rational.

In the conclusion of this chapter I would like to return to Confucianism to search for independent values of lawmaking. Lawmaking should not be a plain fact of authority and procedures. It should contribute to the independent values of law, law as justice, rather than a plain fact of coercion and control. Here I came back to the independent value in Confucianism, the humanity (*Ren*). I believed it was an appropriate conception in Chinese philosophy that could contribute to the thesis of lawmaking. *Ren* (loving the people), was the core of Confucianism. It was not about God's love to the people or vice versa, but the love among people. Loving people means we should take the responsibility of our treatments to other people. *Ji Suo Bu Yu, Wu Shi Yu Ren* (do unto others as you would be done by; do not impose on others; treat others in the same way as you would like to be treated), was the guidance for practice *Ren*, the humanity.[17] If we took this humanity value seriously, the difficulties of justifying Chinese lawmaking could be solved.

The reality, however, was much complex than practicing a few principles. It was difficult or even impossible for the poor to 'represent' the successful persons to make decisions. An opposite argument might be that the elite and successful persons would help the poor, like Bernard Mandeville argued in *The Fable of the Bees or Private Vices* (1732). Or in Confucianism, the elite and successful persons were justified as 'good' persons. However, the plain fact of the contribution of the elite in *The Fable of the Bees*, or the far-fetched connection between success and morality in Confucianism, were different from the principle of 'peer treatment'. For example, a middle class lawmaker might lack understanding of the urgency of curbing housing prices because to him the rising price could bring profits of the whole

[17] The Analects of Confucius, Book XII and XV.

nation. He with other middle class lawmakers overruled the bill of restricting the price of the property. Poor persons had to struggle to buy or rent a place to live. In this case, the middle class lawmaker's 'goodwill' might cause a disaster to the poor. Peer treatments therefore only existed when lawmakers were representing the social class they belonged to. Representativeness should be interpreted under this pre-condition. The value of humanity, and people-oriented lawmaking required that people were able to speak for themselves, and their discourses were seriously treated. The value of humanity should be safeguarded by law rather than rely on the rich persons conscience.

Our contemporary legal system is supposed to provide people a fair arena for exchanging discourses. People should make their own choices, which are rational and could be right at the same time. Now it is a best period for China to set up this fair arena since science and technology are changing with each passing day, and communication among different cultures becomes easier and quicker. With the support of communication techniques, we should cherish people's autonomy. Therefore the period of political tutelage should come to an end. People's rational discourses would contribute to both the rationality and justice of Chinese lawmaking.

Appendix 1

P H's Living expenses at W city in China and E city in the U.K. (average cost in 2005–2008)

1,500 unit income per month	W		E	
	Cost	Cost/income %	Cost	Cost/income %
Rent/month for a two bedroom flat	800	53.33	650	43.33
A McDonald meal	21	1.40	7	0.47
A 8 in. birthday cake	120	8.00	15	1.00
A Nike T-shirt	500	33.33	50	3.33
A local brand T-shirt	100	6.67	20	1.33
A train ticket (for same distance)	200	13.33	90	6
A flight ticket (for local; same distance)	300	20.00	100	6.67
Flight tickets (China-UK return)	7200	480.00	450	30.00
One drink	30	2.00	3	0.20
Medical treatment	10,000 (for cancer treatments in hospital for 1 month)	667.00	Free	0.00
Coffee	20	1.33	2	0.13
Tea	15	1.00	2	0.13
Film	80	5.33	6	0.40
3D film	200	13.33	10	0.67
Hotel (double room/per night)	200		80	5.33
Museum	50	3.33	Most free	0.00
Natural scenery	50	3.33	Most free	0.00
Cultural sights	50	3.33	Most free	0.00
Gallery	Free	0.00	12	0.80

(continued)

P. He, *Chinese Lawmaking: From Non-communicative to Communicative*, Understanding China, DOI 10.1007/978-3-642-39507-9, © Springer-Verlag Berlin Heidelberg 2014

(continued)

1,500 unit income per month	W		E	
	Cost	Cost/income %	Cost	Cost/income %
Concert/musicale	400	26.67	40	2.67
Price of a house/flat	7,000/m^2	466.67	1,000/m^2	66.67
Car (same configuration)	30,000	2,000.00	10,000	666.67
TV (local brand)	3,000	200.00	300	20.00
College fees per year (for locals)	10,000	666.67	3,000	200.00
1,500 unit income per month	Cost	Cost/income %	Cost	Cost/income %

Appendix 2

The official position and occupation of the 11th NPC representatives (from major provincial groups)

	An Hui	He Nan	Jiang Su	Shan Dong	Hu Bei	Hu Nan	Beijing
Total	114	161	96	181	124	118	58
Official	71	104	46	149	88	51	29
%	62.28	65.00	47.92	82.32	70.97	43.22	50.00
Businessman	35	36	29	27	23	45	7
%	30.70	22.36	30.21	14.92	18.55	38.14	12.69
Scholars	7	11	12	3	4	5	14
%	6.14	6.83	12.50	1.66	3.23	4.24	24.14
Workers	1	1	5	0	5	1	2
%	0.87	0.62	5.21	0	4.03	0.85	3.45
Peasants	0	2	0	0	2	0	0
%	0	1.24	0	0	1.61	0	0
Other	0	7	4	2	2	16	6
%	0	4.35	4.2	1.10	1.61	13.56	10.34
Male	83	130	63	166	96	91	43
%	72.81	80.75	65.63	91.71	77.42	77.12	74.14
Female	31	31	33	15	28	27	15
%	27.19	19.25	34.38	8.29	22.58	22.88	25.86

P. He, *Chinese Lawmaking: From Non-communicative to Communicative*, Understanding China, DOI 10.1007/978-3-642-39507-9, © Springer-Verlag Berlin Heidelberg 2014

Bibliography

1. Anderson, J.S. 1992. *Lawyers and the making of English land law 1832–1940*. Oxford: Oxford University Press.
2. Anliang, G. 1993. *Li Fa Xue (a study of lawmaking)*. Beijing: Law Press.
3. Anyi, L., and L. Yingtian. 2006. Common prosperity is not only an economic concept: A study of the content and realization of common prosperity. *Theoretical Investigation* 6: 52–55.
4. Ashley, D., and D.M. Orenstein. 2005. *Sociological theory: Classical statements*. Boston: Pearson Education.
5. Ashton, B. 1984. Famine in China 1958–1961. *Population and Development Review* 10: 4.
6. Austin, J., and W.E. Rumble. 1995. *The province of jurisprudence determined*. Cambridge: Cambridge University Press.
7. Balkin, J.M. 1987. Deconstructive practice and legal theory. *The Yale Law Journal* 96: 743–786.
8. Bankowski, Z. 2001. *Living lawfully—love in law and law in love*. Dordrecht: Kluwer.
9. Bankowski, Z. 2007. Bringing the outside in: The ethical life of legal Institutions. In *Law and legal cultures in the 21st century: Unity and diversity*. Warsaw: Wolters Kluwer Polska.
10. Bentham, J. 1843. *Deontology or science of morality*. London: Longman, Rees, Orme, Browne, Green, and Longman.
11. Bentham, J. 1871. *The theory of legislation*. London: Trübner.
12. Bentham, J. 1948. *An introduction to the principles of morals and legislation*. New York: Hafner Publishing.
13. Bentham, J., and J. Harris. 1998. *Legislator of the world: Writings on codification, law and education*. Oxford: Clarendon Press.
14. Bifei, Z. 2009. Expecting electronic voting in 'Two Congresses'. *People's Congress Studying* 4: 37–38.
15. Bin, W. 1995. The market economic legal system is becoming complete. *Legal Daily,* October 19, Beijing.
16. Binder, S.A. 1997. *Minority rights majority rule: Partisanship and the development of congress*. Cambridge: Cambridge University Press.
17. Biyao, T. 2008. The development of voting witness democracy. *Guidance for Citizens* 2: 52–53.
18. Bodansky, D. 1999. The legitimacy of international governance. *The American Journal of International Law* 93: 596–624.
19. Bodenheimer, E. 2006. *Jurisprudence. The philosophy and method of the Law*. Cambridge, MA: Harvard University Press.
20. Bowring, J. 1995. *The works of Jeremy Bentham*. Bristol: Thoemmes Press.
21. Bozan, J. 1999. *History of Qin and Han Dynasties*. Beijing: Beijing University Press.

P. He, *Chinese Lawmaking: From Non-communicative to Communicative*, Understanding China, DOI 10.1007/978-3-642-39507-9, © Springer-Verlag Berlin Heidelberg 2014

22. Bracher, M., and W.K. Buckley. 1986. Reader-response theory. *Publications of the Modern Language Association of America* 101: 250–251.
23. Buergenthal, T. 1969. *Law-making in the international civil aviation organization*. Syracuse: Syracuse University Press.
24. Cane, P. 2009. *The hart-fuller debate*. Oxford: Hart Publishing.
25. Chang, W. 2009. On the Chinese legal belief. *Inner Mongolia Social Sciences* 30: 2–4.
26. Chaohui, J. 2006. The principle of justice in a socialistic harmonious society. *Studies of Theories of Mao Zedong and Deng Xiaoping* 3: 41–46.
27. Chunhai, T. 2003. A thought about increasing Gini coefficient in China. *Jiangxi Social Sciences* 3: 183–185.
28. Chunjiao, Q. 1994. Deng Xiaoping's arguments for common prosperity and against polarization. *Journal of China Youth University for Political Science* 4: 1–5.
29. Chuntian, J. 2007. *A study on contemporary Chinese social transformation and legislative transformation*. Beijing: East China University of Political Science and Law.
30. Chunxia, G. 2010. The supply of the rural public goods and the choice of farm land system. Ph.D. thesis, HuaZhong University of Science and Techology.
31. Confucius. 2004. The analects of Confucius. Shandong: Qi Lu Press.
32. The Law Committee of the Standing Committee of the National People's Congress. 2008. *Statistics of lawmaking of the People's Republic of China*. Bejing: Chinese Democracy and Rule of Law Publishing House.
33. Cotterell, R. 1992. *The politics of jurisprudence: A critical introduction to legal philosophy*. Philadelphia: University of Pennsylvania Press.
34. Daming, G. 2001. On the first issue of the communist party of China's proposition to the current political situation. *Journal of Guizhou Normal University (Social Science)* 4: 75–78.
35. Dershowitz, A.M. 2008. *Is there a right to remain silent?* New York: Oxford University Press.
36. Dicey, A.V. 1915. *Introduction to the study of the Law of the constitution*. New York: The Macmillan Company.
37. Dicey, A.V. 2005. *Introduction to the study of the Law of the constitution*. Boston: Adament Media Corporation.
38. Dickinson, M. 2009. Food Fumble, The Wall Street Journal Asia. March 3.
39. Dietrich, J. 2001. Classifying precontractual liability: A comparative analysis. *Legal Study* 21: 153–191.
40. Duanhong, C. 1998. Democratic legitimacy and supremacy of legislation-critiques on Chinese legislation. *Peking University Law Journal* 6: 59–69.
41. Dworkin, R. 1977. *Taking rights seriously*. Cambridge: Harvard University Press.
42. Dworkin, R. 1977. *The philosophy of Law*. Oxford: Oxford University Press.
43. Farwell, H.W. 1988. *The majority rules: A manual of procedure for most groups*. Pueblo: High Publishers.
44. Feizi, H. 1996. *Literatures of historical Chinese legal thoughts*. Beijing: Law Press.
45. Fengge, S. 2008. Pre-Qin Chinese legalism and its influences to posterity. *Journal of XinXiang University* 22: 21–24.
46. Finins, J. 1980. *Natural law and natural rights*. Oxford: Clarendon Press.
47. Floyd, C.R. 1898. *The science of law and law making*. London: Macmillan.
48. Franklin, J.H., and J. Bodin. 1992. *On sovereignty: Four chapters from the six books of the commonwealth*. Cambridge: Cambridge University Press.
49. Freeman, M.D.A. 2001. Marxist theories of law and state. In *Lloyd's introduction to jurisprudence*. London: Sweet and Maxwell Ltd.
50. Freeman, R.E., and A.C. Wicks. 1998. Organization studies and the new pragmatism: Positivism, anti-positivism, and the search for ethics. *Organization Science* 9: 123–140.
51. Fuguo, W., and S. Qixiang. 2003. On the deficiencies and contributing factors of the current 'Pan-Legalism' trend of thought. *Journal of Fujian Education Institute* 4: 79–81.
52. Fuller, L. 1958. Positivism and fidelity to law-a reply to Professor Hart. *Harvard Law Review* 71(4): 630–672.

53. Fuller, L. 1969. *The morality of law*. New Haven: Yale University.
54. Fuming, H. 1978. Practice is the sole criterion for testing truth. *Guangming Daily*, May 11.
55. Gang, C. 2002. The legitimacy of legislation and its rationalization. *Journal of Remin University of China* 4: 85–90.
56. Gang, C. 2003. Royal legislation and its moral limits: A look at the orthodoxy of legislation in history. *Ethics Research* 2: 58–62.
57. Garner, R.T., and B. Rosen. 1967. *Moral philosophy: A systematic introduction to normative ethics and meta-ethics*. New York: Macmillan.
58. Gongquan, X. 2005. *History of Chinese political thoughts*. Beijing: New Star Press.
59. Gu, B. 1962. *Chronicles of the Han dynasty*. Beijing: Zhonghua Book Company Press.
60. Guanghui, W. 1996. The basic principles of local lawmaking. *Studies in Law and Business* 6: 81–85.
61. Guanglin, Y. 2004. A retrospect and analysis of the development trend of the ethical legislation of China in recent year. *Legal Front* 3: 16–18.
62. Guodong, X. 2009. *Humanistic spirit of civil law*. Beijing: Law Press.
63. Guoming, D. 2008. Legislative studies of quality and safety of agricultural products. *Hebei Law Science* 26: 07–111.
64. Guozhong, Z. 2002. The Chinese rich people evade to taxation. *Finance and Economy* 9: 9–10.
65. Gutmann, A., and D. Thompson. 1998. *Democracy and disagreement*. Cambridge, MA: Belknap Press of Harvard University Press.
66. Gutmann, A., and D. Thompson. 2004. *Why deliberative democracy?* Princeton: Princeton University Press.
67. Guye, Z. 2006. Criticisms on the three arcitles of Guan Zi. *Social Science Front Bimonthly* 5: 143–148.
68. Habermas, J. 1984. *The theory of communictative action*. Boston: Beacon Press.
69. Haichao Z. (stated) and Hui, L. (recorded). 2009. The truth of my chest. Shangjie Chengxiang Zhifu 9: 30–32.
70. Hairen, H. 2007. The enemy of the legalists in Pre-Qin Era: The normative theory on ruling the country through the Law. *Tribune of Political Science and Law* 25: 36–50.
71. Handong, W. 2008. *General theories of law*. Beijing: Beijing University Press.
72. Hao, Z., W. Nan, and W. Deqiang. 2009. A study of peasant-labors occupational diseases reality and legal protections. *Legal System and Social Society* 10: 346–347.
73. Harkin, P. 2005. The reception of reader-response theory. *College Composition and Communication* 56: 410–425.
74. Hart, H.L.A. 1970. *Of laws in general*. London: Athlone Press.
75. Hart, H.L.A. 1958. Positivism and the separation of law and morals. *Harvard Law Review* 71: 593–629.
76. Hart, H.L.A. 1994. *The concept of law*. Oxford: Clarendon Press.
77. Hayek, F. 1944. *The road to serfom*. London: Routledge.
78. Hayek, F. 1960. *Constitution of liberty*. Chicago: University of Chicago Press.
79. Hayek, F. 1982. *Law, legislation and liberty*. London: Routledge & Kegan Paul.
80. Hayek, F. 1988. *The fatal conceit: The errors of socialism*. London/New York: Routledge.
81. Hayek, F., and J. Birner. 1994. *Co-ordination and evolution*. London: Routledge.
82. Hayek, F., and S. Horwitz. 2005. Austrian economist. *Journal of the History of Economic Thought* 27: 71–85.
83. Hegao, Y. 2000. *History of Chinese legal thoughts*. Beijing: Beijing University.
84. Hehai, L., and L. Yufu. 2001. *A study of lawmaking*. Beijing: Zhongguo Jiancha Publishing House.
85. Hirst, P. 1994. *Associative democracy*. London: Polity Press.
86. Hobbes, T., and A. Martinich. 2002. *Leviathan*. Toronto: Broadview Press.
87. Hongbiao, Liu, and Zhongping Chen. 2003. Rearch on the forming process of theories of the road of village surrounding the city. *Journal of Chongqing University (Social Science)* 4: 67–70.

88. Honglie, Y. 2004. *History of Chinese legal ideology*. Beijing: China University of Political Science and Law Press.
89. Hongyi, C. 2002. Introspect of legalists (Fajia) thoughts. *China and Western Legal Traditions* 2: 108–135.
90. Hui, X. 1997. *The idea and basis of the faith in legal theory*. Shandong: Shandong People Press.
91. Ingram, A. 1994. A political theory of rights. Oxford Scholarship Online. http://www.oxford-scholarship.com/view/10.1093/0198279639.001.0001/acprof-9780198279631 Accessed Feb 2, 2012.
92. James, M.H. 1973. *Bentham and legal theory*. Belfast: Northern Ireland Legal Quarterly.
93. Jiacong, H. 1995. *A new study on Guanzi*. Beijing: China Social Science Press.
94. Jian, H. 2003. The origin of death penalty of China. *Journal of Political Science and Law* 2: 37–40.
95. Jianfei, L. 1992. *A study of lawmaking*. Chongqing: Chongqing publishing house.
96. Jiang, Y., Biao, T. and Zhiyong X. (2003). A proposal on constitutional review of the administrative measures of accept and dismiss vagrants and beggars with no means of support in cities 1982. *Nanfang Daily,* May 17.
97. Jianshun, Y. 2008. On the legitimacy of legislation of economic regulations. *Jurist Review* 5: 48–59.
98. Jinzhao, C. 2003. *The rule of law and legal methodology*. Shandong: Shandong People's Publishing House.
99. Jin, Z. 2009. Statistical indicators of the current effective nation legislation. *Journal of Comparative Law* 5: 147–160.
100. Jingli, W. 2008. A study on the new scheme of individual income Tax. *Economics and Trade Update* 15: 61.
101. Jingsong, J. 2004. Discussion of the representativeness of the standing committee of the national People's congress. *Tribune of Political Science and Law* 6: 18–30.
102. Jingsong, J. 2004. Discussion of the representativeness of the standing committee of the national People's congress. *Tribune of Political Science and Law* 6: 25.
103. Jingtao, H. 2007. The report to the 17th CPC national congress. http://news.xinhuanet.com/newscenter/2007-10/24/content_6938568.htm. Accessed 02 Feb 2012.
104. Jinxue, F. 1997. A study of the trust crisis of law and the rule of law in China. *Shandong: Journal of Shandong Social Science* 6: 48–51.
105. Junhao, D., Luesi, G., and Deming, O. 2005. BCG Chinese wealth markets. http://www.bcg.com.cn/cn/files/publications/reports_pdf/Wealth__Markets_China__Dec2005.pdf. Acessed February 2, 2012.
106. Jun, Y. 1999. The introduction of the cost-benefit ratio of law. *Journal of Gansu Social Science* 5: 62–72.
107. Junguo, Z. 2009. A criticism of belief in law. *Journal of Liaoning Administration College* 1: 32–33.
108. Junxian, F. 2009. Suggestions on intensifying tax collection and management of the high income group. *Chinese Enterprise Accounting of Villages and Towns* 4: 66–67.
109. Kant, I. 1780. The metaphysical elements of ethics. http://philosophy.eserver.org/kant/metaphys-elements-of-ethics.txt. Accessed February 2, 2012.
110. Kelsen, H. 1941. The pure theory of law and analytical jurisprudence. *Harvard Law Review* 55: 44–70.
111. Kelsen, H. 1946. *General theory of law and state*. Cambridge: Harvard University Press.
112. Kelsen, H. 2005. *Pure theory of law*. Clark: The Law Book Exchange.
113. Keyu, Q., and W. Xinyao. 1992. *A study of lawmaking*. Beijing: China University of Political Science and Law.
114. Kley, P. 1994. *Hayek's social and political thought*. Oxford: Oxford University Press.
115. Kohlberg, L. 1981. *Essays on moral development*. New York: Harper & Row.
116. Kui, Z., and W. Zuxia. 2009. Measurement and control of income inequality and polarization. *Statistical Research* 26: 76–80.

117. Laigui, F. 2008. From the localization of Marxism in China to Chinese Marxism-the transformation of the research visual angle and the transfer of the focal point of research. *Journal of Shangrao Normal College* 4: 1.
118. Laiqing, W. 2010. The rise and decline of the first people's communes. *Centuries Appearance* 1: 35.
119. Linfu, L. 1983. *Six codes of tang dynasty (Tang Liu Dian)*. Beijing: Zhonghua Book Company.
120. Liangshu, Z. 1989. *Shang Yang and his school*. Shanghai: Shang Hai Ancient Books Publishing House.
121. Liaoyuan, C. 2008. New legalism and new legalists of late Qing dynasty. *China Legal Science* 5: 30–45.
122. Lijuan, Y. 2004. The relation of legislative competence between national People's congress and its standing committee. *Journal of Guangxi Administrative Cadre Institute of Politics and Law* 19: 44.
123. Lin, L. 1991. *A comparative study on legislatures*. Beijing: People Daily Press.
124. Lin, L. 2005. Insist to and complete the session system of the national People's congress. *Theoretical Trends* 3: 8–18.
125. Lin, L. 2005. *Theory and system of lawmaking (Li Fa Li Lun Yu Zhi Du)*. Beijing: China Legal Publishing House.
126. Lin Y. 2005. A Comparative Study of Pre-Qin Legalism. Ph.D. dissertation of Zhe Jiang University.
127. Lingjie, F.Z.M. 2006. New explanations and test to Sen's entitlements: evidence from China. *Economic Studies* 8: 104–113.
128. Liqun, Z. 2008. The cultural self-realization of Marxists in May fourth Era. *Journal of Shengli College China University of Petroleum* 1: 30–32.
129. Liyu, Z., and Z. Shuguang. 2001. *A study of lawmaking*. (Li Fa Xue) Beijing: China Remin University Press.
130. Locke, J. 1991. *Two treatises of government*. Cambridge: Cambridge University Press.
131. Luoke, Y. 1967. On parentage. Shou Du: Zhong Xue Wen Ge Bao Press, 1.
132. Alasdair, MacIntyre. 1981. *After virtue*. Notre Dame: Notre Dame University Press.
133. Maine, H. 1861. *Ancient law*. London: John Murray.
134. Maitland, F.W., and F.C. Montague. 1915. *A sketch of English legal history*. New York: G.P.Putnam's sons.
135. Maqian, S. 2008. *Historical records (Shi Ji)*. Shenyang: Volumes Publishing Company.
136. Meisner, M. 1999. *Mao's China and after*. New York: The Free Press.
137. Mencius. 2002. *Meng Zi*. Zhuhai: Zhu Hai Publishing House.
138. Mendes, C.H. 2009. Is it all about the last word? deliberative separation of powers 1. *Legisprudence* 1: 69–110.
139. Mengqing, L. 2009. A study of Deng Xiaoping's theory and the practice of common prosperity. *Academic Forum* 3: 5–8.
140. Michelon, C. 2006. *Being apart from reasons: The role of reasons in public and private moral decision-making*. Dordrecht: Springer.
141. Mill, John Stuart. 1906. *Utilitarianism*. Chicago: University of Chicago Press.
142. Min, N., and J. Jie. 2008. The legislative study on the law on protecting against weather disasters. *Future and Development* 29: 45–47.
143. Molivas, G.I. 1997. The influence of utilitarianism on natural rights doctrines. *Utilitas* 9: 183–202.
144. Muyu, X. 2006. Why the Chinese rich people are not benevolent? *Government Legality* 13: 21.
145. Na, Y. Difficulties and solutions of Chinese 'Belief in Law' Theories. MA thesis of Chongqing University (Law School).
146. Nan, S. 2000. *Aspects of the Chinese culture of legalism*. Shandong: Qilu Book Press.
147. Needham, J. 1980. History of scientific thought. In *Science and civilization in China*. Cambridge: The Syndics of the Cambridge University Press.
148. Oliver, I. 1983. The 'Old' and the 'New' hermeneutic in sociological theory. *The Brithish Journal of Sociology* 34: 519–553.

149. Parekh, B. 1993. *Jeremy Bentham: Critical assessments*. London: Routledge.
150. Peilin, L. 2002. An Investigation of Contemporary Social Class Classification and Structure. Advanced Research of Deng Xiaoping Theory Report. Beijing: Social Science Academic Press.
151. Peizhao, H. 2003. Common prosperity and virtuous polarization in wealth. *Theory Front* 22: 27–29.
152. Peizhao, H. 2007. Common prosperity and virtuous polarization in wealth. *Theory Front* 22: 27–29.
153. Peng, H. 2011. Chinese legalism and western legalism. *Frontiers of Law in China* 6: 645–670. Higher Education Press and Springer.
154. Peng, H. 2009. The father of the republican constitution and the shattered dream of establishing constitutionalism in the Republic of China. *Chinese and Western Legal Traditions* 7: 530–542.
155. Peng, H. 2005. The constitutional thoughts, efforts and fate of Carsun Chang. MA thesis of Zhongnan University of Economics and Law (Law School).
156. Peng, X.Z. 1987. Demographic consequences of the great leap forward in China's provinces. *Population and Development Review* 13: 639–670.
157. Perju, V. 2009. A comment on legisprudence. *Boston University Law Review* 89: 428.
158. Pound, R. 1959. *Jurisprudence*. St. Paul: West Publishing.
159. Qiao, Z. 2009. Expose the inside story of official appraisal for occupational diseases. *Law and Life* 19: 35.
160. Qichao, L. 2003. *Political ideology of Pre-Qin period*. Tianjing: Tianjing Ancient Books Publishing House.
161. Qichao, L. 2004. *Legal works of Liang Qichao (Liang Qichao Fa Xue Wen Ji)*. Beijing: China University of Political Science and Law.
162. Qichao, L. 1998. *Biography of Guanzi (Guan Zi Zhuan)*. Shanghai: East China Normal University Press.
163. Qigang, W. 2006. *Theory and practice of lawmaking (Li Fa Li Lun Yu Shi Jian)*. Beijing: Beijing University Press.
164. Qilin, F. 1997. *The real estate Law*. Beijing: Law Press.
165. Qingzhu, G. 2009. A constitutional consideration of the occupation structure of the NPC-a case study of a Xinjiang event of prohibition of official representatives. *People's Congress Studying* 6: 11–15.
166. Quan, T., and Z. Xinning. 2004. The possibility of abolishing the prohibition of fireworks in Beijing. *Engineering Blasting* 3: 86–89.
167. Rawls, J. 1971. *A theory of justice*. Cambridge: Harvard University Press.
168. Rawls, J. 1993. The law of peoples. *Critical Inquiry* 20: 363–368.
169. Raz, J. 1979. *The authority of law: essays on law and morality*. Oxford: Oxford University Press.
170. Roderick, M., and King F. John. 1991. *The Cambridge history of China: The People's republic part 2: Revolutions within the Chinese revolution 1966–1982*. Cambridge: Cambridge University Press.
171. Ronggen, Y. 2000. *History of Chinese legal thoughts*. Beijing: Law Press.
172. Rosenfeld, M., and A. Arato. 1998. *Habermas on law and democracy: Critical exchanges*. Berkeley: Univerisity of California Press.
173. Ross, H. 2001. *Law as a social institution*. Oxford and Portland: Hart Publishing.
174. Rousseau, J. 1968. *The social contract*. New York: Penguin Classics.
175. Rummer, R.J. 1991. *China's bloody century: Genocide and mass murder since 1900*. New Brunswik: Transaction Publishers.
176. Sandel, Michael. 1982. *Liberalism and the limits of justice*. New York: Cambridge University Press.
177. Sandel, Michael. 1984. *Liberalism and its critics*. Oxford: Basil Blackwell.
178. Sandel, Michael. 1984. The procedural republic and the unencumbered self. *Political Theory* 12: 81–96.
179. The Law Committee of the Standing Committee of the National People's Congress. 2008. *Statistics of legislation of People's Republic of China*. Beijing: Chinese Democracy and Rule of Law Publishing House.

180. Shaoqun, H., and L. Hong. 2008. The comment on Mao Zedong's theory and practice of the countryside encircling the cities. *Journal of China Executive Leadership Acadmy Jinggangshan* 1: 76–84.
181. Shao, L. 1989. *Biography of historical figures in Si Bu Cong Kan. (Ren Wu Zhi. Si Bu Cong Kan)*. Shanghai: Shanghai Book Store Publishing.
182. Shearmur, J. 1996. *Hayek and after: Hayekian liberalism as a research programme*. London/New York: Routledge.
183. Shihu, H., and H. Haofei. 2001. Legalization of morality: An important means in current moral construction. *Changbai Journal* 3: 38–41.
184. Shiqun, Y. 1999. Further discussion on rule-by-law in Chinese legalism: A reply to Wu Shuchen. *Journal of the East China University of Politics and Law* 2: 50–54.
185. Shiwei, Z. 2008. The effects of the public policy relating to the recent real estate fever. *Ningxia: Social Sciences in Ningxia* 1: 13–15.
186. Shklar, J.N. 1986. *Legalism, law, morals and political trials*. Cambridge: Harvard University Press.
187. Shuchen, W. 1998. Discussion on rule-of-law in Chinese legalism: A reply to Yang Shiqun. *Journal of the East China University of Politics and Law* 1: 54–63.
188. Shuchen, W., and L. Li. 1998. *Chinese legalism and its spirits*. Beijing: China Radio and Television Publishing House.
189. Shude, C. 1927. *Laws of nine dynasties*. Beijing: Zhonghua Book Company.
190. Shuqin, W. 2007. The moral legitimacy of the legal analyzed in terms of philosophy of Law. *Philosophy Trends* 9: 16–21.
191. Simian, L. 1997. *Ten courses on history of Chinese political thoughts*. Shanghai: East China Normal University Press.
192. Skorupski, J. 2006. Welfare and self-governance. *Ethical Theory and Moral Practic* 9: 289–309.
193. Smart, J.J.C. 1956. Extreme and restricted utilitarianism. *The Philosophical Quarterly* 6: 344–354.
194. Song, W. 2001. *Revised edition of Liang Qichao's works (Ying Bing Shi Wen Ji Dian Jiao)*. Yunnan: Yunnan Education Press.
195. Standen, J.A. 1986. Critical legal studies as an anti-positivist phenomenon. *Virginia Law Review* 72: 983–988.
196. Stoner, J.R. 1994. *Common law and liberal theory: Coke, Hobbes and the origins of American constitutionalism*. Lawrence: University Press of Kansas.
197. Summers, R.S. 1974. Evaluating and improving legal process-a plea for process values. *Cornell Law Review* 60: 1–52.
198. Tamanaha, B.Z. 2004. *On the rule of Law*. Cambrdige: Cambridge University Press.
199. Tao, Y. 2008. New Lawyers Law and the Hidden Rules. Xinjing News. June 02.
200. Tatsukichi, M. 2003. *Public law and private law*. Beijing: China University of Political Science and Law Press.
201. Charles, Taylor. 1990. *Sources of the self*. Cambridge: Cambridge University Press.
202. Teng, P. 2007. Research on the recent problems of polarization of China. *Lanzhou: Journal of Lanzhou Commercial College* 23: 20–25.
203. Touchie, J.C.W. 2005. *Hayek and human rights*. Northampton: Edward Elgar Publishing.
204. Toynbee, A.J., and D.C. Somervell. 1957. *A study of history*. London: Oxford University Press.
205. Tyler, T.R. 2004. *Procedural justice*. Hampshire: Ashgate.
206. Wailu, H. 1947. *History of Chinese thoughts*. Shanghai: Sheng Huo Bookstore Press.
207. Waldron, J. 1999. *The dignity of legislation*. Cambridge: Cambridge University Press.
208. Waldron, J. 1999. *Law and disagreement*. Oxford: The Clarendon Press.
209. Walker, L. 1975. *Procedural justice: A psychological analysis*. New York: L. Erlbaum Associates.
210. Wangsheng, Z. 1988. *A study of Chinese lawmaking (Li Fa Xue)*. Beijing: Beijing University Press.
211. Wangsheng, Z. 1988. To set up a study on Chinese socialistic lawmaking. *Law Review (Chinese)* 6: 21–26.

212. Wangsheng, Z. 1994. *On legislation*. Beijing: Beijing University Press.
213. Wangsheng, Z. 2000. 50 years lawmaking of China 1949–1999. *Legislation Review of China* 1: 1–22.
214. Wangsheng, Z. 2006. *A study of lawmaking (Li Fa Xue)*. Beijing: Law Press.
215. Wanyi, Z., and H. Dawu. 2008. A study of legislation of protection of credit right. *Modern Law Science* 30: 165–171.
216. Wenhua, L. 1999. Economic laws are the result of the thought of economic reform. *Juridical Science Journal* 2: 4–5.
217. Wenyi, H. 2008. *Li Fa Xue*. Beijing: High Education Press.
218. Wilson, B.P., and K. Masugi. 1997. *The supreme court and American constitutionalism*. Lanham: Rowman & Littlefield.
219. Wintgens, L.J. 2002. *Legisprudence: A new theoretical approach to legislation*. Oxford/Portland: Hart Publishing.
220. Wintgens, L.J. 2005. *The theory and practice of legislation-essays in legisprudence*. Aldershot/Hants/England/Burlington: Ashgate.
221. Wintgens, L.J. 2007. *Legislation in context: Essays in legisprudence*. Aldershot: Ashgate Publishing Limited.
222. Wintgens, L.J. 2008. Legisprudence as a new theory of legislation. *Journal of Comparative Law* 4: 144–160.
223. Wintgems, L.J. 2009. Freedom and legisprudence-a more substantial view: A reply to Professor Perju. *Boston University Law Review* 89: 1795–1805.
224. Whittington, Keith E. 2000. In defense of legislatures. *Political Theory* 28: 690–702.
225. Xiaohong, M. 2004. *Rite and law (Li and Fa)*. Beijing: Peking University Press.
226. Xiaoming, D. 2009. A study on lawmaking of Civil Public Welfare Lawsuit. MA thesis of Qingdao Univeristy.
227. Xiaoming, L. 2006. Maybe it is too harsh to force the rich to donate. *Financial View* 4: 35.
228. Xiaoping, D. 2001. *Selected words of Deng Xiaoping*. Beijing: The People's Publishing House.
229. Xiaoru, Y. 2003. Moral legalization: A fictitious and perilous proposition. *Journal of Southwest China Normal University (Humanities and Social Sciences edition)* 29: 51–54.
230. Xiaoyang, Q. 2008. *The talks on the legislative law of People's Republic of China*. Beijing: China Democracy and Rule of Law Publishing House.
231. Xianhua, F., and X. Ruiqing. 2008. Discussion of moral Pan-legalism. *Cards World* 7: 49.
232. Xin, L. 2008. *Legislative law*. Beijing: Beijing University Press.
233. Xinnian, C. 2005. Chen Xinnian's talk. *Beijing Youth Daily,* November 14.
234. Xinyan, W. 2008. The paradigm for research on Marxist philosophy in contemporary china. *Social Sciences in China* 2: 5–16.
235. Xu, H. 2010. Officer returned to His post, Tang Fuzhen ignores law and have only herself to blame. http://news.ifeng.com/society/1/201004/0409_343_1599152_1.shtml. Accessed 02 Feb 2012.
236. Xiaomei, H., and L. Zelin. 2008. Issues of Chinese Marxism philosophy since thirty years of enforcing the opening and reform. *Postgraduate Journal of Zhongnan University of Economics and Law* 3: 91–92.
237. Xiao, X., D. Dong, and X. Youyu. 1999. *Works and memories of Yu Luoke*. Beijing: China Federation of Literary and Art Circles Publishing Corporation.
238. Yanying, Z., and D. Xiaobo. 2003. An analysis of the influence of modern Pan-lawism. *Journal of Yuxi Teachers College* 19: 48–51.
239. Yang, X. 2001. Five-virtues in Chinese culture-a cutural examination of Pan-moralism. *Journal of Yantai University (Philosophy and Social Science)* 14: 207–210.
240. Yanqing, C. 2001. On similarities and differences between Aristotelian rule-of-law and rule-by-law in Chinese legalism. *Gansu Social Science* 3: 19–21.
241. Yi, X. 2008. A historic examination of 'great Leap' and People's commune. *Hebei Academic Journal* 28: 74.
242. Yifu, L., C. Fang, and L. Zhou. 1994. *The Chinese miracle: The development strategy and economic reform*. Shanghai: Sanlian publishing house.

243. Yili, Z. 2010. The ignored infants affected by Sanlu milk crisis. *People Digest* 2: 32–33.
244. Qi, Ying. 2006. *A third concept of liberty*. Beijing: Dongfang Publishing House.
245. Yingsh, Y. 2003. *A modern interpretation of Chinese traditional thoughts*. Jiangsu: Jiangsu Renmin Publishing House.
246. Yinshi, Y. 2003. *Scholars and Chinese culture*. Shanghai: Shanghai Renmin Press.
247. Yong, P. 2009. On cyber-crime legislation in China. *Hebei Law Science* 27: 49–57.
248. Yonghe, Z. 2009. *A study of lawmaking. (Li Fa Xue)*. Beijing: Law Press.
249. Youcheng, T., and L. Lin. 2004. *Theories and practices of lawmaking*, 160–169. Beijing: China Legal Publishing House.
250. Youlan, F. 2000. *Collections of San Song Tan. (San Song Tan Quan Ji)*. Zhengzhou: Henan People's Publishing House.
251. Yu, F. 2008. A criticism of belief in law. *Modern Law Science* 30: 10–17.
252. Yuan, L. 2008. The enlightenment of Marxism in China. *Journal of Ideological and Theoretical Education* 3: 36.
253. Yuan, R. 1980. *Li Ji*. Beijing: Zhonghua Book Company.
254. Yuanpei, C. 1985. *The political works of Cai Yuanpei*. Heibei: Heibei Remin Publishing House.
255. Zedong, M. 1961. *On the People's democratic dictatorship. Selected works of Mao Zedong*. Beijing: The People's Publishing House.
256. Zedong, M. 1990. *Mao Zedong's early works*. Hunan: Hunan Press.
257. Zedong, M. 1991. *Works of Mao Zedong*. Beijing: People's Publishing House.
258. Zeming, J. 2006. *To execute the three represents in a new historical circumstance*. Beijing: The People's Publishing House.
259. Zhang, Zai. 2000. *Zhang Zi Zheng Meng*. Shanghai: Shanghai Ancient Books Publishing House. Wang Fu Zhi (commentary).
260. Zhaogeng, M. 2008. The historical background of the people's daily editorial 'wipe out the black sheep' in 1966. *Culture and History Monthly* 8: 81.
261. Zhen, L. 2009. A study of contemporary Chinese Marxism CPC ideology. *Journal of Xue Xiao Dang Jian Yu Si Xiang Jiao Yu* 9: 14–26.
262. Zhengli, S. 2005. Studies on contemporary Chinese Marxism. *Journal of Henan University (Social Science)* 4: 6–8.
263. Zhenhua, Z. 2004. A study of Deng Xiaoping's theory. *Journal of Xihua University* 3: 18–19.
264. Zhibo, H. 2008. Why is law less useful than documents? *Procuratorial Daily,* June 11.
265. Zhicheng, Z. 2010. Revival of theory of Han Fei and the growth of New legalism in the early and middle of 20th century. *Journal of South China Normal University* 2: 129–135.
266. Zhijian, L. 2001. A study of creative local lawmaking. *People's Congress Studying* 8: 18–21.
267. Zhiping, L. 1997. *Searching for the harmony of the natural order: Studies on traditional Chinese legal culture*. Beijing: China University of Political Science and Law Press.
268. Zhiping, L. 2003. *Death and revival: The dawn of new age (Si Wang Yu Zai Sheng: Xin Shi Ji De Shu Guang)*. Beijing: China University of Politics and Science of Law.
269. Zhiqiang, R. 2008. Taxation and donation. *Resources Inhabitant and Environment* 15: 69–71.
270. Zhong, Y. 2002. Concept and idea of city lawmaking. *Journal of Sichuan University (Humanities and Social Science)* 1: 124–129.
271. Zhong, Y. 2009. *Confucius and Socrates*. Beijing: China Renmin University Press.
272. Zhongqiu, Z. 2008. The moral principle and the value of traditional Chinese law. *Journal of Nanjing University (Philosophy, Humanities and Social Sciences)* 1: 125–134.
273. Zhongxin, F. 2001. *The basic spirit of the tradition of Chinese law*. Shandong: Shandong Renmin Publishing House.
274. Zhongxin, F. 2000. *Believe in the truth of law (Xin Fa Wei Zhen)*. Beijing: China Legal Publishing House.
275. Zhongxin, F., and H. Peng. 2009. The contributions and characteristics of Liang Qichao's legal thoughts. *Journal for Legal History Studies* 12: 329–359.
276. Zhouya, L. 2003. The legal theory of the legalists in ancient China and its influential significance in modern times. *Modern Law Science* 25: 36–39.

277. Zhuoyan, L. 2006. Re-estimate China's urban poor population. *Finance & Economics* 9: 82–89.
278. Kai, C. 2004. The right to work and its realization in the market economy. *China Labor* 6: 4–9.
279. Qichao, L. 1902. Bentham's theory of utilitarianism. (Le Li Zhu Yi Tai Dou Bian Qing Zhi Xue Shuo). Xin Min Cong Kan (15): 11–25.
280. Xiaoyang, Q. 2000. *A bulletin of 50 years law*. Beijing: Chinese Democracy and Rule of Law Publishing House.
281. Yuepeng, R. 2009. *Introduction of western Marxism. Habeimasi:Law in communication)*. Ha Erbing: Heilongjiang University Press.
282. Bing, S. 1998. *Procedure, justice and modernization*. Beijing: The Chinese University of Political Science and Law Press.
283. Nonet, P., and P. Selznick. 1978. *Law and society in transition: Towards responsive law*. NewYork: Harper and Row.
284. Habermas, JÜrgen. 1998. *On the pragmatics of communication*. Cambridge: MIT Press.

Other Resources Include

http://news.163.com/10/1227/07/6OT4LON700014AEE.html
http://blogs.wsj.com/chinarealtime/2010/12/28/a-traffic-death-exposes-government-credibility-crisis/
http://edition.cnn.com/2011/WORLD/asiapcf/01/01/china.village.clash/index.html?iref=allsearch
http://w3.pku.edu.cn/academic/legislation/index_Chinese.htm
http://www.legal-theory.org/?mod=info&act=view&id=269
http://amoylegis.xmu.edu.cn/
http://www.un.org/esa/population/publications/WPP2004/WPP2004_Volume3.htm
http://www.ipu.org/english/home.htm
http://news.sohu.com/20091203/n268635575.shtml
http://news.sina.com.cn/s/2009-07-10/032718191682.shtml
http://news.sohu.com/20090729/n265556646.shtml
http://news.xinhuanet.com/employment/2009-07/22/content_11753354.htm
http://news.sohu.com/20080917/n259590366.shtml
http://news.sohu.com/20090101/n261527075.shtml
http://news.xinhuanet.com/ziliao/2004-11/15/content_2221419.htm
http://paper.dic123.com/paper_144736981/
http://news.xinhuanet.com/politics/2009-06/30/content_11626985.htm
http://www.stnn.cc/global/wg/wg10/t20060511_210361.html
http://www.hudong.com/wiki/%E6%96%87%E5%8C%96%E5%A4%A7%E9%9D%A9%E5%91%BD
http://www.people.com.cn/GB/shizheng/252/8956/8967/20020914/822374.html
http://www.chinadaily.com.cn/cndy/2009-08/12/content_8558038.htm
http://www.bbc.co.uk/worldservice/learningenglish/language/wordsinthenews/2009/07/090710_witn_iron_page.shtml
http://www.theaustralian.news.com.au/business/story/0,,25754321-36418,00.html
http://edition.cnn.com/2009/WORLD/asiapcf/08/11/china.riotinto/index.html?iref=newssearch
http://news.szhk.com/2010/05/27/282749837802150.html
http://chinese.dsturgeon.net/text.pl?node=47249&if=en&remap=gb
http://www.chinacourt.org/html/article/200804/28/298683.shtml
http://news.sina.com.cn/s/2010-06-09/044420438816.shtml
http://www.baolawfirm.com.vn/dmdocuments/Culpa%20in%20contrahendo%20in%20English%20Law.pdf
http://www.gg-art.com/imgbook/index.php?bookid=53
http://news.wuxi.soufun.com/2010-05-06/3314113_5.html
Chinese Political Advisor Calls for Stricter Control in Land Expropriation. from Xinhua News Agency, March 8, 2008.

P. He, *Chinese Lawmaking: From Non-communicative to Communicative*, Understanding China, DOI 10.1007/978-3-642-39507-9,

Chinese Text Project. http://chinese.dsturgeon.net/text.pl?node=11591&if=en&remap=gb
The Rochdale Pioneers. http://www.bbc.co.uk/dna/h2g2/brunel/A2764424
New characteristics and new structure: Changes from 10 NPCs. 2003. *People's Daily,* March 4.
The Inter-Parliamentary Union. 1986. *Parliaments of the world: A comparative reference compendium*. England: Gower Publishing Company.
Sun Zhigang: The milestone of the history of citizen's rights. 2008. *XiaoXiang Morning,* December 19.
The State Administration Taxation. http://www.chinanews.com.cn/cj/cj-plgd/news/2009/06-19/1741312.shtml
Asia Development Bank report 2007: http://web.worldbank.org/WBSITE/EXTERNAL/COUNTRIES/EASTASIAPACIFICEXT/CHINAEXTN/0,,contentMDK:21639761~pagePK:141137~piPK:141127~theSitePK:318950,00.html

Printed by Printforce, the Netherlands